Enter the Superheroes

American Values, Culture, and the Canon of Superhero Literature

Alex S. Romagnoli and Gian S. Pagnucci

THE SCARECROW PRESS, INC.
Lanham • Toronto • Plymouth, UK
2013

Published by Scarecrow Press, Inc.
A wholly owned subsidary of The Rowman & Littlefield Publishing Group, Inc.
4501 Forbes Boulevard, Suite 200, Lanham, Maryland 20706
www.rowman.com

10 Thornbury Road, Plymouth PL6 7PP, United Kingdom

British Library Cataloguing in Publication Information Available

Library of Congress Cataloging-in-Publication Data

Romagnoli, Alex S., 1983-
Enter the superheroes : American values, culture, and the canon of superhero literature / Alex S. Romagnoli and Gian S. Pagnucci.
pages cm
Includes bibliographical references and index.
ISBN 978-0-8108-9171-5 (cloth : alk. paper) -- ISBN 978-0-8108-9172-2 (electronic)
1. Comic books, strips, etc.--United States--History and criticism. 2. Superhero comic books, strips, etc.--History and criticism. 3. Graphic novels--United States. 4. Superheroes--Social aspects. 5. Superheroes in literature. I. Pagnucci, Gian S. II. Title.
PN6725.R666 2013
741.5'973--dc23
2013008376

Printed in the United States of America

Alex: To my Mother and Father, superheroes in their own right, and to Colin, who knew the best superhero stories

Gian: For Cormac and Loughlin and every other kid who ever dreamed of being a superhero, and for Edel, who is the most super person I've ever known

Contents

Acknowledgments

Alyssa Richman for her wonderful cover art.

Stephen Ryan for giving us the chance to write this book.

And Alden Perkins for her invaluable help in completing this volume.

Introduction

A doomed planet explodes, and its last surviving child is rocketed to Earth. The son of a wealthy family watches his parents murdered before his eyes in a dark alleyway. A noble princess is sent from her isolated homeland to a world of alien values. An unpopular high school student with glasses is bitten by a radioactive spider. A scrawny young man volunteers for a super soldier program to help his country fight a great war. Superhero stories have entertained, enthralled, and inspired children and adults alike for over seventy years. These stories are elemental, simple, inspirational, and powerful. Because they tell of ultimate strength, deep despair, unfathomable longing, and immeasurable bravery, superhero stories have been an enduring form of entertainment reflecting American ideals and celebrating the inherent nobility of man.

Though Superman, Batman, Wonder Woman, Spider-Man, and Captain America have never ceased their battles for justice, the place of superhero stories remains relegated to the proverbial slums of literacy, literature, and culture in general. Comic books are looked down upon, banned from schools, ignored by academics, and critiqued as juvenile. As Aaron Taylor notes, "comics remain largely ghettoized in North America after almost a century—popularly regarded as infantile subliterature—their ability to impress upon cultural norms remain quite limited."[1] There was even a time when grandmothers would use comics as liners for kitty litter boxes or as last-minute wrapping paper. Time has brought some change, since today comics are valued as collectibles not gift-wrap. However, few graphic novels are ever taught in schools, and the superhero genre is almost nowhere to be found.

The goal of this book is to establish the importance of the superhero, both as a cultural artifact and as a text to be studied. In this volume we will explore why superhero stories have value, what we could learn from studying superhero comics, and how superheroes shape American culture and values.

Chapter 1 asserts that the concept of the superhero is socioculturally, sociohistorically, and academically significant to our culture. The lessons learned from these characters and stories have become timeless, and the characters themselves have become entrenched in the collective consciousness. From comic books, to television shows, to major motion pictures, superheroes have undoubtedly become culturally significant.

Despite the importance of superheroes to the larger culture, however, academic contexts have yet to honor and privilege superhero stories as significant pieces of literature. In chapter 2, the question of why the academy has made some moves to embrace a limited set of graphic novels while basically shunning superhero literature is examined. We discuss the significance of *Maus* as the most acclaimed graphic novel of all time while also unpacking the ramifications of that recognition and its significance. We then look at other comics and graphic novels traditionally taught in the academy including *Persepolis*, *Palestine*, and others. We also discuss Scott McCloud's work and the absence of superheroes in that work. We conclude by examining why the academy purposefully ignores the superhero.

This volume looks to explore the impact of the superhero genre beyond academic contexts as well. In chapter 3, we broaden the focus of the book from academic usage to popular culture implications. This chapter examines debates over continuity and changes to major superhero characters. We look at the new Ultimate Spider-Man, DC's New 52, and major deaths. The focus in chapter 3 is on how fans react to comic creators' artistic directions. For instance, the death of the second Robin (Jason Todd) is examined, along with how fans literally voted on whether or not the character would live. This chapter concludes with an examination of comics as a publicly engaged medium.

Picking up on the theme of the public's influence, chapter 4 looks at how comic publishers interact with their audiences, specifically through the lens of companies' relaunches. We link the idea of the relaunch/reboot to the larger issue of comic books and superhero stories as evolving mythologies. Specific consideration in this chapter is given to major relaunches in superhero literature including DC's "Crisis" events and Marvel's "Ultimate" series.

Chapter 5 looks at the aesthetics of the superhero and explores how the visuals of the superhero genre inform its themes. We explore the large scope of the cultural significance of superheroes as iconographic figures. Additionally, we look at the enduring nature of these characters and why certain heroes have become so popular and why that popularity persists. This includes discussing the phenomenal success of superhero films in the last ten years as well as examining the lasting imagery of the superhero including capes, masks, muscles, and the symbols emblazoned on superheroes' chests.

Returning again to academic contexts, chapter 6 connects the writing of superhero comics to composition theory. The Stan Lee method of writing is discussed in this chapter, and its implications for the teaching of writing. What teachers can learn about the composition process from the writing of comics is also explored. Finally, we discuss the nature of superhero origin stories and how the writing of these origin stories helps make superhero narratives a unique literary genre.

Children are a major audience to which superhero literature caters. Therefore, chapter 7 explores how children are affected by superhero literature and what role comic books play in defining children's value systems. This chapter looks at the ongoing fascination that superheroes have for children and also discusses the perceived notion of comics as a strictly child-oriented medium. The chapter then discusses the significance of comics creators turning their focus away from children and toward adults as well as more recent efforts by publishers to reconnect with child audiences.

Chapter 8 examines issues of diversity in superhero literature. Because these issues are so complex and far-reaching, this chapter explores questions of race and gender in comics through two case studies: the racially mixed Miles Morales becoming Spider-Man in Marvel's "Ultimate" series and Starfire and Catwoman's depictions in DC's New 52 relaunch in 2011.

The longevity of the superhero is deconstructed in chapter 9 through an examination of superhero literature's "death" stories. Superheroes never truly die, and that trope in superhero literature reflects our own desires to live long and our fears of dying. Since we cannot live forever, our superheroes do that for us. Additionally, the few lasting deaths in superhero literature are discussed to explain why certain characters must remain deceased in order to maintain the power of superhero mythology.

Chapter 10 looks at how technology has impacted superhero literature. The development of technology in superhero literature has been both reflective and prophetic of culture. From Iron Man to Batman, technology has influenced the narratives of superheroes for their entire existences. This chapter addresses how technology in superhero literature has affected our culture and how real technology has affected superhero storytelling.

Chapter 11 provides an argument for the development of a Canon of Superhero Literature. By referencing the literary work of Harold Bloom and the comic studies work of Peter Coogan, this chapter is the culmination of the book's argument about the value of superhero literature. This chapter claims that the best way to promote academic acceptance of superhero literature is to define a canon of the genre's most important and historically significant stories. The chapter then outlines how such a canon can best be constructed.

Enter the Superheroes concludes by presenting an extensive list of super-hero texts meant to constitute a Canon of Superhero Literature. We list the most seminal superhero texts that have helped create and develop the my-thology of superheroes and have fostered their growth into a cultural phe-nomenon. The list discusses historically important works as well as the great-est superhero stories ever told.

Superhero stories have a seventy-year tradition. They represent an American mythology and significant cultural iconography ripe for explora-tion today. Within superhero stories can be found all our hopes, ideals, fears, dreams, and longings. It is time to give these stories their due. The time of the superhero has come.

NOTE

1. Aaron Taylor, "He's Gotta Be Strong, and He's Gotta Be Fast, and He's Gotta Be Larger Than Life: Investigating the Engendered Superhero Body," *Journal of Popular Culture* 40, no. 2 (2007): 346.

Chapter One

The Significance of the Superhero Examined

Superhero stories and characters have withstood the test of time, attempted censorship, and the constant evolution of entertainment forms. Their longevity can be attributed to their universality and relatability. As much as these characters may be all powerful, they're simultaneously representative of the common man and all that he stands for in a world that can be inherently corrupt and dangerous. The fact that superheroes are fictitious does little to diminish their significance since nearly all superheroes' origins are grounded in humble beginnings with normal people doing great and noble feats with the powers they've gained. People know, adore, and glorify these stories. As Grant Morrison says, "We love our superheroes because they refuse to give up on us. We can analyze them out of existence, kill them, ban them, mock them, and still they return, patiently reminding us of who we are and what we wish we could be."[1] The consistent presence of superheroes is their greatest strength. In the remainder of this chapter, we'll explore the cultural importance of the superhero including: Historical Significance, American Perceptions of Good and Evil, Power and Its Appeal, and Superheroes and Mythology.

HISTORICAL SIGNIFICANCE

The history of comic books has been well documented over the years, with numerous historians and authors such as Peter Coogan,[2] Bradford Wright,[3] Gerard Jones,[4] and David Hajdu[5] making a genuine case for their historical precedent. Nevertheless, like all superhero stories, the origin of comics needs to be reviewed, if only in a much abbreviated way.

It's 1938 and the Great Depression has taken its toll on America. Newspapers, magazines, and radio shows are the dominant forms of entertainment for the masses that yearn for distraction from economic turmoil and the rumblings of war in Europe. The children of this era take their allowances (or what little cash they can spare) to corner soda shops and newsstands to buy penny candy, small snacks, or cheap publications depicting daring characters saving damsels in distress.

Before comic books there was what is now referred to as pulp fiction. These publications were not known for their literary brilliance or for their deep social commentary. Instead, these magazine-length novels were as lurid as the publishers were allowed to make them (and sometimes more so). As Gerard Jones put it in his book *Men of Tomorrow: Geeks, Gangsters, and the Rise of the Comic Book*, "The plots were crowded with thugs and sinister Orientals and underdressed molls."[6] Pulp novels were aimed directly at male readers, with boys naturally being intrigued by them. Needless to say, the more salacious the content, the more the boys of this generation yearned for them. Characters such as Doc Savage, The Shadow, John Carter, and the Phantom punished evil-doers with their fists and asked questions later. If the woman the hero was saving had her already scandalous apparel shredded to pieces in the process of her rescue, this was all the better, at least from a sales perspective. These pulp novels were everything a boy of the time (or perhaps any time for that matter) could want.

However, while these pulp novels had quality covers created by some visibly talented artists, their content was prose with very few (if any) pictures. To add imagery to the equation, this same generation of boys who craved powerful men saving beautiful women from the clutches of sinister villains was introduced to the first superhero in June 1938.

Action Comics #1[7] featured a muscular man dressed in a blue jumpsuit with a billowing red cape smashing a car into a building. To boot, men are running away from this mysterious man screaming for their lives. The title of this new magazine blazed across the top of the cover: bright red letters against a white background promising, above all else, "Action." Boys in 1938 were powerless to resist it, and it only cost a dime.

Inside, readers were introduced to Clark Kent, a mild-mannered newspaper reporter for the *Daily Star* (it wasn't the *Daily Planet* yet) who moonlighted as the brightly colored vigilante Superman. In this same landmark issue readers were introduced to Lois Lane, Clark Kent's fellow reporter at the *Daily Star*. As would be expected, Superman saves Lois Lane from a group of thugs hell-bent on killing her. Lois Lane's first reaction to this mysterious man is that of fear, with Superman reassuring the ace reporter whose dress strap has conveniently fallen off her shoulder, "You needn't be afraid of me. I won't harm you."[8] The issue ends with Superman dangling a gangster from a telephone wire with the evil-doer crying for his life. This was completely new to readers of the time and introduced what would become the archetype for the American superhero.

Why was this character successful though? What was the appeal? Looking at the first story of Superman from a modern context yields little reaction because his exploits have become, what some might consider, cliché. Nevertheless, those clichés became the basis for the modern superhero.[9] Superman was successful because he represented what every American male wanted to be. He was handsome, immeasurably strong, wanted by women, and inherently noble. His arrival from a distant world made him the ultimate immigrant extending his appeal to include not only boys, but boys who may have come to America from another land. Superman also wasn't affected by the struggles caused by the Great Depression or worried about the rising tensions in Europe. For all intents and purposes, Superman was just that: super.

The appearance of this hero spawned the creation of a multitude of other heroes as well. DC (then called National Periodicals), thrilled with the commercial success of Superman, started releasing more comic books featuring new superheroes: Batman, Wonder Woman, The Flash, Green Lantern, the Sandman, Dr. Fate, and a multitude of other characters. In response to the success that DC was experiencing, other publishers began creating their own versions, including Timely Comics' Captain America and Fawcett Comics' Captain Marvel. Amazingly, all of these characters experienced commercial success, if only for a limited time.[10]

And these characters, whose roots can be traced to ancient literature and classical models of heroic narratives,[11] became the image of the modern hero. Propelled by the fantastical suits, bright colors, and comic-style storytelling were tales that embraced the elemental conflicts of society, chief among them, the battle between good and evil.

PERCEPTIONS OF GOOD AND EVIL

Why were these comic stories successful, though? Much of their success can be attributed to the colorful nature of the medium in which they were featured: the comic book. It has to be kept in mind that color printing was still relatively new at this time, and anything other than the traditional black and white newspaper print was something to behold. The concept of superheroes was also a novel idea. There had been the pulp heroes of old who fought for the innocent, but theirs was a rougher, tougher, and more controversial style of justice. The same boys who had grown up reading the pulps behind their mothers' backs were the boys who now flocked to the Technicolor of the comic book world with its amazing heroes dressed in bright colors and personifying the most admirable qualities of nobility.

When superhero comics hit the newsstands in the late 1930s, the country had never seen anything like it. While a sequential style of storytelling that seamlessly combined image and text was nothing new, the introduction of brightly clad heroes to this medium using their powers for good was exciting and different. This effect still hasn't worn off on people after seventy years with television shows, movies, children's toys, lunchboxes, and countless other culturally significant aspects of life embracing the unique qualities that superheroes exude.

There is a deeper value to why superhero stories work, though. While the flashiness and the aesthetics of the superheroes are certainly a contributing factor to their appeal, their success can also be attributed to their blatant personifications of society's morals. Specifically, superhero stories embody American culture's dichotomy of good and evil.

Superheroes represent a set of timeless values; their motivation to do good, their passion for justice, and their opposition to evil are ageless, and people have admired the pursuit of such values for nearly all of existence. Pick any superhero. No matter which one is chosen, a superhero is likely to have these characteristics:

1. His/her origins are, in some way, informed by a tragedy.
2. He/she is obsessed with achieving his/her goals.
3. With few exceptions, he/she is a solitary figure.
4. His/her goal is unattainable.
5. He/she has a weakness.

These characteristics humanize heroes who possess god-like abilities. Ultimately, the limitations make them relatable to readers. The perseverance these characters exhibit in pursuing good makes them effective storytelling vessels. As such, superhero narratives can transcend the colorful and admittedly fantastic elements of their stories; this enables them to become vehicles for examining and deconstructing humanity's efforts to balance good and evil.

The line between good and evil is particularly clear in superhero comics. In traditional superhero stories, the heroes are incorruptibly noble and the villains are blindingly evil; Batman is always good, and the Joker is always evil. Granted, more recent comic literature has tested these predetermined notions of good and evil in comic books through character deconstructions. In fact, the stories where a hero's nobility is tested are some of the most powerful and significant stories in comic book history, and these stories will be visited later in this book. For most audiences though, superhero stories draw their line between good and evil very distinctly.

In creating such a clear and present distinction between good and evil, superhero stories reflect the dominant culture's prevailing perceptions of what makes a hero noble. Superheroes, being a uniquely American concept, then reflect what American culture considers the most estimable qualities in a person. There is little room for argument in superheroes' motives and actions because they're so noble. Think of it this way: If Spider-Man saves a child from a burning building, could that possibly be interpreted as a morally ambiguous action? Probably not. It seems logical to assume that most people would consider that feat both commendable and selfless. If the Joker robs a bank simply because he wants money, is that interpreted as morally reprehensible? One would hope so. The point here is that with few exceptions, the heroes and villains in superhero comics represent what mainstream American culture defines as good and evil. The clear-cut nature of this dichotomy is pretty rare in literature.

Take a classic literary example that all American high school students have had to address in survey classes. In John Steinbeck's novel *Of Mice and Men*,[12] the character George kills his mentally impaired friend Lenny by shooting him in the back of the head in order to save Lenny from an inevitable, and likely horrid, fate at the hands of angry farmhands. Earlier in the story, Lenny had accidentally killed his employer's wife, and the angry farmhands are looking for Lenny to exact a brutal revenge and kill him. George's actions can be interpreted in many ways, but most literature classes would look at George's killing of Lenny in terms of euthanasia: was George correct in thinking he had the right to kill Lenny in order to save him from a more miserable and likely painful ordeal? Here is where moral ambiguity comes into play. Depending on the person reading the book, the reaction to George's mercy killing reflects that individual's culture, beliefs, and experiences. Any reaction and subsequent judgment is completely subjective, and either argument (for or against the mercy killing) can be reasonably argued and articulated using evidence from the book, personal life experiences, and studies on mercy killings. There is no clear consensus as to what is right, though.

With superhero stories, there is usually a general consensus as to what is right and what is wrong. Again, there are superhero stories that purposefully blur this line, but the heroes are generally perceived to be correct in their courses of action. This allows for a more concrete discussion of what a culture deems to be "good" and "evil." While *Of Mice and Men* is a powerful and thought-provoking story, the ending calls into question the moral fabric of a man. The discussion is no longer about culture when George kills Lenny; the conversation remains singularly focused on a specific character at a specific time in a specific context. Generalizing George's actions in order to analyze his nobility at a sociocultural level becomes challenging because of the situation's inherent subjectivity. In contrast, superheroes tend to embody American culture's ideals. In essence, when the actions of superheroes are discussed and analyzed, these actions can be used to examine the values of an entire culture.

For traditional superhero stories, superheroes are the carriers of what society views as righteous and just. As Richard Reynolds puts it in his book *Superheroes: A Modern Mythology*, "The superhero has a mission to preserve society, not to re-invent it."[13] Since this preservation of society exists in superhero stories, they become valuable artifacts to study traditional/cultural views of good and evil. While characters have naturally changed over their fictional existences, their moral compasses remain fixed on the true north of morality with one important exception.

Batman, whose original incarnation as the dark and vengeful crusader has morphed over the years since his first appearance in 1939, exemplifies the similar yet dynamic nature of a moral compass. Batman's first appearance in *Detective Comics #27*[14] featured Batman (then called "The Bat-Man") solving and then foiling a murder plot. The story, "The Case of the Chemical Syndicate," shows Batman as a ruthless and terrifying vigilante with no relationship with or formal sanctioning from law enforcement. Additionally, Batman is directly responsible for the death of the villain at the end of the story as the villain is intentionally punched into a vat of acid with Batman stating, "A fitting ending for his kind."[15] Supporting this extreme vigilantism is Batman's point-blank shooting of two people at the conclusion of *Detective Comics #32*.[16] Ask any reader or avid fan of Batman and they're likely to tell you that Batman doesn't kill as part of his moral code. Yet, the Batman of 1939 kills criminals with alarming regularity, and that ruthlessness may have indirectly led to Robin's creation only a few months later in 1940.[17] Despite Batman's ruthlessness as a killer and crossing most people's moral threshold and tolerance of street justice, he does still act to a certain extent in the best interest of the society in which he lives.

Batman's earliest actions, in *Detective Comics #27–38*,[18] can be viewed as morally ambiguous because of his callousness and apparent disregard for human life. However, his moral code was soon changed to match that of the comic's predominantly adolescent audience when an editorial decision was made by DC to ban superheroes from killing villains. This also fit well with DC's decision to add the adolescent character of Robin the Boy Wonder to the comic. Whitney Ellsworth, the editor of the Batman comic books during its first issues, "declared that Batman should never intentionally kill again, and he didn't."[19] In this way, culture influenced the editorial and subsequent creative decisions about these superheroes. This discursive relationship between fans and creators is a major component of the superhero genre, and it is discussed in detail in chapter 3 of this book. The roots of that dialogue began here though, in the late 1930s. Again there exists a link between American culture's view of good and evil and how superheroes view good and evil. The character Batman, because he openly reflected the value system of his culture (America), was made to evolve to better represent the morality of that culture.

Superheroes then have undeniable anthropological and sociological significance both as artifacts and as examples of evolving embodiments of justice. But while their morality is purposefully aligned with society's, the implication of that morality is proportional to the power superheroes possess.

POWER AND ITS APPEAL

All superheroes definitely have one characteristic in common: they're powerful. Yes, exceptions can be cited for characters such as Batman who is essentially an extraordinarily fit and smart human, but he's still a billionaire with the power to fund his vigilantism. Basically, though, all superheroes are powerful, and that power is usually of a physical nature. Superman's original radio introduction even celebrated him as being "faster than a speeding bullet" and "more powerful than a locomotive." These things are impossible for humans to accomplish; no man can run faster than a bullet. But therein lies the value: the superhero enables the reader to examine the nature of power.

What *if* a man could run faster than a bullet? What *if* a man could be stronger than a train engine? What *if* a man could fly through the sky? If there was a man who could really do all of these amazing feats, the societal implications would be astounding. People would need to rethink the limitations of the human body. Science would need to reexamine physics and where Newton and Einstein might have been wrong. The collective psyche of humanity would struggle with the inherent and simultaneous majesty and danger of this extraordinary man. As Grant Morrison said of legendary comic writer Alan Moore's stories addressing this very hypothetical notion, "Moore argued that the arrival of a genuine superhuman being in our midst would quickly and radically alter society forever."[20] Superhero stories provide an outlet for these types of sociocultural and hypothetical scenarios. In examining these hypothetical scenarios, the human condition is put through tests of nobility. For superhero comics the nobility of the character is again usually quite clear-cut. The heroes in the stories are the characters who embrace their new powers while having an awareness of those powers and the inherent dangers of their misuse. Villains are the characters who abuse their power for selfish reasons.

This exercise can even be done on a sociohistorical level. What *if* the United States really made a super soldier serum during World War II? What *if* this new super soldier turned the tide of the war for the Alli
man was then frozen in ice and reawakened decades later? Fo
also known as Captain America, these questions are possibl
historical fiction and a study of the human condition at its f

tion this story then evokes is what would *you* do if you had Captain America's powers?

The truth is no one knows what he/she would do with new powers if they were somehow gained. What is known is how the writers and artists of these stories interpreted the possibility of amazing power and how they thought it should be used. Apparently, to the people who write and draw superhero comic books, the responsibility that comes with being powerful is paramount.

The often cited quote from Stan Lee and Steve Ditko's first Spider-Man story, *Amazing Fantasy #15*, sets the tone for this discussion beautifully: "With great power must also come—great responsibility!"[21] In the story, Peter Parker inadvertently allows a robber to escape from the scene of a crime despite his amazing abilities because he feels the situation doesn't concern him. Upon Peter's return home, he finds his uncle has been murdered by the same man he allowed to escaped only hours earlier. The result of Peter Parker's inaction is tragic and eventually becomes the catalyst for his donning of the superhero's signature red-and-blue suit.

Spider-Man's moral ambiguity in this story was one of the first examples of effectively addressing nobility and the introduction of powers. Unlike Superman, Captain America, The Flash, Wonder Woman, and many other characters who came before him, Spider-Man was faced with deep and significant life choices that would affect him going forward as both Peter Parker and as Spider-Man.

This balance of great power and responsibility becomes the cornerstone of superhero stories. People like to think they'd use super powers for good, and maybe they would, and that is the wonderful nature of Spider-Man and other superheroes. When faced with these new powers and gifts, their altruism shines through personal desires. Spider-Man had to experience a profound tragedy, but his morality after that tragedy becomes paramount. It is impossible to determine whether people in reality would utilize super powers in the name of good, though. Unless a scientist inadvertently gives himself super spider powers in reality, the world may never know the truth. However, the possibility can be explored in psychological, cultural, and sociohistorical contexts with superhero stories.

Stories of power intrigue audiences with their possibilities, their scenarios, and their blatant analyses of power's effect on people. Traditional superhero stories are modern-day deconstructions of the human condition and ultimate power. As with Spider-Man, who selfishly allowed a criminal to continue evil deeds unchecked, power both enhanced and diminished Peter Parker's quality of life; he gained superpowers, but he also lost his father figure, Uncle Ben, in the process. Like many literary characters who struggled with their actions and/or inactions, Spider-Man became a tragic hero a generation of readers could relate to. The fact that Peter Parker/Spider-

Man was a teenager who fought crime was really the commercial appeal of the character. Sure Spider-Man looked aesthetically awesome hanging from spiderwebs in New York and punching super-villains across the panels of comic books, but Spider-Man's real appeal came from his relatability beyond the super powers.

While teens could not possibly relate to fighting Doctor Octopus, they could relate to Peter Parker needing to get home in time so he wouldn't upset his Aunt May. Teenage boys could also relate to Peter Parker struggling with talking to girls on a daily basis at school. More so than other superheroes before him, Spider-Man/Peter Parker lived an actual life that reflected a "real" reality. Could someone possibly relate to Clark Kent? Absolutely, but Clark Kent was an adult with a job, and his superpowers were always a part of his identity development. Could someone possibly relate to Bruce Wayne? One would hope not, as Batman watched his parents being murdered. Could someone possibly relate to Captain America? The Flash? Green Lantern? Wonder Woman? Iron Man? Daredevil? The list could go on for pages, and it seems feasible that every one of the major superheroes are relatable at some level or else they wouldn't be successful franchises, but Spider-Man just seemed to address the reality of power and responsibility in a coherent and semi-realistic fashion: "Peter Parker brought the specky Clark Kent archetype back and gave readers a teenage hero who felt like a teenager."[22]

Since all superhero comics have an underlying theme of power and its effects on people, they also address human desires and experiences, making them essential readings on the human condition for twenty-first-century audiences. For seventy years superhero stories have analyzed, reanalyzed, and critiqued human power. For the twenty-first century, superheroes are the premiere form of literature concerning humans' interactions with powers beyond their understandings.

As one last example, the Silver Age Green Lantern from DC Comics provides yet another dynamic scenario of power and its effects on humans. Hal Jordan was a test pilot for the United States Air Force until a purple alien named Abin Sur crash landed on Earth. As a member of the Green Lantern Corps, Abin Sur was required to pass on his ring of power to a worthy successor. Upon his crashing on Earth, Abin Sur's power ring (the weapon of the Green Lantern Corps) summoned Hal Jordan, as he was the most worthy successor on Earth. Hal Jordan receives the ring and becomes the Green Lantern of Earth and the sector of which Earth is a part: Sector 2814.[23]

It's a great Silver Age story and the brain child of Julius Schwartz's revitalization of many Golden Age superheroes when he was made the editor of DC Comics.[24] Nevertheless, Hal Jordan is given a ring of immeasurable power that could be used selfishly for personal fame, fortune, and power. Of course, Jordan does not use his newfound ring for personal gain and instead upholds the Green Lanterns' values. The question then becomes this: what would you do with a ring of immeasurable power? Even beyond that question and the burden of having immeasurable power, the parallels between Hal Jordan's ring and J. R. R. Tolkien's Ring of Power in *The Lord of the Rings* are evident. The powers of the rings are different, as are the circumstances in which the protagonists gain their respective rings. However, there is still an examination of humans and the lure of power from an object that is endowed with incredible energy. Coincidentally, *The Lord of the Rings* was published in 1954,[25] only five years before Hal Jordan's first appearance in *Showcase Comics #22* (1959).

SUPERHEROES AS MYTHOLOGY

If superheroes are characterized as being near physically perfect and morally incorruptible, then they're worthy of being included in academic and other discussions of culture and society. Viewing these characters through a mythological lens puts a unique spin on the cultural significance of the genre, as mythology transcends generations and audiences. Superheroes achieve this level of significance in culture through both their physical stature and their propensity for being moral compasses.

As gods among normal men, superheroes introduce dynamics into discussions of culture and society that are unique to modern audiences. There are, of course, numerous mythological figures that are similar to superheroes in both stature and personality including Achilles, Hector, Odysseus, and Gilgamesh.[26] While these characters are undoubtedly important and worthy of intense academic analysis, they all have one characteristic in common: they're thousands of years removed from their initial audiences. This point of contention is not intended to diminish the historical, cultural, and social significance of these classic characters. What this is intended to do is make a case for studying the modern-day representations of the ideals these characters hold.

In *Reading Comics: How Graphic Novels Work and What They Mean*, Douglas Wolk discusses the importance of the superhero to comics. While much of Wolk's analysis of superheroes focuses on the academic perception of superheroes (as a necessary evil that needs to be appeased for the greater and economic good of the art form), it does see superheroes as embodying universal concepts. Specifically, "Superheroes are, by their nature, larger than life, and what's useful and interesting about their characteristics is that they provide bold metaphors for discussing ideas or reifying abstractions into narrative fiction."[27] So while the story of *Daredevil* can be read at face value, as that of a lawyer who moonlights as a masked vigilante in New York's Hell's Kitchen,[28] it can also be read in a way that questions the intentions of a lawyer who uses his special powers to fight crime and disrupt the very system of law he has sworn to protect. In such a reading, Matt Murdock's motives and intentions take on a whole new context: he is right in stopping criminals, but he's also wrong in interfering with the law. Duality, hypocrisy, social/professional ethics, and legality are all major themes that can be studied by examining the stories of the blind superhero who secretly doubles as a lawyer in Hell's Kitchen.

Mythology is really a reflection of what a culture values, and superheroes have become, as Richard Reynolds said in 1992, a modern mythology. As a modern mythology, superheroes then take on the burden of being a representation of what culture and society value at a given moment. In the case of superheroes, their temporal influence as culturally significant characters ranges from 1938 (when Superman first appeared) all the way through today. This is not much different than other mythology that has come before. Taking an example from Greek mythology, Achilles is the epitome of physical strength and prowess. While he does have a weakness (his heel), his strength is an inspiration to people, as he is the ultimate in human physique. However, Achilles' propensity for killing and his ruthless tactics much better represent ancient Greek culture than they do modern American culture. This dichotomy can create conflict in studying the character from a modern context, as part of the character's significance can be generalized (his strength) and the other can be purposefully identified as almost anachronistic (his propensity for killing). For ancient Greeks, Achilles was a superhero, but he does not work as well as a superhero in today's society.

For modern audiences Superman is undoubtedly a superhero, and much of his appeal can be attributed not only to his physicality and limitless power but also his moral compass. While Achilles's morality can be called into question by modern audiences, Superman's morality and actions are much more in tune with modern culture's moral standards. When present-day audiences read Superman's stories, their analyses of these stories become much more relatable than those of Achilles because Superman's actions more closely resemble the actions of a person holding twenty-first-century values. In other words, modern audiences relate better to Superman than they do to Achilles. This doesn't mean that Superman is "better" than Achilles though. In fact, people have been studying Achilles for thousands of years, and rightly so. It is just time to promote superheroes to the same basic level of academic respect that ancient mythological characters have.

In the 1978 motion picture *Superman: The Movie*, Lois Lane dies during an earthquake caused by Lex Luthor. Superman becomes so enraged (which looks awesome onscreen by the way) that he races into the sky only to experience conflict about his next course of action. As an audience we don't know what Superman is going to do, but we do know that his actions might be rash because he has just lost the woman he loves. After contemplating for a few seconds, Superman proceeds to fly around the Earth causing it to spin backward and subsequently turning back time to a point where he can save Lois from dying.[29] Ignore the implausibility of this (I know it's hard) and analyze this course of action. Even though Superman is not human, modern audiences can relate to Superman because he shares many of the same ideals. Furthermore, his reaction is uniquely human in that he wants to go back and make things right, something humans cannot physically do. But this is Superman, and he does have the power to change the world in such a significant way. The question becomes this: does Superman have the right to turn back time in order to save the person he loves? This is a heavy question and one that can only be analyzed from multiple perspectives. It taps into the very soul of audiences, as it is something everyone has wanted to do at one point or another: turn back time to save someone we love. We have probably all thought, at one time or another, that if we could just change one little thing to fix a mistake in our past, we would do it in a heartbeat and without hesitation. At that point in *Superman the Movie*, this powerful alien from Krypton becomes so human that he succumbs to his personal desires to save his own sanity; this superhero experiences human emotions despite the powers that separate him from ordinary people.

Superheroes exist because the world needs them to. Superman's actions in *Superman: The Movie* seem omnipotent, but they're probably the same actions we would take in order to save a loved one we had just lost. Audiences need these fictional archetypes to reference, even if only subconsciously. As Peter Coogan says, "The superhero's mission is prosocial and selfless, which means that his fight against evil must fit in with the existing professed mores of society and must not be intended to benefit or further his own agenda."[30] Superman's actions in *Superman: The Movie* are selfish, but that rare scene of Superman being selfish is what makes the film powerful and timeless.

GOING FORWARD

These superheroes are the characters that many children grew up with, learned their morality from, mimicked during play, and followed into adulthood. Superhero stories haven't gone anywhere, either. Instead of disappearing into thin air and becoming a footnote of history in America, they've spread like wildfire into nearly all areas of life and around the globe. Sports stars get tattoos of superhero emblems on their arms, little trinkets in thousands of stores across the country emblazon superhero images across their products, children wear pajamas with detachable capes, and movies are made at an alarming rate designed to ensnare even the most casual of fans into their undeniably entertaining web. Almost no one can escape the influence of the superhero: "It should give us hope that superhero stories are flourishing everywhere because they are a bright flickering sign of our need to move on, to imagine the better, more just, and more proactive people we can be."[31] Instead of losing their influence on society, superhero stories are becoming stronger.

Like the heroic stories of ancient mythology, today's superhero stories refuse to go quietly into the history books, to languish unread for countless years later with little understanding as to why they were even recorded. Instead, the tales of superheroes endure because they represent culture, society, values, hopes, dreams, fears, and humanity all wrapped up in colorful stories that can be effectively explored in any medium. Superheroes aren't going anywhere anytime soon because they are us.

NOTES

1. Grant Morrison, *Supergods: What Masked Vigilantes, Miraculous Mutants, and a Sun God from Smallville Can Teach Us about Being Human* (New York: Spiegel & Grau, 2011), 416.

2. Peter Coogan, *Superhero: The Secret Origin of a Genre* (Austin, TX: Monkey Brain, 2006).

3. Bradford Wright, *Comic Book Nation: The Transformation of Youth Culture in America* (Baltimore: Johns Hopkins University Press, 2003).

4. Gerard Jones, *Men of Tomorrow: Geeks, Gangsters, and the Birth of the Comic Book* (New York: Basic Books, 2004).

5. David Hajdu, *The Ten-Cent Plague: The Great Comic-Book Scare and How It Changed America* (New York: Farrar, Straus and Giroux, 2008).

6. Jones, *Men of Tomorrow*, 29.

7. Jerry Siegel and Joe Shuster, *Action Comics* 1, no. 1 (June 1938).

8. Siegel and Shuster, *Action Comics* 1, 13.

9. Richard Reynolds, *Super Heroes: A Modern Mythology* (Jackson: University Press of Mississippi Press, 1992), 10.

10. Wright, *Comic Book Nation*, 17–18.

11. Coogan, *Superhero: The Secret Origin of a Genre*.

12. John Steinbeck, *Of Mice and Men* (New York: Covici Friede, 1937).

13. Reynolds, *Super Heroes*, 77.

14. Bob Kane and Bill Finger, *Detective Comics* 1, no. 27 (May 1939).

15. Kane and Finger, *Detective Comics* 1, no. 27, 6.

16. Bob Kane and Gardner Fox, *Detective Comics* 1, no. 32.

17. Bob Kane and Bill Finger, *Detective Comics* 1, no. 38.

18. Bob Kane and Bill Finger, *The Batman Chronicles: Volume 1* (New York: DC Comics, 2005).

19. Brian Cronin, *Was Superman A Spy? And Other Comic Book Legends . . . Revealed!* (New York: Plume Books, 2009), 38.

20. Morrison, *Supergods*, 185.

21. Stan Lee and Steve Ditko, *Amazing Fantasy*, no. 15 (August 1962): 11.

22. Morrison, *Supergods*, 94.

23. John Broome and Gil Kane, *Showcase Comics* 1, no. 22 (October 1959).

24. Wright, *Comic Book Nation*, 183.

25. J. R. R. Tolkien, *The Lord of the Rings: The Fellowship of the Ring* (London: Allen & Unwin, 1954).

26. Coogan, *Superhero: The Secret Origin of a Genre*.

27. Douglas Wolk, *Reading Comics: How Graphic Novels Work and What They Mean* (New York: De Capo Press, 2007), 92.

28. Stan Lee and Bill Everett, *Daredevil* 1, no. 1 (April 1964).

29. *Superman: The Movie*, directed by Richard Donner (1978; Iver Heath, Buckinghamshire, UK: Warner Home Video, 2006), DVD.

30. Coogan, *Superhero: The Secret Origin of a Genre*, 31.

31. Morrison, *Supergods*, 414.

Chapter Two

The Academicization of Comics

Where Are the Superheroes?

Superheroes are the public and private shame of American comics. They're the
Peter Pan façade that refuses to grow up, the idiot cousin that the whole family
resents for being the one who supports them and brags about it. They're
omnipresent, they're eternally the same; they're the part that acts like it's the
whole.
—Douglas Wolk, *Reading Comics*

Like the superhero, the work of the comic scholar is never ending. On the
one hand, comic studies has made some inroads toward academic legitimacy.
The field has even reached a level of importance in which there is now a new
reader available: Heer and Worcester's *A Comics Studies Reader* (2009)
published by the University Press of Mississippi. However, while the medium of the graphic novel has achieved a kind of faddish acceptance, one of
the genres that helped create this form still languishes on the outskirts of
academic discourse: the superhero genre.

THE TRADITIONAL COMIC CANON

To be sure, graphic novels have gained some traction in literary studies. In
fact, there are more graphic novels being taught now in at least some English
courses across the country than ever before. However, those graphic novels
are a very select group. While only a handful of literature teachers use graphic novels in their classrooms, if you can find one who does, you'll get some
consistent answers if you ask what graphic novels they teach in their courses.
Most likely the graphic novels the teacher uses will be one of the following:

- *The Complete Maus* (2003) by Art Spiegelman
- *Persepolis* (2007) by Marjane Satrapi
- *Palestine* (2002) by Joe Sacco
- *Pride of Baghdad* (2008) by Brian K. Vaughn & Niko Henrichon
- *American Born Chinese* (2006) by Gene Luen Yang
- *A Contract with God* (1978) by Will Eisner
- *Jimmy Corrigan: The Smartest Kid on Earth* (2000) by Chris Ware
- *Watchmen* (1986) by Alan Moore and David Gibbons

Though not exhaustive, we would argue that the above list, for all intents and purposes, represents a canon of graphic novels. There are a few other major works that could possibly be added to the above list, but this represents a significant portion of the graphic novel canon being taught in the United States today. We include this list to highlight two important facts: First, certain graphic novels have achieved a level of respectability and reverence in academia, which is a promising development for the field of comics studies. Second, and much more problematic, is what is *not* on this list: superheroes.

Among the popular academic graphic novels listed above, only one book, *Watchmen*, focuses on superheroes. And although *Watchmen* is a superhero graphic novel, the goal of *Watchmen* is to deconstruct the entire idea of the superhero. To some extent, *Watchmen* is designed to rethink the superhero genre to the point of oblivion. As *Watchmen* writer Alan Moore says of his book:

> My main concern was to show a world without heroes, without villains, since to my mind these are the two most dangerous fallacies which beset us, both in the relatively unimportant world of fiction and in the more important field of politics. Human instinct seems to categorize the world continually in terms of heroes and villains. [1]

Now to be clear, *Watchmen* is a masterpiece and a graphic novel highly worthy of being taught. *Watchmen* is also one of the finest examples of superhero literature ever created. Nevertheless, because the purpose of *Watchmen* is largely to rethink the entire value of the superhero, this graphic novel does more to eliminate superheroes from the canon of graphic novels than to support their teaching. Ultimately, Moore wants us to realize how bad the world would be if superheroes existed. As Grant Morrison notes about Moore's work in general, "Moore argued that the arrival of a genuine superhuman being in our midst would quickly and radically alter society forever." [2] It's a fascinating idea to explore, but it also works against most of the superhero themes written about in the past seventy-plus years.

Thus, while *Watchmen* certainly merits inclusion in what we are, later in this volume, labeling "The Canon of Superhero Literature," we also become very worried when *Watchmen* is the only superhero book students are taught. *Watchmen*'s gritty deconstruction of the superhero genre is explored later in this chapter, but its content represents a departure from what most people would consider traditional superhero literature. And setting aside *Watchmen* for the moment, one can see that the rest of the most popular graphic novels taught in academia all fall outside the realm of superheroes. These other graphic novels are what the art critic Douglas Wolk labels as "art comics."

Wolk defines the term "art comic" in his book *Reading Comics: How Graphic Novels Work and What They Mean*. According to Wolk, "As an art critic, I can (tautologically) describe [an art comic] as the kind of comic I find it most fruitful to discuss critically."[3] Since Wolk has a vote in the annual Eisner Awards (the comics equivalent of the Academy Awards named after the legendary comic book writer and artist Will Eisner), Wolk is certainly a credible expert in the field of graphic literature. What is surprising about his approach to comics is the way he so ardently separates art comics from superhero comics. While Wolk never specifically says he disapproves of superhero comics, his book certainly devalues the form. One can't help but feel that Wolk is somewhat ashamed of even having to consider superhero comics at all in his book on graphic novels.

Wolk isn't alone in his dismissal of superhero comics, either. Martin Baker's 1989 book *Comics: Ideology, Power and the Critics* doesn't even mention superhero comics. It's rather disappointing that a 256-page book about comics doesn't even mention in passing the impact superheroes have had on the comic book form. It is also troubling that the highly esteemed comics scholar Scott McCloud also generally ignores superhero comics. Scott McCloud is renowned for his work on graphic novels and comic art in general, and McCloud's book *Understanding Comics*[4] has been cited ad nauseam in academic circles as the premiere text for learning how to read and understand comic books and graphic novels. There is no doubting the brilliance and style of Scott McCloud's work; writing about how comics function using a comic book format is quite revolutionary. Additionally, McCloud's work was a pivotal early part of the struggle to make graphic novels more accepted within academia. Even though McCloud's work is commendable, he makes a point of singling out the superhero genre as something shameful: "I've been trying to understand comics for about 15 years. Here's what I've come up with so far. The first step in any such effort is to clear our minds of all preconceived notions about comics. Only by starting from scratch can we discover the full range of possibilities comics offer."[5] The visual that goes along with this narration is a huge panel where Scott McCloud's avatar is standing in front of a vast array of small panels, each depicting a popular comic book character. Sure, there's Archie, Bugs Bunny,

Betty Boop, Blondie, and other Sunday morning staples, but the overwhelming majority of characters present are superheroes. It appears, from the illus-
tration, that McCloud feels superhero comics are a limitation, so he wants
readers to clear superheroes out of their minds.

Claudia Goldstein further contributes to the differentiation many scholars
make between comics worthy of academic study and comics that are strictly
for entertainment. Goldstein's commentary on the subject is geared more
toward art theory and history than literary or English studies. As many scholars do, Goldstein works from the premise that only certain comics are worthy
of serious study: "I ask the class to consider whether all comics are art, or
whether, as intelligent readers, we can begin to distinguish the truly interesting, thoughtful, and creative comic artists from the hacks."[6] While Goldstein
never specifically mentions superhero comics, her distinguishing between
tiers of comic book art is itself quite interesting. There have always been
distinctions made by scholars about art quality, but the natural subjectivity of
that distinction has been artificially standardized. The same could be said for
the traditional literary canon as well, where the value of texts has already
been predetermined through years of repeated usage of certain standard texts
in public schools and universities.

Peter Coogan attributes the lack of academic respect for superhero texts
to the basic characteristics of the superhero genre. Specifically, the genre of
superheroes is, according to Coogan, perceived as a subgenre instead of its
own genre with all the inherent dynamics thereof. In regard to superheroes
and genre, Coogan says, "Despite the attention currently given to superheroes, the superhero genre is little studied. Typically, it is either taken for
granted or dismissed as a genre and marked as a subset of other genres—
science fiction primarily."[7]

As one can see from all of these critics, superhero literature is relegated to
the lowest tiers of artistic and literary recognition. So although studying
graphic novels has become more in vogue within the academy, this trend of
examining graphic novels remains generally limited to the kind of "art comics" that interested Wolk. Superhero stories remain under-studied and devalued. Instead, if a literature teacher chooses to use a graphic novel to teach a
course, he or she usually turns to the kind of graphic novel that meets academic approval, a graphic novel like the award-winning *Maus*.

THE "IMPORTANT" GRAPHIC NOVELS

Maus is the one graphic novel above any reproach. It is a literary masterpiece, untouchable by any critic. If ever there was a comic that was the "part
thinking it was the whole" as Wolk puts it, this is the one. As the first and
only graphic novel to win the Pulitzer Prize,[8] *Maus* has become common

reading for many high school and college students alike who take literature survey courses where the professor adds a graphic novel to the reading list. Art Spiegelman's epic anthropomorphic story of the Holocaust (where the Jewish people are drawn as mice and the Germans are cats) was split into two parts with the first depicting the author's grandfather hiding from the Nazis in *Maus I*, and surviving a concentration camp in *Maus II*. No one would dispute the power of this text, and its visuals depicting the horror of the Holocaust are as heartbreaking and shocking as many of the other premiere texts on the subject such as Elie Wiesel's novel *Night* or Steven Spielberg's film *Schindler's List*.

The major aspect of *Maus* that completely differentiates it from other graphic novels is the predominant opinion in academia that *Maus* is one of the few (if only) graphic novels worthy of being termed literature. What is meant by literature in the case of a graphic novel is, well, not actually quite clear. In Christian Chun's article "Critical Literacies and Graphic Novels for English-Language Learners: Teaching *Maus*" from *The Journal of Adolescent and Adult Literacy*, Chun discusses how *Maus* could be used with ELL students. Chun's article has excellent insight into how using a visual medium such as comic books could be beneficial to students who are learning a new language, but even as Chun elevates the value of *Maus*, he simultaneously dismisses all the rest of graphic literature. Chun says *Maus* "achieves the status of literature with the complexity of its theme, the subtlety of its characterizations, the visual metaphors expressed through its composition, and its seriousness of purpose."[9] Again, it needs to be stressed that *Maus* is an extraordinarily rich text with important symbolism and historical significance. What also needs to be stressed is that *Maus* is one of a very select few graphic novels that literary scholars ever praise.

Gerard Jones even mentions *Maus* as an exceptional piece of comic book history: "In *Maus* he (Spiegelman) wove together the threads of junk culture, satire, fine art, and Jewish history to create the first comic book that fans and literary critics alike agreed was a significant work of art."[10] Within Jones's praise of *Maus* is the implication that most comic books are not significant works of art. Of course comic book fans have always found value (whether it be cultural, social, or political) in comic books, or else they would not continue to read them. Yet though fans may value the medium, few academics do. Superhero comic books, particularly, have yet to prove their worth as a viable medium for academic study. Perhaps that is why when Jones says that *Maus* was the first comic to be genuinely appreciated by both comic fans and literary scholars, his statement isn't very surprising. The hero of *Maus* has no superpowers, no origin story, and no bright costume. Instead, what gives *Maus* emotional power is its raw and unforgiving display of one of the most violent and gut-wrenching atrocities ever to occur in human history.

Another well-respected graphic novel is *Persepolis* by Marjane Satrapi, which tells the story of a young Iranian girl's life during the 1979 Islamic Revolution and her family's struggles. Because it was a culturally significant text that shed light on the life of a young girl who lived through a turbulent and trying time, *Persepolis* quickly became another staple of the traditional academic's library of graphic novels. The success of this graphic novel also resulted in an animated motion picture being produced with the same name in 2007 that was nominated for Best Animated Picture at the eightieth annual Academy Awards in 2008.[11] Like *Maus*, the story of Persepolis is rooted in a historical event through the eyes of someone who experienced it. Also like *Maus*, the celebration of *Persepolis* as a piece of fine literature transcends the perceived limitations and stereotypes of its "sophomoric" graphic novel cousins.

Other esteemed graphic novels, which were mentioned earlier in this chapter but need to be presented here again, include *American Born Chinese* by Gene Luan Yang, *Pride of Baghdad* by Brian Vaughan and Nico Henrichon, *Palestine* by Joe Sacco, and *A Contract with God* by Will Eisner. *American Born Chinese* is an autobiographical story of a boy from China who struggles through school in the United States, *Pride of Baghdad* looks at the American invasion of Iraq through the eyes of lions who lived in the Baghdad Zoo and escaped (based on a true story), *Palestine* explores tensions in Israel during the early 1990s, and *A Contract with God* depicts a man's struggles with his faith after the loss of his daughter. Couple these graphic novels with the two all-stars, *Maus* and *Persepolis*, and one can see a trend begin to emerge.

The graphic novels that are typically accepted by the academy all have stories that are either rooted in historical/significant events through the eyes of a singular person/animal or are commentaries about social/cultural issues. In being elevated to the status of literature, the common thread of academically accepted graphic novels is their focus on reality and people's real-life experiences. Why are stories of reality more valued than those of fantasy when it comes to graphic novels in academia? What are the ramifications of celebrating only one type of story from a medium that is much more heavily indebted to a much different type of narrative?

Imagine studying society, culture, history, or any other field through the medium of television. Now, imagine studying these fields by only looking at television news and completely ignoring sitcoms, reality TV shows, and dramas. Certainly this could be done, but clearly it would give one a very skewed image of television. And while one might feel that sitcoms and reality shows are very crude forms of television entertainment, ignoring them clearly limits what a scholar could learn from the medium. The problem occurs when academics ignore superhero comics and only look at fact-based graphic novels.

Let's be blasphemous here and create a scenario that combines both the reality of academically accepted graphic novels and the fantasy of superhero comics. As it happens, this has been done already. In the comic series *X-Men*, the villain Magneto was given a backstory where he survived the Holocaust and watched his family die in a concentration camp. Even Magneto's burgeoning mutant power (creating magnetic fields and controlling metal) wasn't enough to save his family from the horrors of the concentration camps. Greg Pak and Carmine Di Giandomenico's *X-Men: Magneto Testament* explored this background story even further.[12] It's interesting to note that, despite the book's mature themes, it is categorized in the "Children's Books" section on Amazon.com.[13] Originally released as a four-issue miniseries, *X-Men: Magneto Testament* followed Erik Lensher (Magneto's real name) through his horrible experiences in a concentration camp. While a comic book fan may have expected Magneto to be tearing up Nazis with his powers of magnetism, bending the barrels of their guns and opening up the barbed wire gates of the camp, the creators instead focused on how the young Magneto's motives were heavily affected by his experiences in the concentration camp and caused him to develop his hatred for *Homo sapiens* later in life and become one of Marvel Comics' greatest supervillains.

Stan Lee and Jack Kirby's Magneto from the original *X-Men* comic book series in the 1960s was a far cry from the character who struggles with his morality in the current *X-Men* stories. Instead of having a deep backstory with emotional repercussions and societal implications, the 1960s Magneto was simply a purple-clad supervillain who possessed the power of magnetism and used it to fight an ongoing battle with Professor Charles Xavier's X-Men.[14] The experiences of Magneto in the concentration camp add depth to a character who already represents an extremist point-of-view when it comes to social equality. Because Magneto is a mutant (a person born with an X-gene that causes him to develop superpowers), he feels ostracized from society by "normal" people. He thus favors war between mutants and humans. While Magneto represents a Malcom X type philosophy, his counterpart, Charles Xavier, represents the Martin Luther King Jr. philosophy of fighting bigotry through socially acceptable channels.[15] Once a reader learns how vicious and tragic Magneto's experiences during the Holocaust were, it becomes easier to understand his aggressive viewpoints about creating social equality for mutants.

Returning to the idea of superhero comics not being valued as literature, *X-Men: Magneto Testament* appears to be a noteworthy combination of academic values in celebrated graphic novels and the dismissed elements of the superhero genre. An effective superhero story can be told utilizing both the mythology of a given character and significant historical/social issues that traditionally warrant discussion in academic settings. It is also important to note here that Pak and Di Giandomenico's Magneto story does not trivialize the seriousness or the sanctity of the tragedy that is the Holocaust. Instead, the misery of that historical event becomes the catalyst for the development of a young man into a supervillain.

Of course, *X-Men: Magneto Testament* is a somewhat rare breed of superhero literature. Most superhero stories stick to their traditional formulas and concentrate on adding to the ever-growing mythology of their characters. Superhero stories normally rely on their own traditions to strengthen themselves and further emphasize the sociocultural values they represent. Yet even staying within their normal boundaries, superhero stories still are important vehicles for exploring many important real-world issues. In his book *Supergods*, Grant Morrison addresses how he feels superheroes and realism should be intertwined:

> I agreed that superhero comics could always use a little more realism, but that didn't mean scenes of Batman on the toilet or the X-Men failing to feed the starving millions of Africa. It meant, instead, an acknowledgement that anything we could experience was by its nature real and a corresponding reflection of the idea that fiction had to behave like flesh. The presumption that superheroes could literally show us how to end hunger or poverty seemed as naïve as belief in fairies. [16]

No, superheroes can't set examples for how to end terrorism, and they would be used incorrectly if they were made to address social issues such as failing schools or economic woes. What superheroes can do, though, is present a world where sociocultural values are physically manifested in larger-than-life characters. By using super characters rooted in real-world value systems, comic writers are able to examine ideas that explore and even challenge popular cultural notions.

THE POWER OF SUPERHERO STORIES

Ideas need to be the focus when studying and analyzing stories of any kind. The power of stories to transcend any medium is the universality of the ideas presented in a given story. Take a classic example such as Harper Lee's *To Kill a Mockingbird*. While the story is technically about a young girl named Scout whose father defends an African American man in the Deep South during the Great Depression, the themes and ideas of the story are the core of its significance and value. Those themes are still relevant and reverberate today nearly fifty years after the book's first printing. Through the characters in the story, themes of race, bigotry, poverty, hope, despair, and youth are addressed and analyzed. Students across America read this book annually as part of their high school educations and for good reason. The events of the story take place in the 1930s, but the themes and ideas are timeless.

Literature's strength helps put change into perspective for humans as it brings minds back to the basics of existence. All the technology, political change, and cultural issues can never alter what the words or images on a given page literally are. Interpretations of these texts can change, but literature's influence extends beyond its initial publication period. When Jerry Siegel and Joe Shuster wrote Superman in 1938, those pages of *Action Comics #1* were literally representations of 1930s America and all its subtle nuances. Yet the character of Superman also transcended the comic's time and stretched his influence into the heart of American culture across generations. Superhero comics are simultaneously time-locked and eternal.

Batman's vow to never kill is one superhero characteristic that reflects a socio-cultural value: killing is bad. Nearly all superheroes share this value, though there are some rare exceptions. Batman's struggle with this value is particularly engrossing, however, since he does not possess any super powers. Not having powers gives Batman a disadvantage in his battles. Whenever Batman is in a fight, it's quite possible that a stray bullet or punch to the kidney could kill him. As was discussed in the first chapter, Batman did kill once upon a time, in his earliest issues from the Golden Age, to be exact. That behavior was changed by DC editor Whitney Ellsworth very early on in Batman's stories.[17] Thus, Batman never killing became a core part of his mythology and overall character development.

Despite his vow never to take a life, Batman has come close to killing. His encounters with this moral brink have become a cornerstone of his stories and are brought up on occasion to remind not only Batman, but the audience as well, that killing leads down a horrible path that even the darkest of superheroes should not dare go. One particularly engrossing story had Batman beating his arch-nemesis the Joker almost to the point of death. Jeph Loeb and Jim Lee's *Batman: Hush* depicted Batman being confronted by some of his most ruthless villains in a gauntlet instigated by an unknown antagonist. Needless to say, the Joker was one of those ruthless villains. As Batman pursues the Joker through a stormy labyrinth of Gotham City's back alleys, the Dark Knight makes a case for his frighteningly close, yet drastic, decision: "There is nothing I can do to him that would cause him the agony that he has brought upon others. But I can come close."[18] At the point where Batman is ready to literally kill the Joker for all of his crimes, Commissioner Gordon puts a gun to the back of Batman's head and brings Batman back to his senses by saying, "Batman, if you cross that line—if you kill the Joker tonight—I will lead the hunt to bring you to justice."[19]

The question becomes this: Is Jeph Loeb and Jim Lee's story of Batman nearly killing the Joker merely a story of one man dressed in a costume nearly killing another? Technically, yes. However, like all pieces of literature, value needs to be recognized beyond the literal page. Every child who grew up with Batman, in any of his diverse incarnations, knows that Batman has a moral compass that is always pointed at true north. Batman's methods may sometimes be questionable, but he always comes back to what is socially acceptable. Reading about this noble hero locked in a desperate fight with his most hated nemesis is common, and Batman always wins. When Batman gets to the point of seriously contemplating causing the death of the Joker with his own hands, then all assumptions about this good hero are thrown into a tailspin. Should Batman kill the Joker? Does Batman have that right? What would Batman killing the Joker say about us as a culture if we allowed this character to outright murder his arch-nemesis? Certainly Jeph Loeb and Jim Lee *could* write a story where Batman kills the Joker, but that would spit in the face of all precedents that the character has already established. (The topic of creators' rights and characters' precedents will be discussed in depth in the next chapter.) Instead, Batman's few seconds on the brink of moral oblivion is where this story gains its power and significance; the moral question of killing for the greater good becomes the focus of the reading of the story.

BORN AGAIN: A CASE STUDY

Superheroes, as a literary concept, explore issues of identity more than any other genre. Since so much of the superhero mystique is rooted in duality and coping therewith, examining that duality and breaking it down to its basest components can become an examination of the sociocultural perception of the superhero. Frank Miller and David Mazzucchelli's *Daredevil: Born Again* (1986) takes the superhero Daredevil and puts him through the misery of being destroyed professionally, physically, and emotionally strictly through his secret identity of Matt Murdock. Daredevil was a Stan Lee creation from the 1960s and featured the first superhero with a disability. As a young boy, Matt Murdock was blinded by radioactive material that fell off the back of a truck and hit his eyes while he was saving an elderly man from being hit by the same truck. Although it caused the loss of his sight, the radioactive material heightened Matt's other four senses to superhuman levels. This enabled him to become Daredevil. Using his natural intelligence, Murdock became a noble trial lawyer working hard-luck law cases in New York's Hell's Kitchen. He did this so that he could help people in need using both his superpowers and his legal skills.[20] Daredevil's is a typical Silver Age origin story with radioactivity doing the job of giving the character powers. Frank Miller had reinvigorated this character (who had a sketchy backstory to begin with) in the late 1970s and early 1980s[21] culminating in 1986's *Born Again* story.

Where *Born Again* shines is not with the typical formula of a superhero story but in its examination of the superhero concept through an exquisitely plotted deconstruction of the hero by his arch-nemesis. In the case of Daredevil, this arch-nemesis is the crime lord named Kingpin. Upon discovering Daredevil's true identity (Matt Murdock), Kingpin sets out to destroy Daredevil solely by attacking Matt Murdock through "legitimate" channels. Kingpin clears out Murdock's bank account, gets Murdock disbarred, gets the bank to "lose" Murdock's mortgage payments, blows up his home, and essentially drives Matt Murdock insane. The Kingpin reflects on his accomplishment saying, "He faces **poverty** and public **shame**. He will be **hounded** by doctored **tax** files, deprived of his very **home**. Survival will become his only concern."[22] Taking away everything a superhero has beyond his or her superpowers had never been done so thoughtfully before. Miller's story removed the superhero from his comfort zone. Rather than examine the hero by attacks to his physical presence, the story examines the hero's emotional vulnerabilities.

As a text to be studied, *Born Again* does not harken back to traditional literature or try to be a text that caters to an academically accepted subject. *Born Again* is not a story about real life; it's a story about a superhero. What the story does so well, though, is thoroughly explore the nature of being a superhero. In Miller's hands the artistic constructs of the superhero comic are coupled with brilliant storytelling that not only challenges the superhero as an archetype, but also actually strengthens the genre by empowering a major part of its ideology, the secret identity. This is superhero literature at its finest: taking the preconceived notions and socioculturally accepted perceptions of a hero and analyzing them through character deconstruction in order to strengthen their legitimacy. Miller himself commented on the creative direction he took when writing the story:

> I thought, "Break him down. Destroy him." And then have the real deep hero emerge. And what I thought was the winning idea was I got rid of the costume for a good long time. And so that he wasn't wearing the tights and you realized the hero wasn't the costume. The costume was just dressing around the hero.[23]

What happens when a hero who has a comfortable life is ripped from that life and forced to face an existence of destitution? As a final insult in his plot to destroy Daredevil, the Kingpin even mocks the hero by utilizing Daredevil's Silver Age catchphrase "The Man Without Fear," stating, "And I—I have **shown** him . . . that a man without **hope** . . . is a man without **fear**."[24]

Of course, eventually Daredevil is able to come back from the brink of total loss in order to defeat the Kingpin and restore the nobility of his secret identity, Matt Murdock. Though Daredevil eventually triumphed, the events of the *Born Again* story arc reverberated through the *Daredevil* title for hundreds of issues and became a cornerstone of the character's development for years to come. In more recent *Daredevil* comics, Matt Murdock's identity was published on the front pages of the New York tabloids, again throwing the Man Without Fear into another round of identity deconstruction. [25]

By taking away all of Daredevil's flashiness, Frank Miller and David Mazzucchelli brought the superhero to its barest essence. In doing so, the driving force of the story was not the literal superhero but rather the themes that the genre represents. Even though Douglas Wolk cited superhero stories as being the "private and public shame" of comics, he still recognized that, "Virtually every major superhero franchise, actually, can be looked at in terms of a particular metaphor that underscores all of its best stories." [26] Analyzing superhero stories as cultural constructs of identity, power, and heroism gives them a literary strength to rival that of many other great stories in literature.

Frank Miller has explored the idea of deconstructing superheroes a number of times. In one interview, Miller notes that *Daredevil: Born Again* was "the first of a series of works that I'd been involved with where I've looked at taking the machinery of the hero apart and putting it back together in leaner form so it was more pure." [27] His most famous work, *The Dark Knight Returns* (1986), was an analysis of Batman nearing the end of his life and donning the cape and cowl again after ten years of retirement. At the same time, Miller took a hard look at Superman and examined how Superman's "boy scout" personality might eventually be exploited to further the agendas of the United States government. Miller and Mazzucchelli's *Batman: Year One* (1987) returned to the origin of Batman and followed the caped crusader through his first year learning to be a vigilante. Just like *Daredevil: Born Again*, the story of *Batman: Year One* was unforgiving and gritty, drawing on some of the harshest realities of life in 1980s America.

SUPERHERO LITERATURE AS GRITTY DECONSTRUCTION

One of the most important contemporaries of Frank Miller was fellow comic creator Alan Moore, whose now famous graphic novel *Watchmen* was released the same year as Frank Miller's *The Dark Knight Returns*, 1986. As was mentioned earlier, *Watchmen* was a departure from the traditional superhero. Moore's story brutally critiqued the American superhero and examined how superheroes might actually work if they existed in the "real world." Unfortunately, the reality of *Watchmen* was a bit too real when it came to superheroes, and results of the story are evidence of that. Jamie Hughes points out that "the brood in *Watchmen* choose to do it (be superheroes) for much more mundane reasons—money, power, fame, or to promote their own ideology." [28] The convoluted and interconnected plot of *Watchmen* followed a group of aging superheroes that returns to action to solve the murder mystery of one of their former allies. Along the way, there are multiple reflections on their experiences, and those memories help fill in the gaps of the story as the mysteries of the superhero story are revealed. One can't really do the story justice in trying to summarize it because much of the graphic novel's brilliance is in its exquisitely plotted details.

Looking back at the list of graphic novels that are generally accepted by academia, one finds that *Watchmen* does hold a deserved place on the list. Perhaps it's the grittiness of the *Watchmen* story or maybe it's the beautiful interconnectedness of Dave Gibbons's art and Alan Moore's writing. It could be that *Watchmen* has power in its ability to so viscerally recreate a 1980s America that had lost hope. All of these reasons would be worthy of further analysis, but it can't help but be pointed out that in the world of *Watchmen*, superheroes don't work. There are superheroes in that fictional America, but the root of Moore's story is how characters such as Nite Owl, the Silk Specter, and Rorschach struggle to come to terms with the disdain that the public has for superheroes. Having already pointed out that academia doesn't value or accept superhero stories, it then should not come as much of a surprise that the one superhero story celebrated by academics, *Watchmen*, is a story about the whole world devaluing and rejecting superheroes. It's almost poetic justice: academics accept the one superhero story that gets rid of superheroes once and for all.

Still, there's no denying that *Watchmen* is a great superhero story, one of the best ever written. It also contrasted in an important way with Miller's work. Both writers used a gritty narrative style that explored the craziness that a superhero's existence might inflict upon the real world. However, in Miller's stories, the vitality of the superhero always reemerges. No matter the absurdity or the psychological damage done to the character, the superhero in Miller's stories always finds the will to endure and persevere. Even in a world that may have misunderstood the superhero, people still end up appreciating the hero's self-sacrifice. In Alan Moore's *Watchmen*, things go bad for the superheroes, and they stay that way. Moore's story squashes the happy-ending of the superhero story.

Yet although superheroes fare poorly in Moore's world, this grim fate does not befall the greatest of superheroes. It's not Superman or Batman or Wonder Woman who suffers in *Watchmen*; instead, Moore had to create brand new characters in order to tell his deconstructionist story. Moore's creation of all new superheroes for his story made it easier for readers to disconnect from the concept and examine it through an unaffected lens. For example, Moore's hero Rorschach is very much like *Batman* in terms of having a nonnegotiable style of vigilantism. However, if audiences read Alan Moore's story with Batman in it instead of Rorschach, their perceptions would be impacted by their experiences with Batman's character from their childhoods. *Watchmen* needed to be as disconnected from audiences' preconceived notions of superheroes as much as possible in order for its themes to be fully explored. As a thematic graphic novel, *Watchmen* challenges all the assumptions of superhero literature and presents a harsh world decimated by the good intentions of the superheroes within it.

SUPERHERO LITERATURE AS CELEBRATORY

While Frank Miller and Alan Moore's superhero stories are superb examples of how superhero literature can be deconstructed and analyzed, there are cases where the simplicity of the superhero story is celebrated. Dark and intense themes work well in superhero literature, but so do bright and hopeful ones. Positive stories can sometimes be difficult to find when looking at superhero literature today because as of late, "good" superhero stories have been equated with "dark" superhero stories. There's no doubt that today's more realistic superhero tales are exquisitely produced pieces of art and belong prominently in the pantheon of comic literature, but superheroes were originally intended to be beacons of hope for adults and children alike who found reality a bit too biting at times. When we watch our culture's mytho-logical characters being put through the proverbial ringer, our reflections about those stories focus on how the concept of the hero may be floundering. Deconstruction and analysis of the concept of the superhero works well for a world that has left behind its need for brightly clad heroes. But have we really outgrown our need to be saved? Positive superhero stories engage with humanity's will to thrive and endure. People endure hardships because they know things will get better, and this makes stories about success and hope vitally important to our psyches. Thus all superhero stories, whether grim and realistic or positive and fantastic, deserve scholarly consideration.

Going back again to the list of graphic novels accepted by the academy, one finds that *Maus, Persepolis, Palestine, A Contract with God, The Pride of Baghdad*, and *Watchmen* all offer harsh depictions of reality. All of these great graphic novels deal with real worlds and/or powerful themes, but none of them present a very hopeful world. *Maus* depicts the Holocaust in a powerful way, *Persepolis* highlights the struggles of living through a relig-ious revolution, *A Contract with God* highlights the self-destruction of a rabbi who loses his adopted daughter, *The Pride of Baghdad* examines the United States' invasion of Iraq, and *Watchmen* blows up the superhero through self-analysis. None of those are happy stories. The medium of com-ics, which was born out of the colorful heroes who brightened lives one dime at a time, is now predominantly recognized in academic circles only when that medium purposefully distances itself from its heroic origins in order to explore themes that more typically reflect academic concerns about social equity, the horrors of war, and the troubles of existence. Again, all of those themes are absolutely worthy of being explored through graphic novels and any other medium, but why must the academic value of the comic book be strictly entwined with getting as far away from superheroes as possible? Even as early as 1992, Richard Reynolds stated that, "It may well be (as many critics are now arguing) that the superhero genre belongs to the early days of the comic."[29] From a strictly academic point of view, Reynolds was prophetic, but from a sociocultural point of view, superheroes remain important icons even today. Superheroes are as popular now as they ever have been, and many modern stories remind readers of how superheroes can simultaneously engage and inspire.

Jeph Loeb and Tim Sale made great strides in returning to the basics of the superhero and opting to simply write a superhero story instead of breaking the character apart until the pieces could barely be put back together again. The duo's color-themed graphic novels *Spider-Man: Blue*, *Hulk: Gray*, and *Daredevil: Yellow* took the first issues of these iconic Marvel characters and rewrote them focusing on the inner monologues of the heroes to give insight into their reasoning behind their first adventures and creating a healthy sense of nostalgia. Tim Sale's art in these stories is not dark at all and actually holds true to the graphic novels' colorful titles; the art is Silver Age in style and modern in its application. Jeph Loeb's writing also harkens back to the Silver Age but artfully intertwines the inner monologues with dialogue that feels like it belongs in the Silver Age of comics. The whole series is a reflection on Silver Age characters and making sense of their early adventures for newer audiences.

There are healthy doses of reality in these stories, though. For example, the *Daredevil: Yellow* issues are framed by a letter Matt Murdock writes to a love he lost: Karen Page. The letter doesn't harp on about the tragedy of the event, however; instead, it creates a sense of closure for the character by connecting the character's memories of his love with the burgeoning vigilantism he entered into voluntarily. *Spider-Man: Blue* also focuses on a lost love, but this time it's Peter Parker and his first love interest, Gwen Stacy, who died at the hands of Spider-Man's arch-nemesis, the Green Goblin. Again, the story is about closure and coping with a tragedy. Where many of the darker superhero stories humanize these ultra powerful heroes by stripping away their comforts and barriers until nothing is left, Loeb and Sale's color-themed graphic novels take what the superhero does have and focuses on the differences the character(s) can make and why the tragedies of their lives are so important to their missions as superheroes.

Loeb and Sale took a similar approach with *Superman for All Seasons* by following the Man of Steel through the first year of donning his trademark suit and beginning his never-ending battle. The title pays homage to Robert Bolt's play *A Man for All Seasons*, and each issue of the four-issue miniseries is a season of the year. Like Loeb and Sale's Marvel comics, *Superman for All Seasons* brought Superman back from the brink of his recently depressing storylines. Only a few years earlier, Superman had been brutally killed at the hands of the supervillain named Doomsday in Dan Jurgens's now famous storyline *The Death of Superman*.[30] Superman fans needed a story where Superman wasn't lying bloodied on a pile of rubble with people crying over his decimated body. More than anything, *Superman for All Seasons* embodies the powerful nature of the omnipotent Kryptonian while capturing his human upbringing within the value system that shapes all of his actions as a superhero. The success of the graphic novel became the inspiration for the hit television show *Smallville* (2001) that likewise explored the significance of the Man of Steel's upbringing in a small Kansas farm town. From the high-tech utopia of Krypton to the humble cornfields of Smallville, Kansas, Superman captures the quest for place and purpose that are enduring human themes.

Even Brian Michael Bendis and Mark Bagley's *Ultimate Spider-Man* series, which was designed as a modern-day remake of the character, exhibited a Spider-Man much more youthful, optimistic, and genuinely happy than most of his previous incarnations. Though the series began to get darker as the years passed, initial *Ultimate Spider-Man* stories were a true throwback to the lighthearted, upbeat days of Stan Lee and Steve Ditko's original *Amazing Spider-Man* series of the 1960s. In *Ultimate Spider-Man*, Peter Parker was once again a simple high school student struggling with girls, homework, and the occasional super-powered psycho trying to blow up City Hall.

Optimistic superhero stories like Loeb and Sale's and Bendis and Bagley's seem the least likely type of narratives to make their ways into academic discussions. Earlier it was asserted that the academy likes to focus on the darker aspects of the human condition. It may be true that more questions can be asked about the actions of a character under extreme duress and pressure than about a character that seemingly has it all under control. Admittedly, it is difficult to write "happy" and not make it sound sappy. Yet happiness is as much a part of the human condition as sadness. One might even argue that it's a more important part since it's our happy moments that keep us going. However, one can't help but think that academia resists the inclusion of these sorts of celebratory stories for one major reason: the perception that happy stories, particularly happy superhero stories, are sophomoric and intended only for children.

Chapter 7 will address the impact of superheroes on children, but the common perception that superheroes are strictly for kids is likely a very strong factor in academia's resistance to the genre. There is superhero literature that is intended solely for children, and that is an audience that will always exist for the genre. Stories aimed solely at child audiences would, understandably, not focus on issues that questioned humanity's place in the world or whether heroes are necessary; that isn't the purpose of literature for children. But as was already shown, there are many, many powerful superhero stories that are not written for children. The problem, then, seems to be that superhero stories get ignored by the academy because the genre was *originally* intended for children. The growth and maturing of superhero literature seems to have been missed by too many academics.

The texts that will be presented at the end of this book as part of a proposed canon of superhero literature include texts that are geared for both child and adult audiences because developing a sense of morality and truly connecting with a character, a storyline, or a world is an evolutionary process that is ongoing. The dark and deconstructive superhero texts are a result of writers and artists reflecting on both their childhood experiences with the characters and incorporating newer, serious issues those characters can address. Without the original incarnations of superheroes, though, the early incarnations that were intended for children, there would be no *The Dark Knight Returns* or *Watchmen*. Thus this book argues for taking a very broad view when considering what superhero literature is worthy of study.

A BRIGHT FUTURE FOR SUPERHERO LITERATURE

Frank Miller once said, "In comics, in comic books, in superhero comics, people have wasted an awful lot of creative energy and hard work looking for kids who aren't there."[31] Just because superhero stories were originally intended for children doesn't mean that their value must be limited to that initial incarnation. Take J. K. Rowling's incredibly successful Harry Potter novels. Their original audience was children. From there, though, the stories matured while keeping the original, magical appeal that children find irresistible. The same has happened with comic books and superhero stories. All of the superheroes have grown from their original incarnations into socioculturally significant metaphors for power, heroism, bravery, and social justice. Clearly superheroes aren't just for kids anymore.

Consider one final example from the modern age of superhero stories, Grant Morrison and Frank Quitely's *All-Star Superman*. This story was a twelve-issue mini-series that spearheaded DC's short-lived "All-Star" concept where famous creators would team up to write stories for characters that were completely removed from the continuity of the main issues. This would give the creators absolute free reign to do whatever they wanted with the character(s) and their mythologies. For *All-Star Superman*, Morrison and Quitely wrote an end story for the Man of Steel that had him dying from overexposure to the sun's radiation, thanks to an evil plot by Lex Luthor that finally succeeded. In the story, Superman finds that the radiation gives him only one year to live, so he makes it his mission to secure the future of the world, confront his nemesis for a final time, and consummate (emotionally, not literally) his love for Lois Lane. Along the way he has to complete a gauntlet of tasks, similar to Hercules's twelve labors, which push him to the limit both physically and emotionally. The novel incorporates Silver Age references, utilizes the entire supporting cast of Clark Kent and Superman, and challenges the reader to accept a story that is both outlandishly superheroic but also stunningly emotional. Superman's final act of heroism has him flying into the sun in order to keep it burning so that the rest of the world may survive: a fitting ending for the world's greatest hero.

The value of superheroes is rooted not only in our lived experiences with them, but also in our understanding of what is generally good in our world. Our world, which is ripe with injustices of our own making, is simultaneously inhabited by fictional characters who grace comic books, television shows, and motion pictures and who constantly fight against those very evils. The value of superheroes is not only in their fictional existences but also in their creations by people who can both expose the world to injustices and help bring the world back from the brink of destruction.

THE BEGINNINGS OF A NEW CANON

This chapter has explored how superhero literature can be an effective genre through which to explore important themes that inform the human condition. Although superhero stories began as simple distractions for young children, they have grown into complex, multilayered, socioculturally significant narratives that are ripe for academic exploration.

The characteristics of superhero literature will be further analyzed in the chapters that follow. The complexity of superhero literature is one of its defining characteristics, and this makes it useful to further deconstruct and delve into the fantastic stories, incredible characters, and amazing worlds that make up that literature.

Yet what makes superhero stories most important are their effects on people, on how people perceive right and wrong, justice and injustice, power and humility, and the world, both real and imagined. Almost everything that matters to society is addressed in the pages of comic books. And yes, there are many instances where superhero stories become silly and fantastic, and even some that are absolutely ridiculous, but that is true of any genre. Not every story told can be amazing. Therefore, we need to find the superhero stories that best reflect our concerns and that give us the best glimpses of all the rich potential that superhero narratives hold.

It is for this reason, then, that this book calls for the development of a new canon of superhero literature, one that celebrates and recognizes the superhero as a legitimate and vital component of our culture. Too many years have passed with superhero stories being blatantly disregarded for their perceived sophomoric characteristics. Superheroes are strong characters that have stood the test of time, censorship, and relegation. Many of the socioculturally relevant dynamics of superhero literature are explored in the coming pages, and that relevancy leads to what needs to be done for comic studies and academic studies in general: the time has come for the superheroes to enter.

NOTES

The epigraph is from Douglas Wolk, *Reading Comics: How Graphic Novels Work and What They Mean* (New York: Da Capo Press, 2007), 100.

1. Christopher Sharrett, "Interview with Alan Moore," in *Alan Moore Conversations*, ed. E. L. Berlatsky (Jackson: University Press of Mississippi, 2012), 46.

2. Grant Morrison, *Supergods: What Masked Vigilantes, Miraculous Mutants, and a Sun God from Smallville Can Teach Us about Being Human* (New York: Spiegel & Grau, 2011), 185.

3. Wolk, *Reading Comics*, 30.

4. Scott McCloud, *Understanding Comics* (Allenspark, CO: Tundra Publications, 1993).

5. McCloud, *Understanding Comics*, 198–99.

6. Claudia Goldstein, "Comics and the Canon: Graphic Novels, Visual Narrative, and Art History," in *Teaching the Graphic Novel*, ed. S. E. Tabachnik (New York: Modern Language Association), 256.

7. Peter Coogan, *Superhero: The Secret Origin of a Genre* (Austin, TX: Monkey Brain, 2006), 23.

8. "Special Awards and Citations," The Pulitzer, www.pulitzer.org/bycat/Special-Awards-and-Citations (accessed June 25, 2012).

9. Christian Chun, "Critical Literacies and Graphic Novels for English-Language Learners: Teaching *Maus*," *Journal of Adolescent & Adult Literacy* 53, no. 2 (October 2009): 147.

10. Gerard Jones, *Men of Tomorrow: Geeks, Gangsters, and the Birth of the Comic Book* (New York: Basic Books, 2004), 328.

11. "The 80th Academy Awards (2008) Nominees and Winners," The Academy of Motion Picture Arts and Sciences, www.oscars.org/awards/academyawards/legacy/ceremony/80th-winners.html (accessed June 25, 2012).

12. Greg Pak and Carmine Di Giandomenico, *X-Men: Magneto Testament* (New York: Marvel Comics, 2009).

13. www.amazon.com (accessed June 25, 2012).

14. Stan Lee and Jack Kirby, *The X-Men: Volume 1*, Marvel Masterworks ed. (New York: Marvel Comics 2009), 1–23.

15. Henry Hanks, "The Secret to 'X-Men's' Success," CNN, http://articles.cnn.com/2011-06-03/entertainment/xmen.legacy.go_1_chris-claremont-dave-cockrum-x-men-franchise?_s= PM:SHOWBIZ (accessed June 25, 2012).

16. Morrison, *Supergods*, 220.

17. Brian Cronin, *Was Superman a Spy? And Other Comic Book Legends . . . Revealed!* (New York: Plume Books, 2009), 37–38.

18. Jeph Loeb and Jim Lee, *Batman* vol. 1, no. 614 (June 2003): 17.

19. Loeb and Lee, *Batman*, no. 614, 20.

20. Stan Lee and Bill Everett, *Daredevil* vol. 1, no. 1 (April 1964).

21. Frank Miller, *Daredevil Visionaries—Frank Miller: Volumes 1–3* (New York: Marvel Comics, 2002).

22. Frank Miller and David Mazzucchelli, *Daredevil: Born Again* (New York: Marvel Comics, 2010), 24.

23. "The Men Without Fear: Creating Daredevil," *Daredevil*, directed by Mark Stephen Johnson (2003; 20th Century Fox, 2003), DVD. Documentary on DVD Extras.

24. Miller and Mazzucchelli, *Daredevil: Born Again*, 74.

25. Brian Michael Bendis and Alex Maleev, *Daredevil Ultimate Collection: Volume 1* (New York: Marvel Comics, 2010).

26. Wolk, *Reading Comics*, 95.

27. "The Men Without Fear: Creating Daredevil."

28. Jamie A. Hughes, "'Who Watches the Watchmen?' Ideology and 'Real World' Super-heroes," *Journal of Popular Culture* 39, no. 4 (August 2006): 548.

29. Richard Reynolds, *Super Heroes: A Modern Mythology* (Jackson: University Press of Mississippi, 1992), 118.

30. Dan Jurgens and Brett Breeding, *Superman* vol. 2, no. 75 (January 1993).

31. "The Men Without Fear: Creating Daredevil."

Chapter Three

The Battle Between Fans and Creators

In 2010, *Ally McBeal* creator David E. Kelley was hired by NBC to produce a Wonder Woman television pilot.[1] This seemed like a good plan at the time. Kelley is a savvy TV producer who had already found success reaching a female demographic. Who better to update Wonder Woman for today's television audience? And update the heroine Kelley did, outfitting her in a sleek new costume that included spandex blue leggings. When a photo of the new costume was released, fans criticized the costume. As Andy Khouri of the ComicsAlliance website notes: "The costume as photographed resembled the kind of cheap, rubbery, unlicensed female superhero costumes you see brimming out of Hollywood Boulevard exotic dancer supply stores around Halloween. Although refined for the pilot itself, this costume instilled great fear and sadness in many comic book fans."[2]

Wonder Woman, even for the most casual of fans, is expected to wear blue bikini bottoms with white stars on them. So what's the big deal if they make a television show where she wears pants instead? Because, for many comic book fans, it's just not Wonder Woman if she doesn't wear the right costume. As Khouri elaborates, "geeks are prepared to forgive all manner of televisual sins. Except of course when it comes to Wonder Woman's pants, which as all ComicsAlliance readers know is probably the single most written about topic in the history of sequential art."

Why though? Is it not enough to simply read the stories and enjoy the art and writing or to watch the television show? Why do fans care so damn much whether Superman wears red underwear outside of his suit or if Spider-Man's web shooters are mechanical or organic or if Wonder Woman should wear her traditional star-spangled hot pants? To understand why, we need to first understand the fans who read superhero comics.

SUPERHERO COMIC BOOK FANS

Perhaps the most misunderstood fan base in American culture is comic book superhero fandom. Let's get it out of the way immediately: Not all superhero comic book fans live in their mothers' basements at the age of thirty and count the webbing on Spider-Man's costume for accuracy purposes. In fact, reading superhero comics has come to be more "in vogue" of late, and this has lessened the stereotype that superhero comics are only read by antisocial loners. Nevertheless, many superhero comic fans are very serious about their love of the medium, and some of that passion can even translate into fanaticism. At the same time, though, most superhero comic fans just enjoy the characters and the stories and, rather than being loners, enjoy interacting with other readers of the genre. However, it is important to establish where these limited perceptions of superhero comic book readers came from.

As far back as the 1920s and 1930s, science fiction culture was booming thanks to the growth of pulp fiction publications (as discussed in the first chapter). While many of these pulp fiction titles were "strong man" stories with the hero simply pummeling evildoers using massive arms and bloody fists, other pulp fiction titles were exploring the possibilities of science and its implications for a changing world. These "science fiction" titles were more promising in their views of humanity. Gerard Jones took an extended look at this burgeoning culture and stated, "What set them (early science fiction fans) apart was a passion for a particular packaging of mainstream anxieties and aspirations and an openness to one another's peculiarities so long as the unifying passion was there."[3] As early as the 1920s, there was a culture of reading fantastic stories and sharing that passion with others. Jones also comments that the early cultures of fandom were "overwhelmingly male, mostly middle class, mostly Anglo or Germanic or Jewish, and mostly isolated."[4] Jones's description of these early fans reflects a culture that was very insular. Even at its beginnings, science-fiction culture was a crowd that remained on the periphery of mainstream or dominant culture. In using words such as "apart," "peculiarities," and "isolated," Jones characterizes these early fans as being both pioneers of a burgeoning culture and carriers of a social burden.

Comics grew in popularity over the 1950s and 1960s, and Marvel Comics' rise in popularity only helped to establish the superhero genre as the premiere genre of the comic medium.

One also has to remember that comic books did not become a specialty item until the late 1970s and early 1980s which saw the rise of direct market comic book shops. Prior to this time, kids used to pick up comics at their local grocery stores, corner marts, soda shops, or newsstands. When they did so, these kids' decision to buy a comic was usually dictated by the comic's cover.[5] While there were pockets of fandom devoted to discussing and critiquing comic books, prior to 1980 most superhero comic book reading was viewed only as a casual pastime for children and adolescents.

What then needs explanation is how reading comic books went from being a harmless hobby to a culture of fandom and sometimes obsession. Two major factors contributed to the onset of comic culture as we know it today: the rise of Marvel publishing and the growth of the comic book shop.

MARVEL ENTERTAINMENT, LLC

Stan Lee put Marvel Comics on the map. Lee was a master of creating hype and interest. He was one of the first writers to promote his company's characters using what is now known as a "crossover." In a crossover, a character from one title appears in another character's title and the events of the story affect both characters. Lee's crossover idea was a sales bonanza, propelling Marvel readership into unheard-of spheres of completionism. For example, if you were a collector of the Incredible Hulk's comics, you wanted to read about all of the Hulk's exploits. So Lee would let you know as an Incredible Hulk reader that the Hulk was going to appear in the pages of *Fantastic Four #12* as a guest star and (Shock!) fight The Thing! Even the cover of that fateful issue shouted, "At last!!! The Fantastic Four meet The Hulk!"[6] A reader who would normally only buy his or her favorite character's comic book was now going to buy two issues that month. Marvel's crossovers were epic, too: Daredevil and Spider-Man, Captain America and Iron Man, Thor and The Incredible Hulk. The list could go on and on, and it's safe to say that Stan exhausted nearly every possibility he could think of.

Crossovers had been done before, even as early as in the Golden Age of comics. National Periodicals' (DC Comics) *All Star Comics*, for instance, featured the Justice Society of America. This team combined all of the major heroes from the company into one comic book title.[7] If a reader was a fan of Green Lantern or The Flash, they were likely to also buy *All Star Comics*, effectively doubling the number of comics a reader might buy in a given month. This team concept was revamped in the 1960s when DC created the now household name of the Justice League of America.[8] Again, the same theory applied that the readers of single character books would also buy the team title. Even Marvel had used this concept with its *Avengers* title by combining many of its popular characters on one team. These team titles were crossovers of a sort, but they never had the same appeal and verve as the limited character crossovers because the crossovers where Marvel's characters made only guest appearances in another character's title had special significance in terms of continuity. Spider-Man might reflect many issues later about the fight he had with Daredevil in an earlier issue. And Stan Lee, ever the salesman, would put a little editorial box at the bottom of the panel reminding you, "true believer," that it was back in *The Amazing Spider-Man #16* when the web-slinger had fought Daredevil, and boy, had you missed one hell of a fight if you didn't buy that issue!

With the popularity of Marvel Comics becoming more and more pronounced in the 1960s, fans were jumping on the bandwagon and picking favorite characters to follow. While fans were busy buying their favorite issues and trying to fill in the holes in their collections by trading with other kids or hoping a corner drug store still had last month's issue on its spinner-rack, Lee was adding to the collecting fire by making readers aware of stories they might have missed.

Even as early as 1962, Lee was planting the seeds of this revolutionary concept of creating a multifaceted, multilayered universe where one character's actions could affect other characters. As *The Fantastic Four* was the first superhero book that ushered in the Marvel phenomenon, Lee wasted little time hyping and connecting his new characters. Two pages into *Fantastic Four #4*, the line "THE HULK IS COMING!" sits at the bottom of the page instantly creating interest. Who is this Hulk? What does he want? Just five pages later, on page 7, "WHAT IS THE HULK??" is emblazoned at the bottom again. This continues throughout the rest of the comic: "WHAT IS THE HULK??" on page 12, "YOU'VE NEVER SEEN ANYONE LIKE THE HULK!" on page 17, and "WHO IS THE HULK??" on page 22. The anticipation rises, but the audience never gets to see the Hulk; they have to wait for the first issue of *The Incredible Hulk* to come out.[9]

As an audience nearly fifty years removed from *Fantastic Four #4*'s original publication, most people know that the Hulk is a large, green monster who loves to smash things. For audiences in 1962, however, the Hulk was a completely new and mysterious character no one had ever heard of before. Lee and artist Jack Kirby even went so far as to have Johnny Storm read the first issue of *The Incredible Hulk* in a *Fantastic Four* comic book. In a meta-textual scene, Reed Richards asks Johnny Storm, "What are you reading Johnny?" Storm replies, "A great new comic mag, Reed! **Say!** You know something—! I'll be doggoned if this monster doesn't remind me of **The Thing!**" The Thing responds, "Ver-ry funny! Gimme that mag, squirt! I'll teach ya to compare me to a comic book monster!"[10] While this scene might drive continuity purists crazy as it makes very little sense from the point-of-view of the characters in the Marvel universe, it was excellent cross-promotion for a new comic book that was premiering that same month. In addition, because Johnny Storm is the hot-headed teenage member of the Fantastic Four, his choice of reading material lends credibility to making that literary choice for the audience of adolescents reading his own story. Finally, this scene comes immediately after *Fantastic Four #4* where the Hulk's coming was hyped with bolded text at the bottom of the pages.

Lee didn't stop there with *The Fantastic Four*, though. *Fantastic Four #5* is one of the very early comic book issues that makes editorial mention of a "back issue." On page 20, Johnny Storm (The Human Torch) tells Reed Richards (Mr. Fantastic), "**Reed!** The gems were scattered to the bottom of the sea during the storm!! What if **Sub-Mariner*** should ever find them??!" The asterisk is for a footnote at the bottom of the page where Lee tells the reader, "SUB-MARINER" . . . SEE FANTASTIC FOUR, ISSUE #4, MAY."[11] This editorial note was designed to prompt a reader of *The Fantastic Four* to feel they would need to pick up that previous issue in order to truly understand the current story in his/her favorite book.

One last example of this technique involves Spider-Man and his relationship with the Fantastic Four. While Spider-Man's first appearance was *Amazing Fantasy #15*,[12] his first solo issue, *The Amazing Spider-Man #1*, was a crossover story with the Fantastic Four. Readers who bought the first issue of *The Amazing Spider-Man* in 1963 probably would have been familiar with the Fantastic Four, so the fact that Spider-Man meets the Fantastic Four instantly creates a meta-textual event where both the characters and the readers are thrown into a universe where all the heroes meet each other.[13] Fans of the Fantastic Four might have bought the first issue of *The Amazing Spider-Man #1* just because their favorite superhero team was on the cover along with Spider-Man.

In addition to all of this crossover marketing, Marvel comics in this era included extensive letters sections at the end of each issue where fans wrote in to the editors, writers, and artists of the comics offering input, praise, and criticism of their favorite stories. The dialogue initiated here between reader and creator has not subsided since.

Take *The Amazing Spider-Man*, one of Marvel's most popular books. In the letters section of *The Amazing Spider-Man #25*, a fan wrote to Stan Lee inquiring about the flow of Spider-Man's character through several stories:

> Dear Stan and Steve,
> There is one thing I don't understand, and that is, in one issue, Spider-Man is a hero and is liked by everyone and in another, he is disliked and people fear him as though he were a villain. This happens about every other issue. An example of this is in issues #20 and 21. In #20 Spidey is liked and in #21 Spidey is disliked. I would like to know why.
> Lowell C. Morris, III, 5101 No. Cypress, Kansas City, Mo. 64119

This faithful reader takes the initiative to question how his favorite character is being treated, and Lee, always the humorist, answers the fan's question in a witty (and probably honest) fashion:

> *Okay, Lowell, maybe some of our frantic fans will write and tell you! (And, when they do, drop us a line and clue us in, huh?)*[14]

For a fan to be so aware of a character's personality and characterization would imply a consistent readership that was emotionally invested in the exploits of his favorite superhero. Even more interesting is the expectation that Lee and artist Steve Ditko would answer his letter; readers knew that the creators genuinely cared about what they thought about their characters. The creators at Marvel received thousands of letters, so the chances of being published would have been quite slim. However, the connection between reader and creator is evident in the style of the correspondence. And sometimes the letters sounded like two friends joking with each other, such as this example from *Daredevil #21*:

> Dear Stan,
> Marvels are great! Never again will I read Brand X nonsense. I'm also glad to report to you that most of the guys in our dorm are now reading Marvels. The only problem is that we all get arrested every Thursday (when the new comics are put on the rack at the drug store) for inciting a riot! Then we all take what Marvels we can beg, borrow, or steal, and read them in our cells. Keep up the good work! Oh, by the way, the unanimous favorite here at Andrew College is Daredevil, so keep turning out more and more of him. Spidey is also a chosen favorite.
>> Johnny Blanton, Box 7, Andrew College, Cuthbert, Ga.
>
> *Glad to hear it, John—and if you ever need anyone to post your bond, just whistle for your ever-loving bullpen!* [15]

A generation of comic book readers raised on a healthy diet of Stan Lee's encouraging the buying of "back issues" and soliciting of fan reaction had resulted in a group of young men and women trying to complete sets of their favorite characters. Given that there weren't many (if any at all) comic book shops in the 1970s, collectors of back issues had to get in touch with one another through comic book ads or small conventions where collectors traded and bought comics. As Bradford Wright describes early fandom, "During the 1970s, however, fan culture became a cottage industry in and of itself, complete with proprietary and factional divisions. . . . The disregard that much of the public held for comic books became, in this respect, the secret weapon that saved them from oblivion." [16] It is also important to note here that the young men and women who had read comic books in the 1950s and 1960s had by now become working adults who had incomes that allowed for purchasing comics far above their original cover prices of 10, 12, or 15 cents. In response to this growing demand and the fact that many fans and readers had become adults, comic book shops began opening in the late 1970s to cater to the interests of these maturing fans.

COMIC BOOK SHOPS

What started initially as meeting places for a few fans has become the cultural phenomenon known today as the comic book shop. This was a specialized market for collectors to find back issues and talk about their favorite stories with other fans. In addition, comic book shops became the sites where the market prices for back issues were determined for years to come. In the early 1980s, comic book companies became aware of this burgeoning industry and began selling their comics directly to the comic book shops.[17] Even today, if you buy a comic book from a book store such as Barnes & Noble and compare it to a comic you buy from a comic book shop, you'll notice that under the barcode of the comic book shop's copy are the words "Direct Edition" or "Direct Market." By getting issues earlier than their newsstand counterparts, comic book shops are given incentives to try to attract readers to buy through the shops instead of the traditional grocery store or drug store.

With comic book shops, a culture of collecting new and old issues was created that is as unique as the characters in the comics who don the capes and cowls. The phenomenon of comic book shops has not gone away either. Even with the comic collecting bubble bursting in the mid-1990s due to market saturation and constant publication gimmicks,[18] comic shops were nevertheless able to evolve from the collector's clubs they had been in the 1980s to the socioculturally significant forums for a unique community of readers they are today. Recently the AMC Network has even launched a reality TV series called *Comic Book Men* that focuses on day-to-day business in Jay and Silent Bob's Secret Stash, a comic book shop in Red Bank, New Jersey, which is owned by comic book writer and filmmaker Kevin Smith. Not surprisingly, in one episode Stan Lee even drops by for a visit.[19]

From Lee's early encouragement of readers to buy more comics, to comic shops providing the means to do so, fans became invested in the medium, the characters, and the mythologies both emotionally and financially. And that key word, investment, brings us back to the point at hand: Why do fans care so much about these characters and mythologies that they sometimes openly and vigilantly challenge creative decisions about the characters made by writers and artists?

INVESTMENT

Sure, fans are financially invested in their favorite characters. At $2.99 an issue and over $10.00 for a single movie ticket, a collector/reader/fan has to be. But the financial aspect of fandom has always been present and always will be. Most fans won't complain too much about the price as long as the story and visuals are of a high quality. Where the fans' passion truly comes from, however, is the longtime connection the audience has with the character(s). Most dedicated comic fans have grown up following the adventures of their favorite characters. A kid may not be literally punching the Red Skull and foiling the Skull's plot to hit the United States with a cruise missile, but the kid reading that story definitely has pictured him- or herself as Captain America. That passion never really dies. Instead, over time this passion and connection evolves into a respect for the character, the character's original creators, the character's history (both fictional and nonfictional), and that character's influence on culture. So when that same reader who grew up with a character like Captain America finds out that Marvel plans to kill America's super soldier, he or she can't help but feel personally affected by that decision.

Marvel did indeed kill Captain America in 2007. Ed Brubaker and Steve Epting wrote and drew the story in *Captain America #25*, and it was a culmination of their twenty-five-issue run on that title as well as of Marvel's event mini-series *Civil War*. In the *Civil War* story, Captain America openly resists legislation that would require all superheroes to register with the American government and operate on the government's behalf. The concept of having superheroes fight over their beliefs as self-appointed vigilantes was quite original, and the story works very well until Captain America uncharacteristically starts crying during the final battle and decides to surrender, having decided he has crossed a line and is no longer protecting the American populace he had set out to serve.[20] By giving himself up to the authorities, Captain America must then answer for his crimes against the American government. In *Captain America #25*, Steve Rogers (Captain America) is walking up the steps of the courthouse where his trial will take place when he is assassinated by an unknown assailant.[21] The scene is an undeniably powerful and emotional piece of comic art, but some fans couldn't help but feel cheated by the event.

Brubaker and Epting are certainly credible creators, and their storytelling is among the finest in the industry, but do these creators have a right to kill a character that is older than them, has more cultural significance than them, and has inspired generations of readers? For some readers and fans, the answer to that question is "No." The issue of major deaths in comic books will be explored further in chapter 9 of this book, but it is also relevant here to the question of what rights creators have to take liberties with characters who have existed beyond the creators' tenures.

One particularly engrossing clash between fans and creators was a death story actually instigated by the fan base itself. The death of the second Robin, Jason Todd, was an event that was literally begged for by the fans of Batman. The original Robin, Dick Grayson, had recently left Batman as sidekick and changed his superhero persona to Nightwing.[22] Grayson left because he felt he and Batman had insurmountable philosophical differences. The departure of the Boy Wonder made sense given the newer and darker direction Batman was going in during the late 1970s and 1980s thanks to Denny O'Neil and Neal Adams's reinvigoration of Batman in the early 1970s.[23]

As absurd as it might sound, Jason Todd was originally given a nearly identical origin story as Dick Grayson. Like Grayson, Todd also came from a circus and had a family that was killed.[24] Bruce Wayne took the young Todd in and gave him a chance to be the new Robin. This was all before the *Crisis on Infinite Earths* mini-series occurred in which all of Jason Todd's backstory was rewritten. (*Crisis*-type events will be discussed further in the next chapter.)

As part of the reimagining that DC promised through the *Crisis on Infinite Earths* story, Jason Todd was reintroduced in the new continuity as a street-smart kid whom Batman caught trying to steal the wheels off the Batmobile.[25] Batman then takes the young man into his care the same way he did with Dick Grayson. The major difference this time was that the new Robin was, as many readers perceived him to be, a jerk. The dynamics of the Batman and Robin relationship were redefined to include brazenness on the part of Robin, frustration on the part of Batman, and disagreements that nearly resulted in fist fights between the two heroes. Jason Todd was a far cry from Dick Grayson, and the editorial staff at DC heard about it. Letters flooded the offices from fans requesting that the character either be killed or, at the very least, stripped of his Robin title and privileges.

Denny O'Neil, then the editor of DC Comics, came up with an unprecedented way to decide the fate of the second Robin: The fans would literally vote on whether Robin would live or die. At the end of *Batman #427*, fans were given two telephone hotlines they could call, one for if they wanted Robin to live and the other for voting to finish him off.[26] The votes from readers resulted in the demise of the new Boy Wonder: "The final tally ultimately went against Jason Todd by a margin of only twenty-eight votes."[27] This precedent extends beyond superheroes and even beyond comic books. No other genre had ever given its fans such creative control as to decide the fate of a singular character and thus dictate the creative decisions of a publisher. O'Neil reflected on the fate of Jason Todd by saying, "The immediate effect it had on me was it changed my mind about what I was doing for a living. I thought I was a writer/editor working in this odd little literary backwater. Coming off of that experience I realized I am the custodian of modern folklore."[28] As a creator, O'Neil felt the pressure of his position on a professional as well as a cultural level. Having the authority to dictate the course of events for characters that readers felt they had ownership of gave O'Neil an imposing sense of responsibility.

The biggest surprise here may be that DC caved in to reader demands in this public fashion. DC could have just killed Jason Todd in a story without having the fans vote on his fate. Instead, having readers vote became an embodiment of the power of comic book fans and the symbolic investment of fans in their beloved (or hated) characters. Fans indirectly wrote the story of Jason Todd. Frank Miller said of the event, "*A Death in the Family* should be singled out as the most cynical thing that particular publisher has ever done. An actual toll-free number where fans can call in to put the axe to a little boy's head."[29] As Frank Miller is a creator, his reaction to the event is reflective of a creator who finds fault with the ongoing discourse between fans and creators.

Fans of superhero comics have surprising influence with comics publishers, perhaps more influence than fans have with any other entertainment form in America. Is that a good thing, though? The major problem with giving fans influence over creative decisions in any entertainment medium is that different fans often want different things. When Superman married Lois Lane in the early 1990s,[30] some fans loved it, and some fans hated it. When Spider-Man donned his black suit for the first time in the 1980s,[31] some fans loved it, and some fans hated it. When Bruce Wayne was temporarily replaced with Dick Grayson as Batman (twice),[32] some fans loved it, and some fans hated it. The list could go on because so many creative decisions go into every comic. But one force has done more to call into question the creative decisions of superhero comic publishers than any other: fan postings on the Internet.

THE WEB OF FANDOM

As fandom has moved to the Internet, it has evolved into one of the most powerful tools for influencing superhero stories and their creative directions. With the original fan letter sections printed at the end of older comics, editors were able to censor, edit for content, or completely ignore opinions of readers writing to the publishers. On the Internet, editors have no ability to filter. Letters sections weren't really revolutionary when they arrived in comics because newspapers had been publishing letters to the editors for most of their existences. Comic book letter sections were held in high esteem by fans, though, and actually getting one's letter published was an accomplishment worthy of sharing; it meant that your opinion was well thought-out enough for the editor to consciously and actively put it in the comic magazine. Comic fan letter sections were a forum for mature (for the most part) and spirited debate, praiseworthy feedback, and constructive criticism.

The Internet is great for shopping, finding movie times, checking sports scores, and getting DVDs for dirt-cheap. What it is not great for is gaining measured feedback on the latest editorial decisions of famous comic publishers. The way the Internet works in regard to fans commenting on superhero entertainment is that fans either go to message boards (which can be provided by the publishers themselves) and post comments, or they can go to comic news and fan sites and write their comments at the bottom of the news article in the "Comments" section. Unlike the fan letters in old comic books, the reactions from fans on Internet message boards or comments sections are often true and pure emotion. There is no filtering here. Filtering is for wimps. On the Internet, people feel, if you don't like it, just up and say, "That idea is a piece of #^&%." Is this fair? From some fans' standpoint it is because of the investment these readers have made in the stories. From a creator's standpoint it probably isn't because creators work hard to develop stories they believe fans will enjoy. One thing the Internet does do is that it provides a forum for fans to voice a wide range of reactions to comic storylines, whether those reactions are supportive, questioning, highly critical, or even outright rude.

Comments from readers on the Internet are also extremely relevant in regard to when a comic is published. In the past when letters were written to the publishers and printed in the back of comic books, the comments for a particular issue might be two to three months removed from the comic's initial publication. If you commented on *X-Men #15*, you might not see the comments about that issue until *X-Men #17* or *#18*. With Internet commentary from fans, reactions sometimes arrive months *before* an issue comes out. The influence of fans on superhero stories doesn't end in the pages of comic books either. Since superhero characters have transcended the traditional borders of glossy comic book pages, movies and television shows also now bear the brunt of superhero fans' opinions.

PUBLICLY ENGAGED MEDIA

Most media generates feedback. This feedback is very important on a basic level because it indicates that there is public interest in the media product. Television shows, movies, radio programs, magazines, comic books, and Internet sites all can generate dialogue between fans and that medium's creators/contributors. With superhero fans, that dialogue is crucial to the success of a franchise or a given incarnation of a superhero and his/her stories, and much of this dialogue occurs on web news sites for comic books.

Since mainstream news outlets still predominantly do not recognize comic books as newsworthy, the Internet has become the primary source for news regarding the comics medium. More recently, there have been examples of popular outlets mentioning comic book news such as the cable network G4's *Attack of the Show* news show, but even that is still a very specialized news source. *USA Today* does occasionally run stories about publishing-related events, such as when DC Entertainment launched The New 52, but again, these stories are still few and far between.[33]

Newsarama,[34] Comic Book Resources,[35] and Superhero Hype[36] are popular comic book news sites on the Internet. In addition to exclusive previews of upcoming issues, these sites do Top 10 (or Not Top 10) lists about comic books, conduct interviews with creators about their past and upcoming works, and provide coverage of important conventions such as the New York Comicon and the San Diego Comicon. What these websites also do is provide comment sections for fans to react to news stories. Even more than the message boards provided by the publishers themselves, the comment sections for these comic book websites provide some of the purest fan reactions to superhero comics, movies, and television shows available.

The purity of these comments generally stems from the initial reactions fans have when reading comic stories or news feeds. Message boards and forums provide great venues for reaction, but there is still a degree of filtering that goes on due to some messaging boards requiring a registration of some sort with a consistent username. Additionally, some forum posts are subject to editing. Comments sections provide no such filtering. A quick look at some of the postings about that recently proposed Wonder Woman television series can show just how unforgiving some fan commenting can be.

WONDER WOMAN PILOT

As discussed in this chapter's opening, as part of the hype for the proposed live-action Wonder Woman show, in 2010 a photo of the actress Adrianne Palicki as the warrior princess was released. Much to the dismay of many fans, the actress was wearing blue pants along with blue boots. This was a major break from blue bikini bottoms with white stars that Wonder Woman had traditionally always worn. For superhero fans, the change in uniform was a major deal as it highlighted the beginning of a new chapter in Wonder Woman's story.

Fans place a significant amount of value on the costumes/suits/uniforms superheroes wear. Not only are costumes a major part of a hero's continuity (more on this concept next chapter), they also are part of a character's tradition. When Lynda Carter played Wonder Woman in the 1970s television show, she wore the traditional Wonder Woman suit. For seventy years Wonder Woman wore her traditional costume. Then a television show was developed where the character, who for seventy years had looked the same, was slightly tweaked.

On the website Super Hero Hype, a news story about the new Wonder Woman show was published on March 18, 2011.[37] The following comments (which have not been edited for content) are from fan postings on March 18, 2011, reacting specifically to that article:

Eisbergsalatsus: Oh my g........ holy f**king s**t WHAT IS THIS!?!?!? XDDDD
This looks like a f**king stupid halloween costume! XD
These pants . . . that's really too much for my heart XD

Bobo: That's so bad that it's actually funny. I've seen better stuff walking around at conventions. The above brings up a good question. Which crap show will have received the most shows to hit air before it's canceled with extreme prejudice The Cape or Wonder Woman.

Just awful.

lopez: EPIC FAIL!!!!!!!

Alex Darko: She's hot but i hate that they chose the pants look instead.

Heem: Thats a joke right ahhaha!? This is a joke right? Right?

Christopher: This rocks. Love it!

Our Time Has Co: Yea totally looks like a crappy Halloween costume, my exgirlfriends mother made a better one

Don B.: It looks better than I thought it would, but I still don't like it.[38]

These comments are representative of what a typical comment section at the end of a comic book news site looks/sounds like. There were many more comments than these, but the point is that the fans displayed their displeasure immediately and with extreme prejudice. All the pure emotion that is connoted in these comments is genuine because the comments are fans' immediate reactions to learning about the costume change.

It's extremely important to note that the specific story for the television show was not revealed in the article, only that the woman playing Wonder Woman would be Adrianne Palicki and that this was a preview picture of her in her superhero costume. Therefore, all subsequent comments were regarding the aesthetics of the character and not her personality or the storyline.

There is also an important postscript to note concerning the Wonder Woman pilot. The show was never picked up by NBC or any other network, meaning the pilot that was produced was the only episode of the television show ever made. Super Hero Hype again published a news story about this development on May 12, 2011, saying, "With NBC declining to give the go-ahead, it is unlikely that the comic book adaptation will see the light of day as a series."[39] Again, fans reacted the same day to this piece of news:

pernangchur: yes! f**k YOU

robert: it's because the show looks like a joke!!

Batfan86: This is great news! Everything about this show was wrong from the start.

BCL: Man . . . cancelled before it even got the air . . . no one wants that on their resume. Oh well . . . the costume sucked anyway and it sounded like they were gonna screw up the story. I think it was a good thing! Now maybe they take their time and do it right!

Q: thank hera! [40]

At this time, only the pilot for the Wonder Woman show exists. It can be found on the Internet by using a search engine and looking for "Wonder Woman Pilot." Even more enticing is getting the DVD of the pilot at a comic book convention. A staple of many conventions, dealers often have available for sale stacks of DVDs from television shows or movies that haven't been officially released at major retail outlets. As for the Wonder Woman pilot, it has become one of those shows you'll see at a dealer's table at conventions. And for the record, Wonder Woman's costume was changed halfway through the filming of the pilot due to fan response. When her costume was changed, it went back to the traditional blue bikini bottoms and the tall red boots. However, neither the new costume nor her traditional one was powerful enough to get Wonder Woman back on the air.

TEENAGE "ALIEN" NINJA TURTLES?

An entertainment staple of many children who were born in the 1980s was Teenage Mutant Ninja Turtles. Created by Kevin Eastman and Peter Laird in 1984,[41] the Ninja Turtles were originally conceived as a parody of Frank Miller's legendary run on *Daredevil* only a few years earlier.[42] While the Teenage Mutant Ninja Turtles may not be considered "superheroes" by some fans, they're still major players in the world of popular culture.

In 2012, Michael Bay, the man who directed *Transformers* and its sequels, announced that he was going to produce a live-action reboot of the Teenage Mutant Ninja Turtles.[43] Live-action movies of these characters had been made before, most notably 1990's *Teenage Mutant Ninja Turtles*. However, when Michael Bay announced this new film to a crowd at Nickelodeon Upfront, an annual presentation by the cable network to announce new shows and films, Bay stated that the traditional origin story of the anthropomorphic turtles would be changing: "These turtles are from an alien race, and they are going to be tough, edgy, funny and completely loveable."[44]

The key word in Michael Bay's quote was "alien." Traditionally, the Ninja Turtles were baby turtles that were accidentally dropped into a storm drain by a young boy. In the sewer, the turtles encountered a mutagen that affected their physiology. They were found by a rat named Splinter who was also affected by the mutagen. Having been the pet rat of a Samurai warrior, the rat knew martial arts and taught the turtles how to fight. Additionally, the turtles were given the names of Renaissance painters: Leonardo, Donatello, Michelangelo, and Raphael.[45]

The sophomoric nature of the Turtles' story notwithstanding, fans immediately went into an uproar over Bay's announced change to the origin. As absurd as the original origin of the Ninja Turtles may sound, the heroes were a powerful force in many childhoods, and even though they weren't traditional superheroes with secret identities or super powers, they still held strong moral codes and fought evil in the name of justice. The outrage was so vehement in online communities that Michael Bay issued a statement only days after his original announcement about the film:

> Fans need to take a breath, and chill. They have not read the script. Our team is working closely with one of the original creators of Ninja Turtles to help expand and give a more complex back story. Relax, we are including everything that made you become fans in the first place. We are just building a richer world.[46]

This is the discursive relationship between fans and creators at work. Michael Bay's creative change did not match the source material, and fans of the series berated him for it. Bay's reaction to the fans also reflects a mentality that is removed from the culture of fanboys and/or fandom altogether.

While it is understandable that Bay wanted to produce a Teenage Mutant Ninja Turtles film that would be new and different for audiences, change is not something fans necessarily desire. The concept of a reboot/relaunch will be explored in depth in the next chapter, but changing characters and stories, whether minor or major, can bring out the most aggressive sides of fans. Upsetting fans of an established series is also dangerous from a financial standpoint as the quality of a particular entertainment product is not as important as how much the product earns. Therefore, even though Michael Bay could make an amazing movie about the Teenage Mutant Ninja Turtles in which he gave their origins an extraterrestrial angle, if fans don't like Bay's creative decision, they can protest the film by simply not going to the theater to see it.

In fact, fans were successful in their resistance to Michael Bay's film before it was ever made. Like the Wonder Woman pilot, production for

Bay's Teenage Mutant Ninja Turtles film was eventually shut down.[47] Most interesting of all was the reasoning the studio gave for shutting down production of the film: "The issue is said to be the script."[48] In other words, the issues with production were related to the story, and while fan reaction is never cited in the article announcing the shutdown of the film's production, the fact that the script was given as the issue leaves the door open to speculation. As of December 2012, the film remains in production with a tentative release date of December 2013.

FANS AND THEIR QUIRKS

What is to be made of fan responses? Very often, fan responses are not supportive, productive, or even critical. Instead, they're often pure emotion strictly influenced by only past precedents, personal experiences with characters, and desires to contribute to a character's mythology. Douglas Wolk, who categorizes some comics as "art comics," says, "Over the last half century, comics culture has developed as an insular, self-feeding, self-loathing, self-defeating flytrap."[49] While much of Wolk's analysis of superhero comics is heavily influenced by his background as an art critic and therefore questions the importance of superhero comics in the medium of graphic literature, his commentary about fan culture does serve a critical and necessary purpose.

Fans of superhero stories want their heroes to remain static yet simultaneously dynamic; this is a paradox of profound significance. The investment that fans have in their favorite characters supports and empowers this paradox because fans have a sense of ownership about their heroes. Fans don't legally own characters, copyrights, or trademarks, but they feel they still deserve a say in how these characters are handled. The Wonder Woman pilot, Jason Todd's death, and the delaying of the Teenage Mutant Ninja Turtles film are all examples of fans exercising their ownership over these fictional characters.

There is a battle between fans and creators because fans want to be partial creators who help guide the heroes to their eventual victories. This desire stems from the human experience of which these superheroes are representative. Even changing the tiniest of details about a superhero, changes that would seem ridiculous to a casual reader or viewer of superhero stories, can set a fan off. "How dare they give Wonder Woman pants? They don't have the right to do that." Not only do creators have the creative right to give Wonder Woman pants, they also have the legal right. But when creators make aesthetic changes to characters, they disrupt a story's status-quo. Yes, DC can technically do what it wants to with the characters it owns, but the reasons for making these changes need to be very explicit for fans. With

Wonder Woman, the reasons for changing her costume were never explicitly given. Of course it could be pointed out that there should have been a good reason for giving Wonder Woman a bikini bottom and red boots in the first place. That's a fair assertion, but since Wonder Woman's appearance has been standardized for so long, that standardization now serves as reason enough for fans.

Alan Moore recently stated, "My approach to writing is never 'give the audience what they want' because the audience don't know what they want. That's why they're the audience. It is the job of any artist or writer to give the audience what they need, which is not the same thing as what they want."[50] As an acclaimed writer, Alan Moore reflects a creator's mentality when it comes to writing characters that have years of backstory and continuity issues. By trusting a creator to make decisions about a beloved character, the audience is accepting that the creator is both knowledgeable and respectful of the source material. But Moore also admitted to feeling the "weight" of these classic characters:

> I've worked on Superman, just using that character. If you're a conscientious writer, you can't help but feel the weight of myth and history that is connected. . . . These figures have real weight. They might be just made out of words and paper, but their effect in the world can be massive, if they've got the right kind of mass, the right kind of gravity and momentum.[51]

It all boils down to securing the essence of a character(s) and not straying too far from the core of the character's story. If Wonder Woman suddenly appeared wearing jeans and a T-shirt and it was made clear by the publisher that this was the direction the character was going from now on, there would be an uproar on Internet chat sites. But would it really be that big a deal? Even in jeans and a T-shirt, it would still be Wonder Woman, right? Well, technically yes. However, think of it this way: in the context of Wonder Woman's story, much of the character's power would be lost by taking away her costume. Much of her identity as a superhero is rooted in her costume both textually and meta-textually. In both the context of her fictional story and in real life, Wonder Woman's effectiveness would be diminished if she lost her star-spangled costume. Some might think Wonder Woman's suit looks ridiculous, and maybe it does. Yet, that doesn't mean her costume isn't effective as a storytelling device or as a cultural artifact. The fact that audiences can instantly recognize and connect with the signature design of Wonder Woman's costume warrants continuing to honor that design.

This ongoing tension between fans and creators is one of the most interesting aspects of superhero literature. Even though publishers and creators want to make a distinction between who owns superhero characters and who simply reads stories about them, fans don't fully honor the distinction. To fans, superheroes are a discursive construct, and that discourse sustains the relevancy of the superhero genre within the culture. Ultimately, it is both creators and fans who help maintain superhero literature as a thriving genre. So while fans and creators may not always want to work together, ultimately the two are stuck with each other.

NOTES

1. Nellie Andreeva, "Wonder Woman Returning to TV as Series Written and Produced by David E. Kelley," *Deadline Hollywood*, www.deadline.com/2010/10/wonder-woman-returning-to-tv-as-series-written-and-produced-by-david-e-kelley/ (accessed June 26, 2012).

2. Andy Khouri, "Wonder Woman Costumer from Show You Never Saw Appears on Show You Never Watch, Worn by Actress from Show You Hated," *Comics Alliance*, www.comicsalliance.com/2011/12/30/wonder-woman-erica-durance-david-kelley-trolling (accessed January 13, 2013).

3. Gerard Jones, *Men of Tomorrow: Geeks, Gangsters, and the Birth of the Comic Book* (New York: Basic Books, 2004), 33.

4. Jones, *Men of Tomorrow*, 33.

5. Dale Jacobs, "Marveling at the Man Called Nova: Comics as Sponsors of Multimodal Literacy," *College Composition and Communication* 59, no. 2 (December 2007): 180–205.

6. Stan Lee and Jack Kirby, *Fantastic Four* vol. 1, no. 12 (March 1963).

7. Gardner Fox, *All Star Comics* vol. 1, no. 3 (December 1941).

8. Gardner Fox and Mike Sekowsky, *The Brave and the Bold* vol. 1, no. 28 (February 1960).

9. Stan Lee and Jack Kirby, "The Coming of the Sub-Mariner!" *Fantastic Four* vol. 1, no. 4 (May 1962): 2.

10. Stan Lee and Jack Kirby, "Prisoners of Doctor Doom!" *Fantastic Four* vol. 1, no. 5 (July 1962): 2.

11. Lee and Kirby, "Prisoners of Doctor Doom!" 20.

12. Stan Lee and Steve Ditko, "Spider-Man!" *Amazing Fantasy* vol. 1, no. 15 (August 1962).

13. Stan Lee and Steve Ditko, "The Chameleon!" *Amazing Spider-Man* vol. 1, no. 1 (March 1963): 1–10.

14. "The Spider's Web," *Amazing Spider-Man* vol. 1, no. 25 (June 1965): 22.

15. "Let's Level with Daredevil," *Daredevil* vol. 1, no. 21 (October 1966): 21.

16. Bradford Wright, *Comic Book Nation: The Transformation of Youth Culture in America* (Baltimore: Johns Hopkins University Press, 2003), 252–53.

17. Jean-Paul Gabilliet, *Of Comics and Men: A Cultural History of American Comics* (Jackson: University Press of Mississippi, 2010), 86–87.

18. Wright, *Comic Book Nation*, 283.

19. "Stan the Man," *Comic Book Men*, TV show (AMC, 2012).

20. Mark Millar and Steve McNiven, *Civil War* (New York: Marvel Comics, 2008).

21. Ed Brubaker and Steve Epting, "Civil War—The Death of a Dream, Part One," *Captain America* vol. 5, no. 25 (April 2007).

22. Marv Wolfman and George Pérez, "The Judas Contract, Book 3: There Shall Come a Titan," *Tales of the Teen Titans* vol. 1, no. 44 (July 1984).

23. Denny O'Neil, Len Wein, and Neal Adams, *Batman Illustrated: Volume 1* (New York: DC Comics, 2006).

24. Gerry Conway and Don Newton, "Squid," *Batman* vol. 1, no. 357 (March 1983).

25. Max Allan Collins and Chris Warner, "Did Robin Die Tonight?" *Batman* vol. 1, no. 408 (June 1987).

26. Jim Starlin and Jim Aparo, "A Death in the Family, Book 2," *Batman* vol. 1, no. 427 (December 1988).

27. Les Daniels, *Batman: The Complete History* (San Francisco, CA: Chronicle Books, 2004), 161.

28. "Robin's Requiem: The Tale of Jason Todd," *Batman: Under the Red Hood*, directed by Brandon Viettei (Warner Home Video, 2010), Blu-Ray. Blu-Ray exclusive Documentary on Extras.

29. Christopher Sharrett, "Batman and the Twilight of Idols: An Interview with Frank Miller," in *The Many Lives of Batman*, ed. R. E. Person and W. Uricchio (London: BFI Publishing, 1991), 35.

30. Dan Jurgens et al., *Superman: The Wedding Album* vol. 1, no. 1 (December 1996).

31. Jim Shooter and Mike Zeck, "Secret Wars—Invasion," *Marvel Super Heroes Secret Wars* vol. 1, no. 8 (December 1984).

32. Chuck Dixon et al., *Batman: Prodigal* (New York: DC Comics, 1998); Tony Daniel and Fabian Nicieza, *Batman: Battle for the Cowl* (New York: DC Comics, 2009).

33. Brian Truitt, "DC Comics Turns a New Page This Week," *USA Today*, August 28, 2011, http://usatoday30.usatoday.com/life/comics/story/2011-08-28/DC-Comics-turns-a-new-page-this-week/50166706/1 (accessed January 13, 2013).

34. www.newsarama.com

35. www.comicbookresources.com

36. www.superherohype.com

37. SuperHeroHype, "First Look at Adrianne Palicki as Wonder Woman!" *SuperHeroHype*, www.superherohype.com/news/articles/129048-first-look-at-adrianne-palicki-as-wonder-woman (accessed June 26, 2012).

38. SuperHeroHype, "First Look at Adrianne Palicki as Wonder Woman!"

39. Silas Lesnick, "NBC Passes on Wonder Woman," *SuperHeroHype*, www.superherohype.com/news/articles/167277-nbc-passes-on-wonder-woman (accessed June 26, 2012).

40. Lesnick, "NBC Passes on Wonder Woman" (Comments section).

41. Kevin Eastman and Peter Laird, "Teenage Mutant Ninja Turtles," *Teenage Mutant Ninja Turtles* vol. 1, no. 1 (February 1985).

42. Douglas Wolk, *Reading Comics: How Graphic Novels Work and What They Mean* (New York: De Capo Press), 44.

43. Marc Snetiker, "Michael Bay Says 'Teenage Mutant Ninja Turtles' Are Aliens, Reinvents Origin Story," *PopWatch-Entertainment Weekly*, http://popwatch.ew.com/2012/03/19/michael-bay-teenage-mutant-ninja-turtles-aliens/ (accessed June 27, 2012).

44. Snetiker, "Michael Bay Says 'Teenage Mutant Ninja Turtles' Are Aliens.

45. Eastman and Laird, "Teenage Mutant Ninja Turtles."

46. Marc Snetiker, "Michael Bay Responds to Fan Outrage about 'Teenage Mutant Ninja Turtles' Alien Debacle," *PopWatch-Entertainment Weekly*, http://popwatch.ew.com/2012/03/20/michael-bay-teenage-mutant-ninja-turtles-reponse/ (accessed June 27, 2012).

47. Kim Masters, "Paramount Shuts Down 'Ninja Turtles' Reboot; Release Date Pushed (Exclusive)," *The Hollywood Reporter*, www.hollywoodreporter.com/news/paramount-shuts-down-ninja-turtles-338301 (accessed June 27, 2012).

48. Masters, "Paramount Shuts Down 'Ninja Turtles' Reboot."

49. Wolk, *Reading Comics*, 64.

50. *Inside Out East* (Air date March 21, 2008), Television show, David Whiteley and Alan Moore (BBC, 2008).

51. Daniel Whiston, David Russell, and Andy Fruish, "The Craft: An Interview with Alan Moore," in *Alan Moore Conversations*, ed. E. L. Berlatsky (Jackson: University Press of Mississippi, 2012), 119.

Chapter Four

The Comic Relaunch

The DC universe has just revamped itself . . . again. This is the second time in its seventy-year history that the DC characters, their back stories, and their mythologies have been reimagined. Altering the mythology of an entire universe of characters entails not only challenging the status quo of the given mythology but also confronting the culture that holds these characters in high esteem. As was discussed in the chapter on the battle between fans and creators, fans strongly believe they have a right to defend the integrity of the fiction they love. Since superheroes have been such an ingrained part of America for over seventy years, these heroes' mythologies have lasted through several generations of readership, thereby cementing these stories into the American cultural consciousness.

DC's announcement in May 2011[1] regarding the rebooting and relaunching of all of their titles in September of that same year set off a firestorm of controversy among fans. At that time, Bob Wayne, the senior vice president of sales at DC, sent a letter to all of DC's retailers outlining what changes would be happening. The highlights of his letter include the following:

> Many of you have heard rumors that DC Comics has been working on a big publishing initiative for later this year. This is indeed an historic time for us as, come this September, we are relaunching the entire DC Universe line of comic books with all new first issues. 52 of them to be exact.
>
> In addition, the new #1s will introduce readers to a more modern, diverse DC Universe, with some character variations in appearance, origin and age. All stories will be grounded in each character's legend—but will relate to real world situations, interactions, tragedy and triumph. . . .
>
> Some of the characters will have new origins, while others will undergo minor changes. Our characters are always being updated; however, this is the first time all of our characters will be presented in a new way all at once.

Dan DiDio, Bob Harras and Eddie Berganza have been working diligently to pull together some of the best creative teams in the industry. Over 50 new costumes will debut in September, many updated and designed by artist Jim Lee, ensuring that the updated images appeal to the current generation of readers.[2]

As has already been established, fans' tolerance for changing superhero literature and canon is often very limited. In fact, it seems fairly safe to say that practically any change to any character is generally met with resistance, often resounding resistance. DC's changes in 2011 were revolutionary in many ways, but they're also reflective of a major theme of superhero literature: the reboot and the relaunch. Comic book publishers rebooting or relaunching their titles is common to comic book fans. This phenomenon is fairly unique to comic books, though it sometimes can occur in other media like TV or movies. Even though it is quite common in the comic book genera, reboots nevertheless yield many debates; instances of controversy; and, fortunately, interesting storylines. Rebooting or relaunching a series is primarily linked to the very nature of comic book publishing, which has its roots in serialization.

THE GREAT SERIAL NOVEL

Serialization is nothing new in the world of publishing. As a concept, serializing stories makes sense for both writers and audiences. Serializing a story means releasing segments that, when combined together, create a full-length story. Almost one hundred years before comics became a major benefactor of serialization, Charles Dickens utilized this model of publication to appeal to the masses. Michael Slater, in his extensive biography of Charles Dickens, chronicled Dickens's writing of one such serial publication, *Barnaby Rudge*, as it was released over eighty-eight issues of a magazine titled *Master Humphrey's Clock*.[3]

Not only did it do wonders for his career as a writer, it allowed people to read one of his stories who might not otherwise have been able to due to the price of a typical book of the time. Dickens's stories were released weekly in newspapers, maximizing his audience and giving everyone the opportunity to experience his now legendary stories. It might take a while to complete a story (as evidenced by the aforementioned eighty-eight issues of *Master Humphrey's Clock*), but the periodicals didn't mind selling the copies because of his contribution. Additionally, the seeds of what has now become the collecting of periodicals can be seen here. People scrambled to complete sets of stories in order to have a complete collection. Missing just one part of a serialized story meant confusion, so publishers loved this as audiences would make it a point of traveling to a store to buy the next installment of Dickens's stories.

Gertrude Himmelfarb's analysis of serialization in novels also bears an uncanny resemblance to the qualities of modern comic book publishing:

> The literary effect of serialization on the structure, style, and content of novels has often been noted: the pressure on the author to produce his weekly or monthly allotment encouraging repetition, verbosity, and such stylistic peculiarities as single-sentence or even single-word paragraphs; the predetermined length of each installment requiring suitably spaced climaxes; the plot adapted to readers' reactions, a new character or dramatic episode introduced when sales began to fall.[4]

New characters, quick and accessible narratives, and "suitably spaced climaxes" are all characteristics of superhero literature and comic books in general. Comic books came after the period that Himmelfarb is analyzing, but it is clear that superhero literature and comic books borrow liberally from the culture of serialization. Even as early as the 1800s, audiences demanded that their stories stay entertaining and fresh but also recognizable.

Comic books were born out of this publishing culture due to their roots in pulp fiction. Pulp publishers followed a serial formula releasing stories of the same characters every month and selling them at a dime apiece. It's no surprise to find that most of the comic book publishers started out as pulp publishers. Historically, the reason for superheroes' stories being released in a monthly magazine format is due to their roots as pulp fiction.[5]

However, when superheroes were created in the late 1930s and early 1940s, they weren't expected to have a strong cultural influence. The early comic book superheroes were meant to be, as a title of the time put it, "fun" (*More Fun Comics*). To quote from one of the pioneers of comics studies, Scott McCloud, "When I was a little kid I knew EXACTLY what comics were. Comics were those bright, colorful, magazines filled with bad art, stupid stories and guys in tights. I read real books, naturally. I was much too old for comics."[6]

In the 1960s, however, Stan Lee began writing comics and brought to the medium a sense of the real world. Lee, whose Marvel creations have since become iconic American symbols of strength and heroism, actually had grand aspirations as a writer. Gerard Jones notes that Lee "had always wanted to be more than a pulp hack. He said he'd wanted to write the Great American Novel as a young man, but he'd liked making money too much to drop his comic work long enough to write it."[7]

Lee is best known for creating the troubled real-world teenager Peter Parker who is secretly the masked vigilante Spider-Man. Like many teenagers, Peter Parker suffered immensely from loneliness and a desire to belong to a world he could never infiltrate: the world of the popular kids. But along with creating imperfect heroes came the need for developing relationships that mirrored "real life." If Peter Parker was a real person who attained spider owers through an accident, many of his relationships would be with other super-powered people. Therefore, the relationships of Marvel characters became paramount in Marvel Comics. This need for relationships was exemplified in the "crossover," which was discussed in the last chapter. Not until the 1960s and the rise of Marvel Comics did superhero stories begin to emphasize and carefully construct their own universes and logistics as a form of storytelling. DC had actually created a semblance of this interconnected universe idea during the Golden Age when it introduced the superhero team called the Justice Society of America in *All Star Comics #3*.[8] However, while the Atom, the Sandman, the Spectre, Dr. Fate, Hourman, and several other heroes were all on the JSA team, their actual interactions were usually limited to a few pages in the comic before the team split up into pairs or went solo so that the comic writers could tell individual stories. The links among the characters on the team were thus barely explored. It took Lee's writing at Marvel to really develop the concept of a superhero universe to its fullest.

THE BEAUTY OF THE UNBEATABLE SUPERHERO

Stories can only go on for so long. Even the longest of fictional stories, the great epics, have beginnings and endings. This is not true for superheroes, however. The story of the superhero never ends. Batman has been fighting crime ever since he put on his batsuit in 1939's *Detective Comics #27*. As a medium that was produced cheaply and was originally designed to sell to as many children as possible, comic books became a form of storytelling where true beginnings and endings did not occur. Each issue's story started and finished, but the superhero always had to survive that story so that he could reappear (and be available for sale) the next month. Superheroes did not age, did not change, and did not waver from their moral dedication to doing good. In this way the superhero becomes a timeless mythological figure.

Even as early as 1972 Umberto Eco, an influential Italian writer on culture and semiotics, saw Superman as a character whose strength came from his ability to exist in a world where time was fixed. Eco noted that Superman's world never changes. Superman keeps fighting the same fights over and over with only the most minor of changes in the details. The world always needs saving, and Superman is always there to save it. As Eco observes, "The mythological character of comic strips finds himself in this singular situation: he must be an archetype, the totality of certain collective aspirations, and therefore, he must necessarily become immobilized in an emblematic and fixed nature which renders him easily recognizable (this is what happens to Superman)."[9] According to Eco, if Superman existed in a world where a story began and ended, he would reach "toward final consumption"[10] and possible resolution by a reader. Stories that finish cause readers to resolve the hero's life in their minds. If Superman vanquished all evil or truly died while trying, his story would come to an end. Interestingly, even "death" stories don't mean the end for superheroes either. The fact is superheroes are simply too valuable to their publishers for them to be allowed to come to an end, and that's what readers love about them. DC Comics has been publishing Superman for over seventy years and Marvel Comics has been publishing Spider-Man since the early 1960s. Neither company could ever afford to stop publishing stories about these characters, though they have killed them as we'll discuss in a later chapter on superheroes and death. For the dedicated comic reader, and even the casual fan, the beauty of Superheroes is that they are always there fighting the good fight.

THE PROBLEM OF THE UNBEATABLE SUPERHERO

While Eco's assertion that Superman's cultural strength is in his temporal ambiguity, the eternal nature of superheroes in general creates more questions than it resolves. How old is Superman? There are two answers to this. The first answer is that Superman is (at the point this book is being written) seventy-five because he was created in 1938 and it is now the year 2013. The other answer is that it is impossible to know how old Superman is because Superman isn't real. A safe bet on Superman's fictional age would be somewhere in the range of twenty-five to thirty-five years old, but there is no way to truly know. Since Superman has continuously been in publication since 1938, it would seem to make sense that he would age along with the publications. However, the writers of Superman and all other major superheroes consistently do not pin down the exact ages of these fictional characters. Comic writers deliberately keep their characters from aging, even when they have birthdays. Even Alan Moore, who had a penchant for making superheroes believable, didn't give Superman an age when he wrote a birthday issue for the Man of Steel.[11] Because Superheroes never age, it becomes impossible to end their stories. "Death" stories where a hero or even villain is killed do happen from time to time, but these deaths are never permanent (more on this in a later chapter). Most "death" stories can be interpreted as deconstructions of the heroes and their beliefs. Even the concept of "Alternate Realities" or "Other World" stories where superheroes are older already reference themselves away just by their very name: they're "alternates" and "others," set apart from the real story of the superhero. In an "Alternate Realty," Superman can grow old and pass away, but even as fans read this story, they know the real Superman will be back in next month's issue. The issue that is critical here is the never-ending nature of the superhero and why that nature is so important for both fans and publishers to recognize.

This all leads back to the concept of the reboot/relaunch. Since superheroes never end, it becomes necessary at times to start them over. Complications stemming from overlapping story arcs, diverse creators, changing audiences, and evolving cultures/societies necessitate change. For creators, this change can be invigorating because just how many times can the Flash fight Captain Cold and beat him without the story growing old? Despite the originality of the superhero genre, the monotony of the superhero story can become an issue when studying it from a sociocultural point of view. While superheroes remain important cultural artifacts that represent a society's views of moral values and heroism, superheroes can nevertheless be reinvigorated and reinvented while still remaining the beacons for good that they always have been.

THE REBOOT AND THE RELAUNCH

The phrase "reboot" originates from the terminology used for computers. [12] When a computer is not working properly, sometimes the best option is to "reboot" the computer: reload all the data and start over. This is what writers sometimes do with superhero literature. The phenomenon also happens in other media as well, and the results can instill new life into a franchise that may have lost its way creatively. The new *Star Trek* [13] film and the new James Bond film, *Casino Royale*, [14] are excellent examples of franchises that essentially started over. *Star Trek* replaced the iconic cast of the original television show (they kind of had to given the age of that original cast) with young actors and restarted the story of the Enterprise's exploration of the final frontier. The same thing happened in *Casino Royale* with Daniel Craig replacing Pierce Brosnan and starting the story of James Bond anew. Differences in the reboots went far beyond simple casting changes, however. Both movies employed styles that were completely different from their earlier incarnations, and both of them catered to an audience expecting better action and effects, more serious actors, and more emotionally significant scenes. Both reboots kept their core themes, however, and that's where the concept of the reboot becomes an important framework.

In the world of the serialized story, James Bond always has to be a British spy, Captain Kirk always has to have a good relationship with Bones and Spock, Superman must always come from Krypton, Spider-Man must always be bitten by a radioactive spider, and, saddest of all, Bruce Wayne must always watch his parents be murdered before his eyes. This is of course an extremely brief list of examples, but the essential core of a superhero must always remain the same or else a new character is created. The factors that can change are then up to the creators who initiate the reboot/relaunch, and those changes need to be carefully executed. In the film *Spider-Man* (2001) starring Tobey Maguire, Spider-Man has organic web shooters that are a result of his attained spider powers.[15] This differs from his comic book counterpart who, for his entire existence, had mechanical web shooters that he created in a lab.[16] This type of change is typical for a reboot/relaunch because it doesn't change the nature of the character or drastically alter the mythology. Instead, it introduces an alteration that would slightly impact the storytelling going forward.

If such minor components of a hero's mythology (such as Spider-Man's web shooters) are the only things that can truly change, then reboots/relaunches are really never more than reintroductions of the same characters. If something important in a hero's mythology were changed, then a reboot/relaunch might have resounding cultural implications. Reboots or relaunches need to be extensive and affect "continuity" in order to be significant. For superhero fans, continuity is everything.

CONTINUITY

When Stan Lee was beginning to incorporate the Marvel characters into each others' stories, he was planting the seeds of collecting comics as a hobby and instilling a sense of investment among readers. But something more was happening as well. Along with characters referencing one another and harkening back to adventures that occurred several issues earlier, the idea of "continuity" was created. Continuity, in the traditional sense, simply refers to the events of a story taking place in a logical and/or coherent way. This idea is not so complicated, because life moves along a logical (at least we hope) path where what one person does affects not only himself or herself but others as well. Just like real life, then, the characters in superhero literature interact, react, and grow with one another. Even though humans don't really have super powers, the crossroads that superheroes encounter in their tales mirror the crossroads that real people encounter: "Stories connect us to other people, and we have a responsibility to respond to those stories."[17] The same can be said of characters in a given universe of varying stories.

Of course it is often difficult to track our own lives and keep straight all the events, people, and places that create our unique existences. What gives lives such dynamism is that variation and change that we are both responsible and not responsible for creating. So when a genre that prides itself on interconnectedness begins to reflect a life-like web of cause and effect, problems of logic and consistency are bound to develop. Imagine one author writing a story and trying to make sure all of the events, people, and places in the story are consistent the entire way through with no mistakes. Now imagine eight different authors writing eight different stories every month and making sure the events, people, and places in each of their stories match not only the individual story the author is writing but also match all the events, people, and places included in the other seven writers' stories. And, by next month, that the eight follow-up stories match all the events from past months' issues too. These are the problems superhero comic writers have when it comes to maintaining continuity.

In an episode of the BBC science-fiction show *Doctor Who* titled "Blink," the Doctor, who is a time traveler, describes time as a "big ball of wibbly-wobbly, timey-wimey stuff."[18] This is a perfect analogy for how superhero comics work because even though everything in a given universe is supposed to be interconnected, it often isn't connected very cleanly. As comic writer Grant Morrison puts it, "in place of time, comic-book universes offer something called 'continuity.'"[19] Continuity is the interconnectedness of the characters, stories, places, and contextual temporality in comic stories, and there is so much to be maintained that continuity often becomes a big mess. At the same time, continuity is a beautiful and unique trademark of the superhero genre.

When reading a comic and seeing Iron Man or any other character refer to an event from his past, this moment of continuity is meta-textuality at its finest. Not only is the reference for the character in the story to base his future actions upon, the reference is also simultaneously an inclusion of the reader in the progression of the story. The reference helps integrate the reader personally into the story by triggering certain thoughts in the reader's mind: Do I have that issue? Where can I get it? Was that the story where . . . ? The possibilities are endless because that interconnectedness is present and utilized in comics all the time.

These days in comics, there are far fewer editorial boxes than the multitude Stan Lee used to include in nearly every reference a character made back in the 1960s and 1970s. Currently, when a superhero makes a reference to a past event, readers are expected to simply know what the character is talking about or they are left to wonder. This is similar to moments in current television shows when a character will reference what happened many episodes ago; the producer never stops the show to remind viewers that the event being mentioned occurred back in the fourth episode of the TV series. Viewers and readers have to supply their own knowledge of the continuity, which makes continuity part of the inside pleasure of being a "true" fan.

Even though superhero continuity is unique in its complexity, it is, as Richard Reynolds, claims, a necessary element of superhero mythology:

> If superheroes are to have any claim at all to be considered the bearers of a "modern mythology" and in some ways comparable to the pantheons of Greek or Native-American or Norse mythology, then this extra-textual continuity is a vital key to the way in which the mythology of comic books is articulated in the mind of the reader.[20]

For this reason, Reynolds separates continuity into "serial continuity"[21] (where stories line up), "hierarchical continuity"[22] (how characters' strengths match up), and "structural continuity"[23] (how stories can be affected by implied possibilities such as "Does Bruce Wayne have an uncle?"). Reynolds's dissection of continuity is interesting in that he includes real-life possibilities for continuity. Reynolds observes that in comic book shops across America there are fans having conversations about continuity at any given moment, and fans look forward to discussing these types of issues with other fans at conventions as well. However, the continuity that is of most importance to the present discussion is "serial continuity" because it addresses how stories literally line up with one another.

Without serial continuity, characters in a given universe would simply exist in their own isolated spheres of narrative, making "crossovers" have little to no effect going forward. In essence, continuity prevents what would be considered "stand-alone" comic issues where the events of the story have no impact on future or past events. Early superhero stories (from the 1940s and 1950s) were inundated with comics that were bound to the singular issues in which they occurred. Villains would of course return, and the heroes would recognize them every time, but the specific events of the issue were almost never referenced later.

Current comic culture thrives on the interconnectedness of its narratives. However, as has already been stated, that continuity can easily become convoluted. In fact, as early as 1985, one comic publisher realized that despite the passion of the fans regarding continuity, there needed to be some regulation of the publisher's superhero universe in order to continue having stories impact each other in significant ways.

THE FIRST SIGNIFICANT COMICS REBOOT

The *Crisis on Infinite Earths* occurred in 1985[24] and was designed to streamline the convoluted continuity of DC's superhero universe. As one could imagine, nearly fifty years of interwoven storylines, diverse creative decisions, changing artists, and evolving audiences had taken their tolls on the fictional universe that manifested itself in the monthly exploits of DC Comics' characters. For a genre that was revolutionary in its presentation of heroic themes, making editorial decisions that promoted better understanding and revamping its entire line seemed like common sense. The creators were on board with the concept, and the twelve-issue *Crisis on Infinite Earths* mini-series made George Perez a superstar creator and sold millions of copies.

Even though the series *Crisis on Infinite Earths* (what a cool name for a series!) was written and drawn in the 1980s, it was born out of the reimagining Julius Schwartz was responsible for in the 1950s when he reintroduced the Flash, Green Lantern, and other Golden Age DC characters, giving them new origins, powers, and personalities. As Bradford Wright explains in his history of comics, *Comic Book Nation*, the Flash, Green Lantern, The Atom, and others were given scientific origins instead of the magical ones used when the characters were first introduced in the 1940s.[25] In addition, the heroes' costumes were altered and the secret identities of the heroes were changed. At first, this doesn't seem too difficult to accept: times change and so do the heroes. In fact, this is one of the first events in superhero literature that resembled a reboot. Where the continuity gets convoluted is when the original Golden Age characters who had been reimagined by Schwartz were brought back to join their new Silver Age counterparts. For example, *The Flash #123* (1961) featured the Golden Age Flash (Jay Garrick) racing against the Silver Age Flash (Barry Allen).[26] For comics, characters crossing over is no big thing, but when it's one character from a new era with a new origin racing against that same character from a different era with a different origin, then things can get a little confusing.

Quite simply, how is that possible? Even by science fiction standards, the same character racing himself is bound to raise some temporal issues. This scenario, along with countless others, is why *Crisis on Infinite Earths* was initiated in the 1980s. Without getting too complicated, the idea was that there are multiple universes/Earths where the DC heroes live. Earth 1 is where the commonly known versions of Batman, Superman, and Wonder Woman live, and Earth 2 is where their Golden Age counterparts live. According to the writers, each Earth's molecules were vibrating at a different speed so that they never touched or were visible to each other. This idea was based on a theory developed by physicist Alan Guth about the existence of parallel universes.[27]

Add to this parallel universe stuff a villain named the Anti-Monitor and countless other Earths, and you have *Crisis on Infinite Earths*. The story was bombastic, it was convoluted, and it was revolutionary. Here were the seeds for what would later become the comic book "event" series where, every once in a while, the comic publishers would throw their entire superhero universes into turmoil leading to major ramifications for characters and major sales.

The *Crisis* title even stuck for DC as it reintroduced the concept in the 2000s not once, not twice, but three times: *Identity Crisis*,[28] *Infinite Crisis*,[29] and *Final Crisis*.[30] Each one of these "event" series had major ramifications for the heroes in the DC universe. They were met with skepticism by some fans and confusion by others, but, fortunately for DC Comics, excellent sales for all. In particular, *Final Crisis* by Grant Morrison and J. G. Jones pushed many casual fans to their limits by throwing the DC universe into such a drastic and overly convoluted story that one needed a PhD in DC history to follow the storyline.

Despite the complicated nature of a reboot, publishers seem to believe that this is what fans want. Fans want their superhero stories to connect seamlessly, logically, and technically. Perhaps this desire stems from the desire to validate one's own investment in the comics medium, its characters, and its stories. Reboots/relaunches may change aspects of a comic, but they also emphasize the value of both the given character and the medium. In other words, if no one cared about these characters, there would be no need for reboots at all; characters would just slowly fade into oblivion.

The implications of the superhero comic reboot extend beyond mere story, though. Altering stories and characters that have such a prominence in society can create a change not only of stories and storytelling but also a change of culture.

HOW COMIC CULTURE INSTIGATES CHANGE

It's bizarre really to think of comic culture as being one that strives for change. As was discussed before, change is what comic book fans like least, as evidenced by their disdain for simple wardrobe changes (see chapter 3). Despite this reluctance, superhero literature is an ever-evolving genre that caters to the fans more than they realize. At a basic level, fans primarily want their stories to do four things:

- make sense in the context of character's history
- link to earlier stories and incorporate those events into future tellings
- keep the core of the character(s) intact
- make temporal and literal sense (for a fantasy story)

If these criteria are met, then most fans will tend to be satisfied with what occurs next. This all goes back to the investment fans have with superhero characters both emotionally and financially. Imagine you've been dedicatedly reading a comic like *The Amazing Spider-Man* for the past five years. You've bought every issue, followed every storyline, gone through every plot twist, and then you hear that Marvel is going to change the characters in the comic drastically. While this will not directly affect your life (hopefully), it will affect both the history you've now been intimately reading about for years and the collection of comic books you've accrued. This sort of change actually happened to Spider-Man's character at the end of 2007 when Marvel decided to break up Mary Jane and Peter Parker.

In an effort to relate back to the original narrative style of Spider-Man (where he was single and not married to Mary Jane), Marvel decided to break up Peter Parker and Mary Jane, who had been married since 1987.[31] For a genre that prides itself on mixing the fantastic with the logical, this didn't seem like a horrible idea. Where the story became overly convoluted was when the breakup was instigated by a minion of the Devil named Mephisto who forced Peter to choose between the life of Aunt May, who had recently been shot by one of the Kingpin's thugs, and his marriage to Mary Jane. Simply put, if Peter chose Mary Jane, he would keep his marriage to her but Aunt May would die. If he chose for his Aunt May to live, then his marriage with Mary Jane would cease to exist, and they would effectively never have met each other.[32]

Of course, noble hero that he is, Spider-Man chose to save Aunt May's life rather than his marriage to Mary Jane, and the next issue of *The Amazing Spider-Man* opened with the storyline titled "Brand New Day" where Peter simply woke up and wasn't married to Mary Jane anymore.[33] This story change had the effect of throwing the whole of the Marvel universe into disarray. Remember continuity? Remember how important that is for super-hero comics to have? For a character, Spider-Man, who is a major factor in the lives of all the other Marvel characters, this changes the entire universe. Now the writers of *Captain America*, *Daredevil*, *Thor*, *Iron Man*, *Black Widow*, *X-Men*, and all of the other Marvel titles have to acknowledge that Spider-Man isn't married to Mary Jane anymore.

This borders on the "So what?" side of the spectrum for many fans, but it is an example of how the genre tries to fix itself through reboots. Was it really necessary to make Peter Parker lose Mary Jane through a deal with the Devil? Wouldn't it have been infinitely simpler if Peter Parker and Mary Jane had just gotten a divorce? That would have actually been a wonderful plot device. Perhaps Peter Parker would have had to hire Matt Murdock (who is secretly the superhero Daredevil) as his divorce attorney, live with Tony Stark (whose alter ego is Iron Man) in Stark's apartment for a while, or try dating a few superheroines after a complicated separation. This leads back to why a reboot is done at all and why it is done in a certain way.

Reboots and relaunches have to occur in a fashion that doesn't affect the core of the character. The relationship of Peter Parker and Mary Jane has always been one of limitless bliss, so a divorce would imply that Peter Parker and Mary Jane have the same problems that normal couples have. But to make the characters highly troubled and imperfect enough to want a divorce might weaken them too much in a genre that demands that characters follow a higher form of morality. Instead, creating a scenario where Peter Parker has no choice but to selflessly sacrifice the love of his life in order to save his aunt changes the breakup into a moral question rather than a social one. In the "Brand New Day" storyline, Spider-Man is able to preserve his strong sense of morality, Mary Jane stays pure, Aunt May lives, and the story can continue with all of the characters not having to change their basic natures. Fans want their superheroes to be real, but not too real.

For a mythology that considers itself an evolving one, there is an incredible amount of concern about the characters changing too much. Audiences demand that their heroes remain static and reflect the same virtues for their entire existence: from the 1940s, 1950s, 1960s, all the way through to today. It's a paradox of profound proportions. But what if the same character wasn't *actually* the same character?

ULTIMATE UNIVERSE

Creating the Ultimate Universe was one of the smartest editorial moves Marvel ever made. Stan Lee, Jack Kirby, Bill Everett, Steve Ditko, Jim Steranko, Gene Colan, and all the rest had incredible ideas, but the Ultimate Universe was, as its title implies, the ultimate idea.

Marvel's Ultimate idea in 2000 was simple: what if the Marvel superheroes began today instead of in the 1960s? Boom! Forty years of convoluted continuity problems solved. Now the stories could start anew and make use of contemporary sociocultural influences that reflected a civilization that had just entered a new millennium. All of Marvel's traditional comics would continue unabated without missing a step; the Ultimate universe would just be another option for the Marvel reader. As one would expect, Marvel launched the Ultimate Universe with Spider-Man.

Brian Michael Bendis and Mark Bagley's *Ultimate Spider-Man* took Peter Parker back to the elemental nature of his character. Instead of having to reflect on all the tragedies, adventures, and relationships a forty-year-old character would naturally accrue through his publication lifespan, this new Spider-Man was simply the unpopular high school kid who struggled in life until he was bitten by a radioactive spider. In *Ultimate Spider-Man*, Peter once again meets Mary Jane for the first time, experiences the loss of his Uncle Ben, and dons his trademark superhero suit. The only aspect of the mythology that changed for the character in *Ultimate Spider-Man* was the time period, which had been updated to take place in the present.[34]

Ultimate Spider-Man was a big hit for Marvel, and fans showed their support by snatching up the first issues of the series. At the present time, *Ultimate Spider-Man #1* is a relatively expensive book on the secondary/collector market with "Near Mint" copies of the issue being listed at $90.[35] Seeing that the book was released only twelve years ago, its value is reflective of the passion fans have for the series. And as much as *Ultimate Spider-Man* was a reboot for a modern audience, it still kept its core characteristics of nerdy Peter, the red and blue suit, a beautiful Mary Jane, a worrisome

Aunt May, a friendly Harry Osborn, and web-slinging at its most pictu-
resque.

The series also showed that Spider-Man could and did work in a modern
context. In 1963, when Spider-Man first appeared, the character was revolutionary, and 1960s America was the perfect proving ground for the wall
crawler. In 2000, the concept of secret identities was put to the test with the
advent of changing technology, and Peter Parker was no longer a freelance
photographer working for the *Daily Bugle*. Instead Peter was a web designer
for the newspaper's website. These were subtle changes, but they contributed
to the changing style of storytelling necessary for a different era; they reflected a changing and evolving culture.

Marvel continued their Ultimate idea with *Ultimates*, another modern-day
retake on a Marvel tradition. *The Avengers* was Marvel's "team" book where
individual heroes came together to fight evils that required more power than
one lone hero could possibly handle. As a title, *The Avengers* was responsible for reintroducing Captain America to the world in the 1960s,[36] and *The
Avengers* became a cornerstone of the Marvel universe. Mark Millar and
Bryan Hitch's *Ultimates* reimagined the Avengers for modern audiences in a
way that revolutionized how people tell superhero stories. More so than any
other series to that point, this series examined the functionality of the superhero in the modern world. In *Ultimates* Captain America was resurrected
from a glacier that he had been frozen in since World War II, Tony Stark
needed his Iron Man suit to keep him alive while he was simultaneously
boozing and schmoozing, and Thor was depicted as a misunderstood eco-
terrorist who no one believed was really the Thunder God of Norse mythology. Working together despite differing philosophies and values was a Marvel
tradition ever since the publisher started their superhero team stories with the
Fantastic Four in 1962. *Ultimates* simply took that formula, updated the suits
and contexts, and invited the reader to follow the fireworks.[37]

Above all else with reboots, it needs to be established that every reimagining remains both faithful to and reflective of the original incarnation of
the superhero. No matter how radical the reboot, the superhero's morality
never falters. Even if Batman were redesigned wearing a red cape with a
green suit, the character would remain the same: seeking vengeance for the
murder of his parents. With the change in appearance would no doubt come
important cultural ramifications in regard to fans' views and general perceptions of the revised character, but even in a new costume Batman, as a
mythological figure, would remain the same.

It is in the nature of superheroes that they must remain consistent. Since
they were born out of a cultural need and desire to have a brightly clad moral
compass, drastic changes to a hero's code of morality would reflect a drastic
change in the culture's morality. Granted everyone has diverse opinions as to
what constitutes morality, but superheroes represent noble morals at their

most elemental. If Spider-Man were rebooted today in comics but was reimagined carrying a gun and simply shooting evil-doers, he wouldn't work as a superhero. Spider-Man's essential character is being a fun-loving, friendly neighborhood superhero. Characters that are "friendly" don't kill criminals no matter what wrongs the criminals have committed. Instead, friendly superheroes strive to not only stop the criminals but also to influence the villains to become better people.

RETROACTIVE CONTINUITY

Superhero literature changes at such a blistering pace that keeping the stories logical from narrative, sociocultural, and sociohistorical perspectives often becomes difficult for the writers. One of the results of the profusion of superhero stories is that the stories in a given universe are constantly recycled, referenced, or even changed as time progresses. When this happens, a concept called "retroactive continuity" is sometimes used. "Retroactive continuity," or retcon/retconning, is when past events in a superhero story are clarified through a revisiting of the past events in a new comic. In the retconned comic, important new details about a past key event are revealed or the event is altered through new information provided by a current writer. What retroactive continuity does is alter the landscape of the superhero story in order to create new narrative opportunities for creators. Retconning can sometimes be met with disdain from fans of superhero literature who resist change to the stories they love.

One of the most famous retroactive continuities in superhero literature was the "death" of Jason Todd, the second Robin. The character was killed by the Joker in *Batman #428* (1988) after fans literally voted to have the character killed (see chapter 3).[38] Nevertheless, the character of Jason Todd was reintroduced fifteen years later at the end of *Batman #617*, but now the character was a villain determined to make Batman pay for not saving him years before. Judd Winick then took the character and filled in the history of how Jason Todd had come back to life.[39]

This is a retroactive continuity situation because it took a storyline that was established and canonized and then changed it in order to advance a given story at a later date. Judd Winick brought Jason Todd back from the dead partially through the event series *Infinite Crisis*. In *Infinite Crisis* the villain Superboy Prime punches a hole in the fabric of time and space, making certain events in the past change. One of those events was Jason Todd's death at the hands of the Joker. Todd is resurrected from the dead a mere six months after he is buried because of this. After being taken in by one of Batman's deadliest foes, Ra's al Ghul, Todd takes up the mantle of the Red Hood, one of the Joker's earliest aliases.[40]

The only way to justify the return of Jason Todd into the DC Universe's continuity was to change what actually happened to the character close to twenty years earlier. Retroactive continuity displays how the work of one creator in superhero literature can be altered at any time by any other creator at a future date. The characters in superhero literature are a communal pot from which any creator can pull, and Jason Todd's resurrection supports such a claim. There are, of course, some events in superhero comics that could, conceivably, never be retconned such as the death of Batman's parents and the death of Spider-Man's Uncle Ben because those events are the literal foundations of their given universes. When Jason Todd's death was told by Jim Starlin and Jim Aparo in 1988, that appeared to have been Todd's final story, but Winick employed retroactive continuity to bring the character back and advance Todd's story further.

Retroactive continuity is representative of superhero literature's evolution as a genre. Bringing characters back from the dead is an exotic creative move to begin with, but superhero literature demands that an explanation be given to have it make sense within its own timeline. Also, since these characters exist in a genre where death is treated as a storytelling vehicle to advance a story and not necessarily as an ending, retroactive continuity then acts as a way to bring characters back from the dead and/or life-threatening events, typical storytelling tropes in superhero literature.

THEN WHY REBOOT AT ALL?

Reboots are restricted by both the tradition of the character and the current moral compass of the culture. If both of these requirements are not met, then the character being rebooted no longer remains the same character. Say Green Lantern was reimagined as a street-tough, leather-wearing, no-nonsense-taking enforcer who pummeled criminals so badly that they needed to go to the hospital. The question of whether or not this new direction really worked would likely be raised. The odds are that fans of the traditional character would cry "foul" and reject the reimagined character as not even being close to the intergalactic policeman Green Lantern has always been. Additionally, unless the character is Batman, brutally pummeling evil-doers in back alleyways is not what a superhero does. Even when Batman acts with extreme violence, he is generally shown to experience an inner conflict about his actions; Batman is always portrayed as using violence because he feels he needs to not because he wants to. From this perspective, a street-tough violent Green Lantern would most likely be an epic failure (although it probably would make for an interesting "Else-Worlds" story).

If reboots, as a publishing phenomenon, are so restricted by their previous incarnations, then what is their point? Well, one reason is financial. Fans love to buy *#1* issues because they are seen as "a jumping on point"[41] and are usually considered to be collectors' items. The term "jumping on point" refers to when a book's continuity has been so dense that reading any issue of a given character in a casual manner might lead to not understanding the story because the reader would have to be familiar with too many previous storylines. With a reboot, new readers are given the chance to "jump on" and join the ride from the beginning. There would of course be a background page for new readers, but the story would focus on continuing a new story-line instead of rehashing and referencing old storylines. Marvel Comics even promotes some of their books as being "Point One" books, which they describe as, "A great jumping on point for new readers setting up new stories and conflicts for Marvel's top heroes!"[42] Marvel titles that are "Point One" will literally be numbered as such: *Daredevil #10.1.*[43] Such titles are clear attempts by publishers to gain new readers.

A "collectors' item" refers to when a comic book is bought simply because it is a #1 issue. These collectors' items are generally considered an investment for possible future earnings. For publishers, both new readers and collectors are key audiences for improving sales and promoting their comic books. With every reboot, new readers and collectors alike (paying $2.99, $3.99, or more for every issue) are brought back to their favorite characters.

A second reason for reboots existing is the creative sphere of the medium. As was noted earlier, just how many times can the Flash beat Captain Cold? Technically, DC could have every issue be the Flash defeating Captain Cold, but audiences naturally and understandably would get bored with that approach. Reboots and relaunches reflect a culture's need to evolve and change. Since comics are so intimately woven into the fabric of American culture and ideals, they need to evolve with that culture and feed off the necessity for change, not fight it.

THE DC NEW 52

All of this leads back to the most recent reboot and relaunch in the industry's history. The beginning of this chapter outlined DC's new comics line which was launched in September 2011. This was a move unparalleled in comics history, and that unprecedented move was reflective of the dire state of DC Comics at the time of its announcing the reboot and relaunch.

Marvel has traditionally been the champion when it comes to market share in comics. Like most market analyses, comic sales are analyzed using market shares (the percentage of comics sold in relation to the entire market). According to Diamond Comic Distributors, the industry's primary source of distribution, Marvel Comics has come in first place and DC Comics has come in second place for the past decade. This trend is based on sales figures noted in Diamond's "Year End Retail Market Share" sales information.[44]

DC eventually became tired of coming in second. When DC decided to launch the New 52, it had come to a point where the stories of its characters were no longer making the impact the publisher wanted. While its flagship characters Superman and Batman had continued to sell well (Batman has always sold well), the rest of its line was experiencing creative and economic doldrums. DC's solution to this problem came in the form of a relaunch perpetuated by an event mini-series titled *Flashpoint*[45] where the Flash inadvertently alters time slightly and affects everyone in the DC universe. In *Flashpoint #5*, the Flash is forced to fix a mistake he made years ago (saving his mother's life by going back in time to save her) instantly altering all of reality. Upon completion of this, he returns to what he thinks is the world he originally left, but it turns out that the DC universe is now slightly altered.[46] Again quoting Bob Wayne, the senior vice president of sales at DC, "'Some of the characters will have new origins, while others will undergo minor changes. Our characters are always being updated; however, this is the first time all of our characters will be presented in a new way all at once.'"[47]

Thus far, the changes in the DC universe have been slight. For example, Superman no longer wears red trunks on the outside of his uniform and instead is now nearly entirely blue; Superman also has a "popped" collar of sorts. A similar change of uniform was made for Batman, where his dark blue trunks were eliminated making him almost entirely gray. Slight alterations to other heroes' suits were also made, but few drastically different changes were made. One major change was Batgirl's identity. Since Alan Moore and Brian Bolland's brilliant Batman graphic novel *The Killing Joke* (1988), the original Batgirl, Barbara Gordon, had been paralyzed because of the Joker shooting her. However, the New 52 made Barbara Gordon Batgirl again, restoring her to full health and eliminating her role as the character of Oracle.

Although some fans cried foul about the New 52, and a few fans even staged a poorly attended protest at the 2011 San Diego Comicon, the changes to DC's characters have been relatively minor in the scheme of superhero stories. Superman is still from Krypton, Batman's parents were still murdered, Wonder Woman is still an Amazon, Hal Jordan is still the main Green Lantern of Sector 2814, and Barry Allen is still the Flash. But what's most important is that DC's heroes are still the same beacons of light in their universe, and they still uphold the morals that the culture values in its heroes.

However, the DC New 52 was also designed to breathe new life into DC's second place position behind Marvel, so how well the new line has sold also has to be taken into consideration. As of the writing of this book, Diamond Distributor's statistics have been updated to March 2012. In the month the New 52 began (September 2011), DC was in first place in "Retail Market

Share." It held first place in this category in November and December of 2011, but in January 2012, Marvel took the lead back and has held that lead since. This means that DC Comics experienced a surge in sales due to the New 52 but hasn't been able to sustain that lead over Marvel Comics.[48]

This won't be the end of reboots and relaunches, of course. Publishers continue to experiment with the genre to attract new readers and maintain their old ones. Marvel may be the next to really revamp its titles, or maybe DC will wait until its flagship title *Action Comics* reaches 1,000 total issues. To do that, DC would have to address the nature of the reboot they've just initiated, as *Action Comics* started over at #1. Despite the seemingly trivial nature of issue numbers, the fact that DC's flagship title, which has been in constant publication since 1938, has been renumbered to #1 reflects a publishing direction that is looking forward to new narratives instead of reflecting on the comic's past stories. Right now, the strategy seems to be working for DC as its reboot has been a financial success. What is yet to be determined is what readers will think of the new initiative as it continues to grow, evolve, and challenge readers' preconceived notions about superheroes. One thing is certain, though: this is not the last time DC or Marvel will reboot or relaunch their titles. It is only a matter of time before a publisher once again decides to reimagine its heroes.

NOTES

1. Brian Truitt, "DC Comics Unleashes a New Universe of Superhero Titles," *USA Today*, www.usatoday.com/life/comics/2011-05-31-dc-comics-reinvents_n.htm (accessed June 28, 2012).

2. Kevin Melrose, "DC Announces Post-'Flashpoint' Details, Relaunches All Titles," *Comic Book Resources*, www.comicbookresources.com/?page=article&id=32563 (accessed June 28, 2012).

3. Michael Slater, *Charles Dickens: A Life Defined by Writing* (New Haven, CT: Yale University Press, 2009), 154–73.

4. Gertrude Himmelfarb, *The Idea of Poverty: England in the Early Industrial Age* (New York: Vintage, 1985), 412–13.

5. Gerard Jones, *Men of Tomorrow: Geeks, Gangsters, and the Birth of the Comic Book* (New York: Basic Books, 2004), 72–75.

6. Scott McCloud, *Understanding Comics* (Allenspark, CO: Tundra Publications, 1993), 2.

7. Jones, *Men of Tomorrow*, 299.

8. Gardner Fox, *All Star Comics* vol. 1, no. 3 (December 1941).

9. Umberto Eco and Natalie Chilton, "The Myth of Superman," *Diacritics* vol. 2, no. 1 (Spring 1972): 15.

10. Eco and Chilton, "The Myth of Superman," 22.

11. Alan Moore and Dave Gibbons, "For the Man Who Has Everything . . . ," *Superman Annual* vol. 1, no. 11 (1985).

12. Dictionary.com, "reboot," http://dictionary.reference.com/browse/reboot?s=t (accessed January 6, 2013).

13. *Star Trek*, directed by J. J. Abrams (2009; Paramount, 2009), DVD.

14. *Casino Royale*, directed by Martin Campbell (2006; Sony Pictures Home Entertainment, 2007), DVD.

15. "A Big Change," *Spider-Man*, directed by Sam Raimi (2002; Sony Pictures Home Entertainment, 2002), DVD.

16. Stan Lee and Steve Ditko, "Spider-Man!" *Amazing Fantasy* vol. 1, no. 15 (August 1962): 6.

17. Gian Pagnucci, *Living the Narrative Life: Stories as a Tool for Meaning Making* (Portsmouth, NH: Heinemann, 2004), 76.

18. "Blink," *Doctor Who: The Complete Third Series*, directed by Hettie MacDonald (BBC Worldwide, 2007), DVD.

19. Grant Morrison, *Supergods: What Masked Vigilantes, Miraculous Mutants, and a Sun God from Smallville Can Teach Us about Being Human* (New York: Spiegel & Grau, 2011), 114.

20. Richard Reynolds, *Super Heroes: A Modern Mythology* (Jackson: University Press of Mississippi, 1992), 43.

21. Reynolds, *Super Heroes*, 38–40.

22. Reynolds, *Super Heroes*, 40–41.

23. Reynolds, *Super Heroes*, 41–43.

24. Marv Wolfman and George Perez, *Crisis on Infinite Earths* (New York: DC Comics, 2001).

25. Bradford Wright, *Comic Book Nation: The Transformation of Youth Culture in America* (Baltimore: Johns Hopkins University Press, 2003), 183.

26. Gardner Fox and Carmine Infantino, "Flash of Two Worlds!" *Flash* vol. 1, no. 123 (September 1961).

27. "Parallel Universes Theory: The Basics," *Quantum Jumping*, www.quantumjumping. com/articles/parallel-universe/parallel-universes-theory (accessed January 13, 2013).

28. Brad Meltzer and Rags Morales, *Identity Crisis* (New York: DC Comics, 2006).

29. Geoff Johns, Phil Jimenez, and George Pérez, *Infinite Crisis* (New York: DC Comics, 2008).

30. Grant Morrison, J. G. Jones, and Doug Mahnke, *Final Crisis* (New York: DC Comics, 2010).

31. David Michelinie and Paul Ryan, "The Wedding," *Amazing Spider-Man Annual* vol. 1, no. 21 (1987).

32. J. Michael Straczynski and Joe Quesada, *Spider-Man: One More Day* (New York: Marvel Comics, 2008).

33. Don Slott and Steve McNiven, "Brand New Day, Part 1," *Amazing Spider-Man* vol. 2, no. 546 (February 2008).

34. Brian Michael Bendis and Mark Bagley, *Ultimate Spider-Man: Volume 1* (New York: Marvel Comics, 2003).

35. Robert M. Overstreet et al., *The Overstreet Comic Book Price Guide: 41st Edition* (Timonium, MD: Gemstone Publishing, 2011), 945.

36. Stan Lee and Jack Kirby, "Captain America Joins . . . The Avengers!" *The Avengers* vol. 1, no. 4 (March 1964).

37. Mark Millar and Bryan Hitch, *The Ultimates: Ultimate Collection* (New York: Marvel Comics, 2010).

38. Jim Starlin and Jim Aparo, "A Death in the Family, Book 2," *Batman* vol. 1, no. 427 (December 1988).

39. Judd Winick et al., *Batman: Under the Red Hood* (New York: DC Comics, 2011).

40. Judd Winick, Shane Davis, "Daedalus and Icarus, The Return of Jason Todd," *Batman Annual* vol. 1, no. 25 (May 2006).

41. Marvel Comics, "In-Comic Events: Point One," *Marvel*, http://marvel.com/comic_ books/events/304/point_one (accessed July 2, 2012).

42. Marvel Comics, "In-Comic Events: Point One," *Marvel*.

43. Mark Waid and Khoi Pham, *Daredevil* vol. 3, no. 10.1 (June 2012).

44. Diamond Comic Distributors, Inc., "Industry Statistics," *Diamond Comic Distributors, Inc.*, www.diamondcomics.com/Home/1/1/3/237?articleID=100122 (accessed July 2, 2012).

45. Geoff Johns and Andy Kubert, *Flashpoint* (New York: DC Comics, 2012).

46. Geoff Johns and Andy Kubert, "Flashpoint, Chapter Five," *Flashpoint* vol. 1, no. 5 (October 2011).

47. Melrose, "DC Announces Post-'Flashpoint' Details, Relaunches All Titles."

48. Diamond Comic Distributors, Inc., "Industry Statistics."

Chapter Five

The Iconography of Superheroes

"Look, up in the sky, it's a bird, it's a plane, it's . . . Superman!" In the late 1930s, radio audiences were introduced to one of the most iconic images in all of popular culture: Superman flying across the sky with his red cape billowing out behind him. Ironically, it was on radio that this image was seared forever into the cultural landscape.[1] Today this may not sound too impressive, as we're bombarded with HD 1080p television images, but that's the beauty of Superman flying over the city. No matter the medium, no matter the time period, no matter the audience, Superman lets us believe that a man can fly.

The producers of the Superman radio drama also knew what they were doing. Although superhero comics were predominantly a visual medium, the radio show was designed to help listeners visualize the Man of Steel streaking across the sky. This description helped highlight the majesty of the world's first superhero. And even though the radio drama introduced Superman's now famous catchphrase out of necessity, that catchphrase has since been utilized in almost every other format in which the hero's adventures have been told. The iconic imagery of Superman is unmistakable. Without even naming the character, most people will know who is being referred to when they hear, "Look! Up in the sky . . ." In fact, the phrase is so memorable it doesn't even have to be said in its entirety for most people to instantly picture the figure of Superman when they hear it.

This instant recognition is due in large part to the iconography in the superhero genre, and that iconography is forever linked to the aesthetics of the superhero. More so than any other genre in literature or popular culture, superhero iconography is heavily influenced by its heroes' appearances in print, on film, and in audiences' minds.

WHAT IS ICONOGRAPHY?

What is relevant and important to a society is what that society deems valuable. Identifying what those literal things or concepts are is an exercise in reflection. From this perspective, iconography is a representation of what a society deems important to its collective consciousness and what it values.

Since the superhero genre is visual, most of its iconography is rooted in its images. Before discussing superhero iconography, though, it is important to address how one reads iconographic images.

John Lucaites and Robert Hariman deconstructed what it meant for an image to become iconic. Not surprisingly, the process of an image becoming iconic has little to do with the image itself and more to do with a group's mental discourse with the image. In recognizing specific images, a cultural identity is created that can be understood and identified by various peoples. It's important to note here that Lucaites and Hariman focus on photographic images and not drawings and/or paintings, but the potential effects of the image (drawn or photographed) appear comparable. Visuals for Lucaites and Harriman are really about developing "the individual aggregate," which "is a trope whereby the population as a whole is represented solely by specific individuals."[2] Therefore the mental discourse held with an image is not just limited to an image; instead, the mental discourse is really being held with culture. The rhetoric described here and represented by imagery is profound, as Lucaites and Hariman are suggesting that mental discourse with an iconic image transcends the bounds of the literal picture and pushes into people's cultural and sociohistorical views.

Consider an example of this from pop culture: Apple's iPod commercial using white silhouettes that was aired on television a few years back. Eric Jenkins analyzed these now famous commercials focusing on the power of the commercial's appeal. In the iPod commercial where people are merely silhouettes, the discourse between the viewer and the image actually forces the viewer to create his/her own image out of the blank space. For Jenkins, this is iconic: "The icon was considered a hypostasis—a concrete embodiment of an underlying spiritual message. Thus the icon was neither wholly secular nor sacred, neither body nor spirit, neither concrete nor abstract, neither mere appearance nor mere representation, neither grossly material nor solely symbolic."[3] With Apple centering its product on a figure that can be morphed into whatever a viewer conceives, the company holds a discourse where all inner dialogical possibilities are passed on to the consumer. Jenkins's analysis of the silhouettes in Apple's commercials may not be exactly like superheroes, but his recognizing of the images in these commercials as being iconic can facilitate this discussion of the iconography of superheroes.

Since American audiences have been exposed to superheroes for over seventy years, this has resulted in a current culture that is generally familiar with the genre, its characters, and their intricacies. Like other famous images, superheroes have melded into the cultural consciousness of America, resulting in the recognition of a superhero not only eliciting literal reactions ("Oh, that's Superman.") but also cultural reactions ("Oh, that's Superman. He's a hero."). This equating of the imagery of the superhero with a broader cultural concept is what makes superheroes iconographic. Instead of simply seeing a superhero in a comic book, movie, or television show, the audience is really seeing what is valued by its collective consciousness.

THE IMAGE OF THE SUPERHERO

The iconography of superheroes exists in their imagery. That imagery has been developed, changed, and perfected since the genre's creation in the late 1930s. Aesthetics is where superheroes achieve their dominance. Granted, the inner struggles and sociocultural commentaries about power are enticing themes to explore in superheroes (as has been the case for most of this book), but the aesthetics of superheroes are where they gain their power upon immediate glance:

> Early comic books used a four-color printing process in which alchemic, elemental red, yellow, blue, and black were combined to create a processed spectrum. Superman, of course, was the first character to take full advantage of this technology, and these fundamental building blocks of the comic-book universe gave superhero comics a luminous, spectral radiance that had never been seen before in a democratic, popular form.[4]

This "spectral radiance," as Grant Morrison calls it, has persisted in the seventy-plus-year history of the genre.

As heroes developed, the maturing audiences of comics necessitated changes to superhero suits and general aesthetics. However, certain aspects of the characters have remained truly and understandably static. This static tendency, as we're calling it, is in no way intended to demean the importance or significance of superhero iconography. Instead, the consistency of superhero iconography is what has empowered these Technicolor heroes as they have graced countless media in their never-ending battles.

SUPERMAN THE ICON

As the first superhero, it is important to discuss Superman as the true archetype of the superhero genre. It may sound jaded to rehash the point, but as Reynolds points out, "Today, many aspects of the first Superman story and its narrative approach have the appearance of cliché: it is necessary to keep in mind that the origin of what later became clichés lies right here."[5] With Superman, flight, strength, muscles, tight-fitting clothes, perfect morality, and a secret identity all became the standard for superhero stories. Almost overnight, other publishers began copying Superman because it worked as a concept.[6]

The last son of a dying planet, forced to adopt his new world, struggling with powers beyond human comprehension: this was the formula for the ultimate story for a culture that often craves for its heroes to be bigger than life and to literally embody the intangible qualities of its conscience. Superman does just that. From a pop-culture perspective, Superman is the ultimate hero, so much so that his traits and appearance have become the recognizable standard for heroism in America.

But why Superman? There have been so many heroes created since his first appearance in 1938. Is his significance so linked to his first appearance that it becomes impossible to differentiate his precedent from his aesthetic value? There is more to the Man of Steel than the precedent he is so fondly recognized as. Let's take a hypothetical situation: If Batman had been created before Superman (they were only created one year apart from each other), would Batman be the standard for American heroes? Some might say Batman is anyway, but as much as Batman is an incredible pop-culture phenomenon and a supremely productive story-telling vehicle, Batman isn't very inviting. Superman, had he been created second, would still likely be the juggernaut of superheroes.

Even though Superman lost his biological family on Krypton, he still had a family that loved and cared for him deeply. On Earth, the Kent family developed Superman's sense of morality and became his guiding light in the human world. Giving Superman the ordinary name of Clark and focusing on how he was raised as a regular human boy helps make the character resonate strongly with audiences. Add to this the fact that Superman was raised in a midwestern farming town, and his humble roots are overshadowed only by his magnificence as a flying demi-god. And Superman's suit, which was made out of the blankets that he was wrapped in on his trip from Krypton to Earth, rationalizes his appearance. The "S" on Superman's chest has also been explained as his family's crest on Krypton.[7] That "S" emblem has become a symbol of hope, strength, and inspiration for both the characters who exist in Superman's world and for real-life audiences. Mark Waid even stated that the "S" symbol was a symbol for "hope" in Kryptontian.[8] We share Superman's family crest as our own symbol of righteousness; this is meta-textuality at its most beautiful.

Compare all of this to Batman, who experienced tragedy at a young age and vowed to avenge his parents' murders. Bruce Wayne became a boy raised by his family's butler and obsessed with the nightmare that shaped his life. If Bruce Wayne had not become Batman, it seems reasonable to assume that he would have ended up in intense therapy. Instead, being Batman is Bruce Wayne's therapy. In addition, while some people consider Batman as psychotic as the villains he delivers to Gotham City's Arkham Asylum, Batman establishes his own code of morality that keeps him in check. Batman's uniform is as iconic as Superman's, but it has changed from a suit designed solely to inspire fear, to one that is designed to also be practical. The practicality of Batman's suit will be discussed later in this chapter, but for the present it needs to be established that Batman is self-made.

Going back to why Superman would still have become *the* icon of superheroes even if he hadn't been the first superhero created, Superman would still have become the premiere hero because he's an abstract concept in which people enjoy believing. Batman is really just an ordinary person, a man who reacted strongly to a personal tragedy and had the means to finance his obsession with righting that wrong. We could, in a strictly technical sense, become Batman, but we can never be Superman, and that's why Superman will always be a greater inspiration and icon.

Subsequent superheroes have only added to this mythology, and each one has brought a uniqueness and a personality that reflects not only the time of his/her origin but the American perception of what a hero is. But what if superheroes had never existed?

ICONIC SUPERHEROES TODAY

If the first superhero were created today, he would probably not look like Superman. Superheroes were initially a product of a 1930s/1940s cultural perception of what a strong-man hero would look like. Those images of the early superheroes have remained with us for seventy years and continue to be the popular archetype for heroes in general. Is it because they look so awesome in their spandex? Is it because the bright colors of their suits make them stand out? Is it because the world needs heroes who wear their values, beliefs, and perspectives colorfully and proudly on their sleeves? Or is it because there is now a sense of nostalgia that causes audiences to want their heroes to stay the same? Roger Rollin addressed the role of nostalgia in hero-worshipping:

> The escapism provided by pop romance involves not only emotional catharsis, the purgation of pity and fear, but also what might be called "value satisfaction," that confirmation or reaffirmation of our value system which results from our seeing this value system threatened, but ultimately triumphant. [9]

Superman was created in the late 1930s, and this character's initial value system is a reflection of the 1930s. Rollin is suggesting that the value of the superhero narrative is in the hero's victory over villains who represent distortions of the hero's and society's value system. With the hero's victory over the villain comes a validation of society's values. Rollin observes that as time passes, a superhero created in an older era may end up representing values that are no longer relevant to today's audience. Rollin argues that this makes hero worship a dangerous prospect because it allows no advancement or growth in values. This can be particularly problematic because superheroes may artificially validate an outdated value system through their fictional victories.

Admittedly, traditional superhero stories have often represented an overly simplified value system of "good guys" versus "bad guys." It was not until creators began writing superhero stories for adult audiences in the late 1970s and 1980s that traditional perceptions of heroism in superhero literature began to evolve. Additionally, Rollin wrote his article in 1970, which was a period of superhero literature where Marvel had only recently entered upon the comic book scene, and superheroes were just beginning to transition into a more mature narrative style. However, embedded in Rollin's analysis lies an interesting possibility to consider.

Imagine if superheroes were created in the late twentieth or early twenty-first century and there was no preconception of the popular superhero as it is known today. Specifically, take away the aesthetics of the famous superheroes: no tights, no capes, no emblems. What would be left? Neo, played by Keanu Reeves in *The Matrix*, comes to mind. As much as that film was an analysis and deconstruction of power and the strength of the mind to resist control, it also featured the formula for a typical superhero. Neo comes from a humble beginning, experiences a loss, is trained to become a hero, and is perceived as being a last hope for a group of people struggling to attain freedom.[10] This is all quite standard for a superhero narrative. Although many elements of *The Matrix* made the film highly original and unique, such as Neo's slow-motion fight scene, *The Matrix* does at least in part also represent an update and/or reinvention of the superhero aesthetic.

Keanu Reeves's character Neo is not overly muscular, and his clothes are extremely muted: stylistic, but muted. Dressed in all black and wearing a leather trench coat, the hero of the film looks more like the traditional perception of a villain instead of a hero. There's no bombastic speech scene, no "suiting up" scene, and no explanation as to why he wears the clothes he does. And in the context of the film, the fact that Neo wears clothes that are all black resonates strongly, as the construct of their environment, the matrix itself, allows a person to look however he or she wants. So why does a hero, who is designed to inspire hope, take it upon himself to dress entirely in black?

Of course one reason Neo dresses in black is because he is an anti-hero. While Neo still holds values that are praised by culture (strength, bravery, perseverance, etc.), he doesn't *literally* embody them. In this way, Neo genuinely becomes an "every man" rather than an iconic hero like Superman. For a generation of adolescents that had grown up with superheroes colorfully influencing their lives, Neo was a realistic slap in the face, and his film blew audiences away. Like the Neal Adams and Denny O'Neil Batman of the early 1970s,[11] *The Matrix* was a new take on a tried-and-true formula.

Going back to the question at hand, though, why do we love our heroes to remain consistent? One possible answer comes directly from the Neo character: Neo represents the new (literally) and Superman, Batman, Spider-Man, and all the others represent the old. Old ideas make people nostalgic even if those old ideas don't necessarily correlate with new perspectives. Superman's appearance in his traditional suit makes people remember what superheroes have looked like since 1938. In many ways, Superman's image is the chain that continues linking generations. Yes, Superman has been tweaked since his first appearance, but he still wears the blue suit, the red cape, and the big red "S" on his chest.

While traditional superhero suits would likely be quite impractical in real-world contexts, in comics they work magnificently, as the visual characteristics of the medium lend themselves to characters embodying heroic themes. In real life, the actual logistics of the superhero suit become much more questionable.

THE CHALLENGE OF BRINGING HEROES TO LIFE

Consider the challenge filmmakers have faced in bringing comic book heroes to life. To dress a person up as a superhero forces consideration of the actual physical nature of the superhero's costume. The first Batman film by Tim Burton in 1989[12] crystallizes this challenge. Rather than use the blue-and-gray Batman costume that had become a staple of Batman comic books, Burton changed the costume to pure black with the yellow encircled bat emblazoned on Batman's chest. Burton himself said, "From the beginning I just felt he was black. You know, there was no question about it: not blue or dark gray or whatever. Obviously the leotard is ridiculous."[13] While the leotard is characterized by Burton as "ridiculous," leotards are nevertheless the classic image of the superhero. However, it does seem logical for a director who revels in the darker aspects of his imagination to dress in jet black a superhero who operates entirely at night.

Batman's retooled suit made literal sense. If a vigilante who roamed a city at night were to dress up as a bat, it would make more sense for him to wear pure black and also to wear protective body armor, because spandex isn't very good at stopping bullets. Burton's film-making style also has to be taken into account here, though, and anyone familiar with his work knows that

Burton has a very macabre sense of style. Films like *Beetlejuice*,[14] *The Legend of Sleepy Hollow*,[15] and *Edward Scissorhands*[16] often elicit as much dark energy as they do entertainment. The batsuit from the 1989 film, and the sequel *Batman Returns*,[17] kept the physical basics of the suit with fins on the gloves, the utility belt, the cape with a clipped bottom, and the cowl with the signature bat ears. While the suit was changed for the film, these changes were limited enough to make the film version stylized but not completely different from the comic version. While today's audiences have by now become accustomed to Batman being dressed completely in black on the movie screen, film audiences in the late 1980s and early 1990s were very surprised by the dark attire of the caped crusader.

What is crucial to recognize in the Tim Burton suit is its consistency. Yes, the suit is entirely black, but the character was still recognizable mostly because of the ears on the cowl and the bat symbol on the chest. Even with drastic changes to the color of the suit, the character needed to remain recognizable to audiences. Christopher Nolan's Batman films *Batman Begins*[18] and *The Dark Knight*[19] also continued the tradition of keeping Batman in a black, armored suit. However, Nolan's films made a point of clarifying why the suit was designed that way; everything in the Nolan Batman films was given a reason for being there. The costume designer for *The Dark Knight*, Lindy Hemming, said of the batsuit, "We just set about redesigning the suit as a much airier, much more modern, and much more subtle piece of equipment, like a suit of armor instead of a rubber suit."[20] In Nolan's films, Batman's suit was an experimental body armor made by Bruce Wayne's company for the military that was scrapped because it was too expensive to build. Bruce Wayne takes the suit, paints it black, and adds other gadgets that Wayne Tech had created in order to build the suit from the ground up. In having the character Bruce Wayne work at building the suit, it gives both the man and the suit a depth of character. Bruce Wayne no longer wears the signature suit simply to fight crime; he wears it to inspire fear while also making the suit as safe and practical as possible. In the comics, Batman is quoted early on saying, "Criminals are a superstitious cowardly lot, so my disguise must be able to strike terror into their hearts. I must be a creature of the night, black, terrible."[21] And so Batman created a uniform meant to feed upon criminals' fears.

Other superheroes brought to the screen received similar realistic alterations. The X-Men shed their multicolored comic book costumes for their first film. Their suits had reached their colorful zenith with Jim Lee's Technicolor gatefold cover for *X-Men #1*,[22] a cover that virtually explodes in color. Yet when the X-Men were first brought onto the silver screen in 2000, all of this color was exchanged for black leather uniforms with a faint gold-colored "X" outlined on the chest.[23] The advantages of the revised costumes are again multifold. First, the leather offers some protection for the hero's body. Second, and more importantly, these muted suits shift the emphasis from the visual icon to the human actor in the hero role. Rather than be overshadowed by his costume, Hugh Jackman's Wolverine roars to real life in the film. The X-Men series had always relied on the depth of its characters as evidenced by the internal conflicts of Wolverine and the team's struggle to cope with the tragedy of the death of Jean Grey/Phoenix. *X-Men* film director Bryan Singer emphasized the potential of the characters' interactions and deemphasized the traditionally colorful aesthetics of the characters that had been established in the comics by Stan Lee and Jack Kirby and later expanded upon by Chris Claremont and John Byrne.

The X-Men suits were still stylized in the films, though, and one can't help but think that their new suits were also influenced by *The Matrix*, which had hit theaters only a year earlier. What is to be made of this trend? The list of heroes' suits that have been altered to reflect a real-life context is extensive, and an explanation/analysis of each film's decisions would become redundant. *Captain America: The First Avenger*,[24] *Iron Man*,[25] *Thor*,[26] and *Green Lantern*[27] have all made points of establishing where their hero's suit came from and why it is the way it is. These altered suits still remain true to the source material though. Even Captain America's uniform, which would have been completely impractical in a war situation, was adjusted in the film to present a man who would be a military leader but also stand out just enough to inspire those around him. And perhaps that's where the challenge for filmmakers comes into play when bringing superheroes to life: how do you keep the hero's tradition and iconography intact while updating it for movie audiences? Answers to this are various, as every filmmaker needs to analyze this challenge in the context of making his or her specific film. Nevertheless, superhero films create their own new iconography by honoring and updating a superhero's established iconography.

The appearance of the hero needs to be made both iconic and practical, thereby satisfying both the nostalgia and realism that fans now demand. As Frank Miller says of comics, "In an artistic sense, everything is narrative. What's done by the hand in comics is something movies cannot approach,"[28] so there's no reason to even try to make films literal comic books. What films do instead is try to respect and represent the ideals that comic book characters embody in a way that is both plausible and visually pleasing.

The iconography of superheroes becomes complicated, however, when superheroines are involved. Superheroines are socioculturally loaded when it comes to their iconography because the history of the female form in superhero literature has been, for the most part, sexualized.

SUPERHEROINE ICONOGRAPHY

Alan Moore discussed in 1983 how women are portrayed in comics. His analysis sums up many of the stereotypes for women in comic books:

> Because of the way comics have grown up, a line on a woman's face makes her look old or ugly. She's got to be totally plastic and smooth—as few lines as possible—perhaps a bit of cheekbone if you're John Byrne. Long eyelashes, little tiny mouth, stuff like that. They've got no character. They are totally interchangeable.[29]

Despite this interview with Moore being more than twenty years in the past, his descriptions of how women look in comic books have not changed much. The depiction of women in superhero comics and superhero media in general has been consistently sexualized for years. Grant Morrison echoed Moore by noting this same problematic focus in the way women are traditionally portrayed in superhero literature: "Superhero stories were written to be universal and inclusive, but often they've been aimed, it must be said, at boys and young men."[30] That "aim," as Morrison calls it, has created an iconography of female superheroines that privileges hypersexualized physicality over crime-fighting practicality. In that hypersexualization is a view of the human figure that is both supremely impractical as well as often physically impossible.

For all the machismo that superheroes exude (and there is a lot of machismo there), the women of superhero comics have become a socioculturally loaded aesthetic ideal. But before female superheroes are discussed, one point needs to be established: as much as the women in superhero comics are physically idealized, the men are equally as idealized. Male superheroes look like professional wrestlers with massive arms, bulging necks, and tight clothes that appear as if they're about to rip because they can't contain the muscles that lie underneath. No normal man looks like Superman, even though it seems fair to assume that all men would *like* to look like him.

The distinction between the idealization of male and female superheroes is in the details of that idealization. Female superheroes have fallen prey to over-*sexualization*, and the discussion for female superheroes, in particular their attire, can probably be best deconstructed by examining its practicality. Mike Madrid asserted in his book *The Supergirls: Fashion, Feminism, Fantasy, and the History of the Comic Book Heroines* that the major difference between male and female superhero attire is not necessarily in the literal clothing (or lack thereof). Instead, it is the meaning behind the lack of clothes that yields the most interesting analysis:

> Male superheroes are usually presented as being unquestionably more powerful than women. Yet, they wear costumes that cover and protect most of their

bodies. Women, on the other hand, are written as weaker, and presumably less able to protect themselves. Yet they charge into battle with most of their bodies exposed.[31]

Madrid equates superhero attire with the abstract idea of power in superhero literature. In addition, Madrid compares the world of superheroes to the world of business where women wear clothes that are more revealing than their male counterparts, and, in that world as well, this is considered to be the cultural expectation and norm.[32]

Superhero attire really comes down to the practicality of the design. Superhero suits exist for a reason, and that reason is almost never practical unless the character is Batman, whose mythology has been adjusted over years of continuity to address this very matter. With superheroines, the reason for their attire is almost entirely aesthetic.

WONDER WOMAN'S UNIFORM

Let's face it, Wonder Woman's suit is totally impractical. While many fans, particularly male ones, may think the uniform looks awesome in the comics and looks even more iconic as worn by Lynda Carter on the *Wonder Woman* television show in the 1970s,[33] Wonder Woman's suit just would not work in a fight. As much as Batman's and Superman's suits have been praised, Wonder Woman's might generate praise too, but not for its value in a battle. What Wonder Woman's appearance does do is establish her as the premiere female superhero. However, her origins are a bit more scandalous than many readers may realize.

William Moulton Marston created Wonder Woman at the request of DC Comics in the 1940s. Acclaimed for his status as a popular psychologist who invented one of the first lie detectors, Marston created a character that melded ancient Greek mythology and culture with a superhero formula that was ripe for consumption by audiences.[34] Wonder Woman's origin was that of a princess named Diana who lived on an island, Themyscira, inhabited entirely by Amazonian women. After winning a gauntlet-like contest, Princess Diana was appointed the representative of Themyscira and literally became the island-nation's emissary.[35] What happened to Wonder Woman after this is something else entirely, though.

Wonder Woman became subject to depictions of bondage and punishment that were as kinky as they sound. Multiple issues depicted Wonder Woman tied up and bent over in suggestive poses. It's questionable whether this sort of content was suitable for many adults, let alone the children who were reading the comic.[36] Mike Madrid described the bondage of Wonder Woman as, "a healthy, or unhealthy, dose of bondage. Wonder Woman's bizarre, kinky rogue's gallery of villains was constantly finding new and elaborate ways to restrain the Amazon, which she always overcame with great resolve."[37] This is how Wonder Woman's initial iconography developed. As Richard Reynolds puts it, "Wonder Woman's iconography of whips and chains became the jumping-off point for the sub-genre of 'Good Girl' art-superheroines as exciting for their looks as for their villain-bashing exploits."[38] As the title progressed, though, the character began to level out and come into her own as a crime fighter.

All of the bondage issues with Wonder Woman were primarily rooted in Marston's depiction of the character he'd created, and later comics have deemphasized this suggestive material. That doesn't mean that Wonder Woman isn't a sexualized character, however.

Wonder Woman's attire consists of a red bustier with gold fringes that are shaped like an eagle and give her cleavage a plunging look. Additionally, the bustier pushes her waist in, giving her an abnormally thin midsection. She wears blue bikini bottoms with white stars on them, red boots that almost touch her knees, silver bracelets, and a gold tiara with a red star on it. All in all, Wonder Woman wears an extremely stylized bathing suit. Add to this her glowing lasso, which can be used to force people to tell the truth when they're wrapped in it, and you've got the traditional Wonder Woman uniform.

Richard Reynolds again makes an excellent point about female superheroes and their costumes, saying, "So, whilst for the superhero the transformation into costume can best be achieved with something as instantaneous as Billy Batson's 'Shazam,' which calls forth the invincible Captain Marvel, for the superheroine the process can (at least potentially) be viewed as the performance of an uncompleted striptease."[39] Wonder Woman definitely fits into this characterization of superheroines and their suits because her arms and legs are completely exposed. The tradition of the character dictates that she remain dressed the way she always has been, and the previous chapter delved into why fans so strongly demand that traditions be followed. A Wonder Woman movie has never been made, but there have always been rumblings of one, and the character would probably work extremely well in a film format. But considering what film directors do with superheroes' appearances in films, speculating what Wonder Woman would look like in a film makes for an intriguing conversation. Would the filmmakers completely scrap the traditional Wonder Woman suit? Would they literally copy the suit from the comics? Would they simply update the traditional suit to make it more practical? All of these approaches are definitely feasible, but Wonder Woman is not as well known as her male counterparts from a narrative perspective. Casual audiences would certainly recognize Wonder Woman's name and appearance, but the details of her story are not as culturally prevalent as other superheroes' stories.

This means that Wonder Woman's power as a cultural artifact and her iconography are primarily rooted in her appearance. All the male superheroes are bound by their appearance as well, but their ability to move away from their source material is much easier. Wonder Woman would have a tougher time doing so. Wonder Woman is only the most famous of superheroines, though, and there are many others who share in the impracticality and perceived cultural necessity of a superheroine suit.

Batgirl, Catwoman, Poison Ivy, Harley Quinn, Vixen, the Black Widow, Storm, Huntress, Shadowcat, Rogue, Jean Grey/Phoenix, and She Hulk are just a few of the many heroines in comic literature. Casual audiences might only be familiar with a few of these characters, but that's often the fate of superheroines: they're usually completely overshadowed by their male counterparts. It should also be noted that villains are mixed into the list of heroes above. This is not by accident. Though villains differ from heroes because of their value systems in superhero literature, their appearances are strikingly similar, especially for the female characters. In fact, it's rather difficult to think of a super villain that has the same aesthetic appearance as a superhero. Where the heroes wear tight-fitting clothes, many villains are characterized by their plain clothing (such as Lex Luthor's business suits) or by their extravagant overdressing (Green Goblin, the Penguin, or Captain Cold). Villains in superhero comics many times personify their corruptness or their ugliness in their appearances. Unlike the superheroes who are all handsome, beautiful, and physically idealized, supervillains usually appear to be physically awkward. The female villains and superheroines, however, both share the same sexualized costuming.

And who did design these suits for female characters? It is difficult to trace who actually came up with the design of a given character because comics are a combination of writers, artists, and editorial boards, with each of them having significant input into the final creative decisions. What seems universal, though, is that the female figure is consistently depicted as an exaggerated "hour glass" figure. Again, it has to be kept in mind that even though female figures are idealized in superhero stories, the male figures are as well. Aaron Taylor says, "The superhero comic is a literature that represents a site of departure for typical ways of thinking about and categorizing the body."[40] That is one of superhero comics' characteristics and one that defines the genre as a unique literary and art form. Wonder Woman remains a strong and respected cultural icon, and her appearance has become a slice of Americana, sometimes being utilized as a symbol for strength and bravery. However, as a character, she is quite archaic in her values. She is sometimes depicted as militaristic, ruthless, and even anti-male. Nevertheless, for most of her storied history, Wonder Woman has been the central flag bearer for all female superheroines, and she is as iconographic as heroes come in regard to superhero literature. To explore how female heroes have changed though, we need to jump to the present.

THE DEVELOPMENT OF CATWOMAN

Selena Kyle (Catwoman) has become the modern representation of the female superheroine. Wonder Woman is still around, of course, but she represents the old guard of the superheroine. Catwoman is defined by her independent nature and her moral conflicts. Traditionally, Catwoman is a cat burglar who flirts with and seduces Batman in order to execute her mischievous and elaborate plots. Usually placed in a swanky museum or ultra-posh apartment, Catwoman's grace as a burglar is unparalleled. She is never out to purposefully kill, never out to damage, and never out to cause mindless chaos; Catwoman steals because she needs the money and also because she loves to live on the edge.

Does this sound like a hero at all? From a strictly moralistic perspective, no it doesn't. Young children are taught that stealing is wrong, which makes Catwoman's stealing morally wrong from society's perspective. However, Selena Kyle's conflict with Batman is more of a sexually charged game of cat and mouse than it is hero and criminal. Even as far back as the 1960s Batman television show, the tension between Batman and Catwoman was palpable, and that tension has defined their relationship up through today's stories. Why does it work, though? Batman vows to uphold justice, and Catwoman seeks to undermine that same justice by taking what isn't hers and getting away with it. The two are oil and water.

This relationship benefits both parties, though. Through Batman, Catwoman is made to question her actions and see in the Caped Crusader a potential life that has meaning via altruism rather than criminality. Through Catwoman, Batman is made to question his life's path and the possibility of having a person in his life give him meaning instead of only an endless mission that must inevitably end in Batman's serious injury or death. In short, the two keep each other close in order to maintain balance in lives that are already lonely. However, the two do not *need* each other; they *want* each other. In that distinction is the value of Catwoman.

Catwoman never hints at needing anyone to fill a void (emotional or otherwise) and is extremely careful to not let the Dark Knight in. For the past few decades the tension-laden relationship between Batman and Catwoman was never completely resolved until DC's New 52 reboot had Batman and Catwoman consummate their relationship with a not-so-tacit implication on the last page of *Catwoman #1*.[41] The events of this particular issue are discussed further in chapter 8 of this book.

All of this discussion of Catwoman and Batman leads back to how Catwoman is iconographic in modern contexts. Since the tension between the two characters has never subsided, the role of Catwoman in Batman's mythology has shifted from the role of villain to one of ally. Instead of being a cat burglar, Catwoman has become one of Batman's closest confidants and shares in his never-ending mission. However, she never totally "buys into" his brand of justice and will tell him how she feels about his courses of action throughout various stories. Since Batman is such an emotionally and psychologically unstable superhero, he always needs voices of reason to balance and ground him, but these voices usually come in the form of Robin, Alfred, or Superman. Catwoman speaks to Batman in an even more candid way. Selena Kyle is emotionally strong, driven, and self-sufficient, never relying on Batman or anyone else to help her. When she wants Batman is when she goes to him, not when he wants her. Catwoman always does things on her terms.

Physically, Catwoman is as idealized as any of the other superheroines in superhero literature. She has the exaggerated hourglass figure and tight-fitting clothes, but her suit has become the most functional and stylized of all the female characters in comics. While her old costumes were very "comicy" with some costumes being elaborate ball gowns with cat ears or skin-tight purple with a fake tail hanging out the back, her new suit is something more akin to high-tech espionage gear than it is a comic book costume. Dressed in black leather with a tight-fitting hood and night-vision goggles, Catwoman wears her suit because it aids in her ability to camouflage herself at night and to work in the shadows. There are of course sexualized aspects to the costume. Most notable is the zipper on the front of her costume that is often pulled down very low revealing a great deal of her cleavage (depending on the artist). Additionally, Catwoman wears high-heeled boots that would probably make it difficult to walk, let alone jump from building to building.

Superheroines' attire has been historically determined by audiences and creators who are overwhelmingly male. And as noted earlier, it is difficult to pinpoint exactly who created the specific costumes for female characters in comic books. There are precedents from the early days of pulp fiction where women were scantily clad and often had their clothes torn to shreds by a mad scientist until characters such as Doc Savage or The Shadow could come to their rescue. In contrast, though, characters like Wonder Woman and Catwoman are not "damsels in distress." Instead, they're strong characters with their own motives, personalities, tragedies, and passions.

The predominance of males in the comic book industry is evident in the imagery of the female superheroes and their iconographies, though. That imagery is dominated by cleavage, long legs, thin waists, and beautiful faces all wrapped up in a crime-fighting persona that shows no mercy. That imagery has only become more prominent in recent years, and the iconography of superheroines is highly influenced by socioculturally loaded depictions of the female form.

HEROES WITHOUT COSTUMES

Superhero attire has always been a point of contention in popular culture because of its gaudiness and flamboyance. Superhero literature is one of symbolism where the emotions, values, and desires of the characters are usually embodied in a highly visual way. Captain America is the All-American superhero, so he wears a stylized American flag as his suit. This is blatant, but it is also effective for a medium, comics, that relies on the visuals to communicate. Nevertheless, there are instances where superheroes have been portrayed effectively without the suits that visually represent them. The television show *Smallville* was famous for its "no flights, no tights"[42] rule which held true all the way through the show's final episode, and Wolverine has recently become a superhero known as much for his casual attire as for his animalistic tendencies.

Overall, though, a certain sociocultural strength is gleaned from superhero attire, and it definitely helps in establishing the characters as American icons. In chapter 2, Frank Miller was quoted as saying of Daredevil, "The costume was just dressing around the hero."[43] For a creator who prides himself on being a deconstructionist of the superhero, taking away a costume makes sense. But let's take a step back. Frank Miller's "Born Again," which Miller is referring to when he says the costume is just "dressing around the hero," is a thought-provoking superhero story, but in that provocation Miller's statement casts doubt as to whether the costume adds, even slightly, to the effect of the superhero. Daredevil is a relatively minor character, so taking away his suit might not affect the character's iconography all that much. And, in fact, Daredevil survived his stint without a costume, though he eventually returned to wearing his red devil outfit.

Let's take this to another level, though. Superman could never lose the traditional suit for an extended period. When this was tried in the late 1990s in comic books by having Superman appear in an electrified blue suit,[44] it was difficult not to raise an eyebrow. *Smallville*, despite its casually dressed Clark Kent, never presented itself as a show about "Superman"; the show always claimed to be about Clark Kent. However, even that show, in its later seasons, began to suffer from Tom Welling not being in full Superman garb because Superman, Batman, Spider-Man, Wonder Woman, Captain America, and most other superheroes are defined by the very things that a filmmaker like Burton feels are "ridiculous": their brightly colored costumes. To a great extent, superheroes are what they wear.

Superhero costumes are, almost by purposeful design, impossible. This is part of what makes them iconic and appealing. To engage with the idea of the superhero, one must willingly suspend disbelief. Suspending disbelief is an established literary concept, and it is credited to Samuel Taylor Coleridge. In his *Biographia Literaria*, he states:

> In this idea originated the plan of the "Lyrical Ballads"; in which it was agreed, that my endeavours should be directed to persons and characters supernatural, or at least romantic, yet so as to transfer from our inward nature a human interest and a semblance of truth sufficient to procure for these shadows of imagination that willing suspension of disbelief for the moment, which constitutes poetic faith.[45]

It takes some poetic faith to accept a superhero costume and to read about the adventures of a hero with unnatural abilities. Thus, for comic readers, the bright and garish costumes of their heroes are acceptable, even necessary. The iconography of superheroes is what makes them unique and even appealing.

The iconic nature of the superhero works both for and against this suspension of disbelief. We allow ourselves to imagine a super-powerful being dressing up in an otherworldly costume. But at the same time, the costume reminds us that no such person can ever exist outside our imagination. Superheroes are, in the end, only icons. They represent a flight of fancy, a person one might wish to be in a dream: "They were what we all might become."[46]

Yet, even though they are fictitious, superheroes are more real than we think they are. Superheroes embody the ideals that culture holds dear: that good will triumph over evil, that with great power comes great responsibility, and that the hero will always save the day in the nick of time. They are a metaphysical representation of our desire for a world that is better than the one in which we live. And, perhaps, they also embody our own efforts to make that world come to life through our own, everyday efforts to be good people. Superhero stories offer us a meta-textuality: if we can create a good place in the world of superheroes, then there is hope that we can also someday make our own world a better place than it is now.

NOTES

1. Bradford Wright, *Comic Book Nation: The Transformation of Youth Culture in America* (Baltimore: Johns Hopkins University Press, 2003), 13.

2. John Louid Lucaites and Robert Hariman, "Visual Rhetoric, Photojournalism, and Democratic Public Culture," *Rhetoric Review* 20, nos. 1–2 (Spring 2001): 38.

3. Eric Jenkins, "My iPod, My iCon: How and Why Do Images Become Icons?" *Critical Studies in Media Communication* 25, no. 5 (December 2008): 473.

4. Grant Morrison, *Supergods: What Masked Vigilantes, Miraculous Mutants, and a Sun God from Smallville Can Teach Us about Being Human* (New York: Spiegel & Grau, 2011), 11.

5. Richard Reynolds, *Super Heroes: A Modern Mythology* (Jackson: University Press of Mississippi, 1992), 10.

6. Wright, *Comic Book Nation*, 18.

7. *Superman: The Movie*, directed by Richard Donner (1978, Warner Brothers, 2006), DVD.

8. Mark Waid and Leinil Francis Yu, *Superman: Birthright* (New York: DC Comics, 2005).

9. Roger B. Rollin, "Beowulf to Batman: The Epic Hero and Pop Culture," *College English* 31, no. 5 (February 1970): 432.

10. *The Matrix*, directed by Andy Wachowski and Larry Wachowski (1999, Warner Brothers, 2007), DVD.

11. Denny O'Neil, Len Wein, and Neal Adams, *Batman Illustrated: Volume 1* (New York: DC Comics, 2006).

12. *Batman*, directed by Tim Burton (1989, Warner Brothers, 2009), DVD.

13. "Beyond Batman: Designing the Batsuit," *Batman*, directed by Tim Burton (Warner Brothers, 2009), DVD. Documentary on DVD Extras.

14. *Beetlejuice*, directed by Tim Burton (1988, Warner Brothers).

15. *Sleepy Hollow*, directed by Tim Burton (1999, Paramount Pictures).

16. *Edward Scissorhands*, directed by Tim Burton (1990, 20th Century Fox).

17. *Batman Returns*, directed by Tim Burton (1992, Warner Brothers).

18. *Batman Begins*, directed by Christopher Nolan (2005, Warner Brothers).

19. *The Dark Knight*, directed by Christopher Nolan (2008, Warner Brothers).

20. "The New Bat Suit" *The Dark Knight* directed by Christopher Nolan (2008, Warner Home Video, 2008), Blu-Ray DVD. Documentary on Blu-ray DVD Extras.

21. Bob Kane and Bill Finger, "The Batman Wars Against the Dirigible of Doom," *Detective Comics* vol. 1, no. 33 (November 1939), 2.

22. Chris Claremont and Jim Lee, "Rubicon," *X-Men* vol. 1, no. 1 (October 1991).

23. *X-Men*, directed by Bryan Singer (2000, 20th Century Fox).

24. *Captain America: The First Avenger*, directed by Joe Johnston (2011, Paramount Pictures).

25. *Iron Man*, directed by Jon Favreau (2008, Paramount Pictures).

26. *Thor*, directed by Kenneth Branagh (2011, Paramount Pictures).

27. *Green Lantern*, directed by Martin Campbell (2011, Warner Brothers).

28. "The Men Without Fear: Creating Daredevil," *Daredevil*, directed by Mark Stephen Johnson (2003; 20th Century Fox, 2003), DVD. Documentary on DVD Extras.

29. David Roach et al., "Garry Leach and Alan Moore," in *Alan Moore Conversations*, ed. E. L. Berlatsky (Jackson: University Press of Mississippi, 2012), 22.

30. Morrison, *Supergods*, 40.

31. Mike Madrid, *The Supergirls: Fashion, Feminism, Fantasy, and the History of the Comic Book Heroines* (Exterminating Angel Press, 2009), 290.

32. Madrid, *The Supergirls*, 289–90.

33. *Wonder Woman: The Complete First Season*, directed by Dick Moder and Stuart Margolin (1976; Warner Home Video, 2004), DVD.

34. Gerard Jones, *Men of Tomorrow: Geeks, Gangsters, and the Birth of the Comic Book* (New York: Basic Books, 2004), 207–11.

35. William Moulton Marston and Harry G. Peter, "Introducing Wonder Woman," *All Star Comics* vol. 1, no. 8 (December/January 1942).

36. Jones, *Men of Tomorrow*, 209–10.

37. Madrid, *The Supergirls*, 45–46.

38. Reynolds, *Super Heroes*, 34.

39. Reynolds, *Super Heroes*, 37.

40. Aaron Taylor, "'He's Gotta Be Strong, and He's Gotta Be Fast, and He's Gotta Be Larger Than Life': Investigating the Engendered Superhero Body," *Journal of Popular Culture* vol. 40, no. 2 (April 2007): 347.

41. Judd Winick and Guillem March, "And Most of the Costumes Stay On," *Catwoman* vol. 4, no. 1 (November 2011): 22.

42. Ken Tucker, "TV Review: Smallville (2001)," *Entertainment Weekly,* www.ew.com/ew/article/0,,181747,00.html (accessed July 5, 2012).

43. "The Men Without Fear: Creating Daredevil," *Daredevil*, directed by Mark Stephen Johnson (2003; 20th Century Fox, 2003), DVD. Documentary on DVD Extras.

44. Dan Jurgens and Ron Frenz, "Superman . . . Reborn," *Superman* vol. 2, no. 123 (May 1997).

45. Samuel Taylor Coleridge, *Biographia Literaria* (New York: The Macmillan Group, 1926), 191.

46. Morrison, *Supergods*, 104.

Chapter Six

Superhero Storytelling

Mort Weisinger, a notoriously vicious DC Comics editor in the 1960s, was known for his cruelty, his demand for perfection, and his questionable treatment of creators.[1] This harsh demeanor fit well with Weisinger's demanding views about how to write comic books. Weisinger insisted on a writing style that limited the number of panels on a page, the number of words on a page, and the layout of the panels on the page. Weisinger's rules were as follows: no more than six panels on a page, no more than 35 words per panel, no more than 25 words in a thought/speech balloon, and a maximum of 210 words on a given page.[2] Comic books in the 1960s were more formulaic than they are today, and Weisinger's formula is evidence of that. However, his strict requirements were designed to keep readers from being overwhelmed. To put this in perspective, a typical Microsoft Word document double-spaced with Times New Roman Font and a font size of 12 has about 250–300 words per page, a number quite similar to Weisinger's standards. The point here is that Weisinger realized there are aesthetic considerations to be made about the composition of comic books, and those aesthetic considerations complement the multimodal nature of comic books.

Weisinger's formula has since fallen out of style, but it remains an effective method for comic writing nonetheless. Even the acclaimed creator Alan Moore admits to utilizing Weisinger's formula when outlining and scripting his graphic novels because Weisinger's standard provides an effective amount of content based on what a given reader is likely to be able to handle when interacting with a text.[3]

So, why and how do comic creators design superhero comics the way they do? Given the multimodal nature of the superhero comic genre that incorporates both textual and pictorial elements, the possibilities are nearly endless when it comes to this style of storytelling. Superhero comics also present a chance to examine composition and storytelling in a unique way, as the writing is dependent on an artistic dynamic. In every comic, the words and the art must work in tandem, necessitating a creative give-and-take between writers and artists. In regard specifically to superhero comics, the standards of the genre require a style of composition that reflects not only the sociocultural nature of the characters but also the serialized nature of the superhero genre and the comic book medium. Because of these unique characteristics, superhero comics hold some important implications for composition studies.

THE MARVEL METHOD

Stan Lee has already been mentioned in this book multiple times, and his contributions to superhero culture, mythology, and storytelling are legendary; he isn't called Stan "The Man" Lee for nothing. As an editor, writer, and publisher at Marvel Comics during the 1960s and 1970s, Stan Lee was involved with the creation of nearly all of the major characters from that time period including Spider-Man, Iron Man, The Incredible Hulk, Thor, Daredevil, the X-Men, and many others. To keep up with all of these proverbial irons in the fire, Stan Lee developed a writing style that has since become both legendary and controversial.

The Marvel Method of writing is really collaborative in nature with much of the process being cooperative. First, Stan Lee would go to the artist of a particular title that he was responsible for writing. These artists included John Romita Sr., Jack Kirby, Steve Ditko, Gene Colan, and others. Since Stan was so busy with all of his other duties as editor/publisher/writer, he left it up to the artist to draw the pages and provide a simple outline for the story. Then Stan would fill in the blank caption boxes, speech balloons, and thought bubbles with text. The credits for these final pieces would then read "Writer: Stan Lee." Mark Evanier, whose biography of Jack Kirby is titled *Kirby: King of Comics*, addressed the Marvel Method in regard to Jack Kirby:

> Sometimes Stan would type up a written plot outline for the artist, sometimes, not. Later, some of the artists (including Kirby and Ditko) would insist that Stan had contributed very little—sometimes nothing—to the plots of the comics. Since he received the total writing fee and (usually) the total writing credit, that would be a sore point in years to come.
>
> But at the time, everyone was happy just to have work and the "Marvel Method," as it would come to be known, produced some fine comics. [4]

In addition to creating problems of authorship, the Marvel Method could also produce some creative problems. Artist Garry Leach, who worked with

Alan Moore on multiple occasions, said of the Marvel Method of writing, "It's horrible, because basically the artist is like the director of photography of a film, and if you've got someone who's inept, incompetent, and doesn't know about basic emotions, then the comic is ridiculous."[5] While the Marvel Method had its problems, it did have one major benefit: producing lots and lots of comic books. Given the pressures he was under, it's clear Lee needed a writing method that could produce as many comics as possible in a given month. At that time, Marvel Comics was allowed to distribute eight monthly magazines or sixteen bimonthly magazines through their distribution arrangement with Independent News, which was owned by DC Comics.[6] Aside from the startling notion that Marvel's biggest competitor would distribute Marvel's comic books for them, this gives insight into just how many books Stan Lee was responsible for releasing every month. The sheer enormity of Stan Lee's monthly publication requirements necessitated a style of expedited production. Even working under these time pressures, Lee's method still managed to produce some of the most memorable stories in superhero history. Without this method, the world might not have had Spider-Man fighting Doctor Octopus, The Incredible Hulk fighting The Thing from the Fantastic Four, and the Avengers thawing Captain America out of the Arctic ice. However, there are certain inherent issues with the Marvel Method that have legal, moral, and compositional implications.

In terms of legality, the estate of Jack Kirby has challenged the Marvel Method of writing. Kirby, whose nickname was "The King," was infamous for his muscled-up characters, flowing action sequences, and dramatic depictions of superheroes. In fact, many of the pictures seen even today on T-shirts, lunchboxes, and other superhero toys/collectibles are from Jack Kirby's 1960s superhero art. Over time, Kirby has become an iconic artist in the world of superheroes and comic art in general.

In 2009 Kirby's family sued Marvel over not receiving creator rights to characters Kirby claimed he had significant input into creating. Eventually Marvel won the case against Kirby's estate: "Ultimately, the court decided that since Kirby was under a work-for-hire freelance contract at the time, he has no entitlement to the copyright for these characters."[7] However, the Kirby estate filed an appeal in August 2011 hoping that the ruling would be overturned.[8] As of the writing of this book, that appeal is still pending in the courts. Additionally, the lawyer who is representing the Kirby estate, Joe Toberoff, is also representing the Jerry Siegel and Joe Shuster estates in their lawsuits with DC over Superman and the ownership of the character.

When Jack Kirby's biographer stated, "that [Marvel Method] would be a sore point in years to come,"[9] he wasn't exaggerating. The Kirby estate's lawsuit with Marvel is proof of that, and the inherent creative confusion of the Marvel Method of writing reflects a style of composition that feeds off collaboration, cooperation, and communication. This constant give-and-take of ideas could create friction between creators, as it blurs the lines of what each writer or artist has responsibility for doing. What this method also does is highlight how superhero comics are often created in a fashion reminiscent of the writing for deadlines done by newspapers. This deadline style still exists in monthly comics, but it has subsided in recent years. The shipping schedule of current superhero titles is still bound to monthly standards, but affordances are sometimes made to allow for shipping delays if particular titles merit it.

What Stan Lee did in the 1960s with the Marvel Method made sense for the industry at that time, but today even more emphasis is placed on the quality of both story and art in comics. Nevertheless, the Marvel Method is an important aspect of the history of superhero comics. It not only established an efficient way to produce copious amounts of stories, it also helped keep artists employed in an entertainment industry that was, and still is, as cut-throat as any other. The creator issues notwithstanding (and those creator issues are extremely significant and worthy of being challenged), the Marvel Method does hold some valuable lessons for composition studies.

THE MARVEL METHOD AND COMPOSITION THEORY

Like the Justice League or the Avengers, the groundbreaking creators of superheroes came together to produce stories that thrilled children, adolescents, and adults. All brought their unique styles of composition, whether they were visual or textual. Steve Ditko's bizarre and unique contortions of Spider-Man melded with Stan Lee's interpretation of a troubled youngster gaining super powers. The straining muscles of Jack Kirby's heroes in fierce battles reflected his own experiences as a streetwise kid, which worked well with Lee's tension-laden dialogue. John Romita Sr.'s art provided Lee with the ability to advance stories through characters' emotions. The point here is that Stan Lee couldn't have created all of the great Marvel stories without these artists, and the artists couldn't have generated such iconic images without the input of Stan Lee's writing. The Marvel Method fed off each creator's ideas, strengths, and visions. It was a creative method built on collaboration.

So what does this mean for composition studies? The central assertion of this book is that superhero literature is worthy of being included in academic discussions. Therefore, the ways in which these classic tales of heroism, longing, and passion are created should also be a part of that discourse. Specifically, the way the Marvel Method works, and comic collaborations in general work, can provide interesting ideas for how to approach the teaching of composition.

Leading composition scholars have, over the years, asserted that composing is primarily a solitary endeavor that involves reflection on one's experiences and how those experiences inform writing. One of the most widely cited composition essays is by the scholar Peter Elbow, entitled "Closing My Eyes as I Speak: An Argument for Ignoring Audience."[10] In his essay, Elbow asserts that writers need to be true to themselves before they can ever hope to be effective when their writing reaches reader's eyes. From Elbow's viewpoint, writing is best viewed as a means of self-discovery and personal reflection. The implications for writers are profound, as Elbow's commentary on writing is really about empowering writers by instilling confidence in themselves and their work.

Another important composition scholar, Ann Berthoff, discusses in her book *Reading, Thinking, Writing* how composition is really about forming relationships with others' interpretations of those relationships: "The continuum of the composing process depends on the fact that we can see one thing—shape, event, concept—*in terms of* another."[11] For Berthoff, composing is all about getting readers to understand what a writer's perceptions are of specific events, ideas, and emotions. In this view, how a writer understands a concept such as "happiness" needs to be composed in a way that enables a reader to understand the relation the author has to the term "happiness." This is challenging because many of the themes or concepts people experience are emotional, passionate, or very difficult to define in writing because they are so abstract.

Being able to express emotions in writing is extremely difficult because not everyone feels emotions the same way. One way to help express abstract concepts is through art, and comics are a medium that utilizes art in a unique way. Scott McCloud's seminal work *Understanding Comics* explains that comics are unique in their ability to share a story through both art and text.[12] McCloud argues that readers of comics must interpret not only what is written and drawn, but also what exists between the panels. McCloud demonstrates how the reader must be an active participant in this meaning-making process.

McCloud's work helps one understand the nature and importance of multimodal literacy. Essentially, as contemporary life has become completely saturated with both textual and visual media, scholars have begun to see a need for helping people to gain multimodal literacy skills. This idea was first put forward by scholars in the New London Group, who argued that literacy education needed to shift away from an overemphasis on the reading and writing of pure text.[13]

Today one of the most important scholars writing about multimodal literacy is Gunther Kress. Kress's book *Literacy in the New Media Age* argues that "The materiality of the different modes—sound for speech, light for image, body for dance—means that not everything can be realised in every mode with equal facility, and that we cannot transport mode-specific theories from one mode to another without producing severe distortions."[14] Essentially, Kress is stating that it may be easier to understand happiness by seeing a person smile as opposed to seeing dialogue that says, "I am happy." There is a natural dissonance in communication when switching between modes. Kress's work urges educators to develop methods for teaching people how to understand the many different modes of literacy they will encounter in today's world.

All of this theory leads back to the Marvel Method of writing that was empowered by the combined efforts of both the artist and the writer. Elbow encourages being true to oneself through reflection, and Berthoff stresses creating strong connections between experiences and how those experiences are translated to the page. Being able to tap into one's own experiences and being able to share them then leads into both McCloud's commentary on comics working with both art and text and Kress and the New London Group's insistence that not all of humanity's thoughts, ideas, and emotions can be contained in one mode (text only, art only, audio only, etc.). The creation of superhero comics is all about navigating these important aspects of creation. These include relaying emotions of characters, expressing why these superheroic characters do what they do, and why audiences connect with them. What superhero comics have evolved into, in terms of their creation, is a discursive relationship between writer and artist working in tandem to tell a particular story. Through the constant give-and-take of writer and artist, the complicated nature of superheroes is brought to life.

Alan Moore wrote some of the most groundbreaking graphic novels in the history of superheroes and comic literature in general. During an interview in 2001, Moore was asked, in regard to *Watchmen*, "Was Dave Gibbons involved in creating the narrative?" Moore replied, "Oh, absolutely. . . . Now, I'd worked with Dave before. I knew that he did have this surveyor's precision when it came to placing objects into a panel, fitting them in somehow, with lots of filigree and detail. So, with *Watchmen*, I was able to exploit that."[15] Here is the relationship between creators that makes superhero comics, and comic literature in general, thrive as a unique form of composition. When creating comic books, the writer must recognize the strengths of the artist, and the artist must link his or her unique skill set to the goals of the writer and the joint project. The complicated political and social themes developed in the highly acclaimed *Watchmen* series were thus the result of the combined compositional styles of both Moore and Gibbons.

Alan Moore commented on the unique narrative style of *Watchmen* in another interview from 2009:

> With *Watchmen*, I wanted to find those things which were unfilmable, that could only be done in a comic. So, for example, we had split-level narratives with a little kid reading a comic book, a newsvendor going into a right-wing

rant next to him, and something else going on in the background in caption, all at the same time and interrelated.[16]

The difference between this collaborative composing process and the Marvel Method is the communication that occurred between the writer and artist when Moore and Gibbons were working. Gibbons isn't mentioned by name in this quote, but it is clear that Moore valued the multimodal nature of their composition. Whereas Stan Lee's Marvel Method was designed to produce comics at high-speed rates, Alan Moore and David Gibbons worked in a complementary manner, empowering each other as they went along.

And while Moore's prowess as a writer extends far beyond the genre of superheroes into historical fiction (*From Hell*),[17] political commentary (*V for Vendetta*),[18] and even pornography (*Lost Girls*),[19] his collaboration with artists still exhibits what all creators in any medium wish to do: meaningfully communicate significant ideas.

Superhero stories present unique challenges since they are tied so intimately to a highly visual medium in order to communicate their messages. In many ways superheroes embody ideas that are difficult to put into words. That's why superhero stories rely on the visual medium of comics. Superhero stories help explore concepts and emotions that only these larger-than-life characters can fully possess. For example, we can't necessarily write what "justice" means because it's an abstract concept that is constructed through our multiple lived experiences. But when we see Superman stop Lex Luthor from blowing up the world, we are offered a defined view of what the cultural idea of justice is. Superman doesn't have to say, "I saved the world from an evil man. That, citizens, is justice." That's not necessary because we know, as an audience, that what Superman just did represents justice. The concept is worked out for us in the visions we are shown. The drawings of these super beings help give meaning to the words both on the page and in our minds: words like *justice* and *heroism* that often defy concrete definition in our own life experiences.

IMPLICATIONS FOR THE ACADEMY

How can all of this discussion about the creation of superhero literature be applied to academic settings, though? Aside from the argument for reading and studying these texts in academic contexts, the ways in which these stories are created have bred controversies and censorship. The uniqueness of their style, from both a structural and a narrative perspective, requires a view of authorship that is unique to comics.

As the Marvel Method has shown, collaboration is both essential to writing superhero literature and inherently controversial in how it makes authorship elusive. The lawsuit that the Kirby estate brought to Marvel over Jack

Kirby's contributions to Marvel's premiere characters is really about authorship and who is responsible for creating some of the most important and iconic superheroes in history. There is, clearly, lots of money at stake, since the superhero industry is worth billions of dollars. But there is more to this that has implications for people who look to read superhero literature and analyze it in a more thorough fashion.

Specifically, the idea of authorship in superhero comics can help inform the concept of authorship for both teachers and students alike in academia. Lisa Ede and Andrea A. Lunsford have written about the idea of authorship in academia and how that concept has evolved over time to value the individual over the collective. In other words, in schools, collaboration is usually devalued while individual work is praised. In superhero comics, and comics in general, much of the material is created through a joint effort involving writers, artists, inkers, letterers, colorists, editors, and others. Because comic books are produced at a fast pace, usually once a month, creating an entire comic is too much work for any one person.

To produce a comic requires multiple collaborations. Yet for the most part, schools teach students that the vast majority of their work should be done independently. Students are almost always tested individually, and most teachers require students to write their papers individually. Even group work often concludes with students being given individual grades. And when students are praised, it's mostly for their independent thinking, not for their collaborative skills. That's why at graduations schools select a valedictorian, the best single student in a class, rather than showcasing the best group of students as a team.

Lisa Ede and Andrea Lunsford have written about this problem at length: "Everyday practices in the humanities continue to ignore, or even to punish, collaboration while authorizing work attributed to (autonomous) individuals."[20] In fact, this view of authorship as one that values the individual over the collective may have contributed to the very tension that existed between Stan Lee and the artists who worked at Marvel. Rather than think of Spider-Man as a joint creation of Lee and artist Steve Ditko, Spider-Man is often viewed as Lee's individual creation. This is how the world mostly thinks about creativity; ideas are seen as belonging to one person, even though that person had many interactions with other people, which likely had an impact on the idea.

Ede and Lunsford argue that everyone could benefit greatly from learning how to collaborate effectively. They point out that much of the world's work is done collaboratively, but not just in the comic industry as we've noted already; this is common in a wide array of other industries as well. Ede and Lunsford claim that much has been lost by education's overemphasis on individual learning, and that students could be better prepared for the demands of their future careers if they were taught how to collaborate, both in writing and in other areas of work. They observe, rightly, that "Collaborative projects can extend beyond the humanities and indeed beyond the academy,"[21] and this makes teaching about comics and how comics are created a valuable option for developing students' collaborative skills. Since superhero literature is a genre that thrives on collaboration, and the value of a given work is rooted in the working relationship between the writers, artists, editors, and other members of a creative team, the inclusion of superhero literature into academic contexts can help redefine traditional views of authorship.

THE ORIGIN STORY

Continuity is a characteristic of superhero stories that gives them much of their unique personality and power and, as a genre, also fuels another important aspect of superhero literature: the origin story. Superhero literature has become so convoluted over the years that keeping track of all the stories, characters, issue numbers, and historical contexts has become a complicated endeavor. Wikis have been created by fans on the Internet to serve as reference sources for nearly every character in the superhero universes. Because wikis enable multiple contributors to add to or edit a particular webpage, these superhero wikis have created a dialogue among fans that serves as a checks-and-balances system to help provide accuracy of information about these characters.

Superheroes get very complicated when it comes to their histories, but one part of their stories remains forever constant and important. Even more than "death" stories, crossovers, event stories, and attire changes, origin stories are the core of superheroes' existences. Origins not only reflect the sociohistorical contexts in which heroes were created, but they also reflect a culture's understanding of what makes superheroes unique storytelling vehicles. Superhero origins fall into what Coogan (2006) called "resonant tropes":

> Every superhero, particularly the ones who have been around for decades, has certain tropes—familiar and repeated moments, iconic images and actions, figures of speech, patterns of characterization—that have resonance; that is they embody or symbolize some aspect of the character, and have gained this resonance through repeated use by storytellers.[22]

Since superhero literature is serialized and traditionally bound to its monthly publication schedule, the countless stories of the characters can get lost in the minds of readers due to the sheer amount of material that exists. The origin stories of these characters then become the basis for a reader's understanding of who these characters are, where they came from, and how they'll reflect on the character going forward. For readers of superhero literature, the stories of how the heroes came to be are familiar and constant.

Origin stories, then, become the most important stories for superheroes as socioculturally significant characters. While most people won't know who the villain was in the Batman story *The Long Halloween*,[23] they will most likely know the story of how Batman came to be. There is so much ambient noise in superhero literature that focusing in on how the heroes got their start is essential to gaining a general understanding of the genre.

The sheer number of repeated tellings of origin stories per character is astounding as well, but that redundancy also represents the importance of those origins. In Hollywood superhero films, this trend is particularly telling. The Tim Burton film *Batman* had an origin sequence explaining how Batman came to be.[24] A few years later, *Batman Forever*[25] revisited the origin of Batman in a more abbreviated fashion. In 2006, Christopher Nolan's entire film *Batman Begins* explored the Dark Knight's origin in detail.[26] Add to this list *Batman: The Animated Series* and various other incarnations of Batman over the last twenty-five years and there's a trend of revisiting this same origin story over and over again.

Like Umberto Eco's assertion of Superman not ending because this would cause audiences to reach "final consumption,"[27] superheroes are bound to a style of writing that is genre specific, and the origin story is the genesis of that genre. Origin stories are also continually revisited in order to reaffirm the importance of the superhero in changing times and to reference a character's present actions against his or her origin. In other words, based on the origins of a given character, the subsequent actions the character takes must make sense in the context of his or her reason for being a superhero. For example, Batman's origin may be revisited in the middle of a story where he is having a moral dilemma. Looking back at his origin story, if only for a page or possibly even just one panel, can create a meta-textual event where the reader is able to consider the potential next course of action along with the character.

This, going back to Ann Berthoff, is creating relational understanding. Readers can understand why Batman acts the way he does through this metacognitive referencing of the character's origin. The same referencing needs to be done by the creators who continue the serialized stories of superheroes; it's a continual collaboration between creator and reader that preserves continuity, ensures the sanctity of the character, and develops an underlying discourse between creators even if they're generations apart. C. W. Marshall stated in an essay concerning the inclusion of ancient mythology into superhero literature that "authors adopt figures for their own narrative ends, are aware of what has gone before, and situate their creative work in an ever-evolving continuum."[28]

Origin stories are part of Marshall's "ever-evolving continuum" and inform future stories. It would be very difficult for a creator to write a superhero story without knowing the character's origin, and it would be virtually impossible to write a story that fans would value in such a case. Because of the vital nature of the origin story as a point of reference for all future stories, origin stories become, as Doctor Who would say, "fixed points" in the composition process.

A FIXED COMPOSITIONAL POINT

In an episode of the science-fiction show *Doctor Who*, the Doctor, who is a time-traveling adventurer, says, "There are fixed points throughout time where things must stay exactly the way they are."[29] For creators of comic books, these "fixed points" are the origins of each major superhero. Peter Coogan's "resonant tropes" are similar to this, and Coogan cites the pearls of Martha Wayne as being a resonant trope for Batman's origin[30] and Superman's Fortress of Solitude[31] as being an example of Superman's origin. Stories can be told about these characters going forward, and subtle changes can be made, but some things must remain consistent, particularly the character's origin.

For creators, this presents a challenge that was already hinted at in this book in chapter 4 on the nature of the reboot/relaunch: creators can only change so much without significant reader response and/or negative ramifications for the characters. This makes the writing of superhero literature a unique compositional process.

Especially in regard to the origin stories, creators *must* keep in line with what has come before. Even when Spider-Man was reimagined for Marvel's Ultimate line in 2000, Peter Parker still gained his super powers after being bitten by a radioactive spider.[32] It is conceivable that Brian Michael Bendis could have changed the origin; maybe Peter Parker could have been endowed with magical spider powers instead of being bitten by that radioactive arachnid. However, drastically changing Spider-Man's origin would have been problematic because much of the mystique behind Spider-Man, and Marvel's characters in general, is the scientific accident. Bendis needed to keep the Fixed Compositional Point of Spider-Man's origin as it had been established by Stan Lee and Steve Ditko in 1962's *Amazing Fantasy #15*.[33]

Brian Michael Bendis and Mark Bagley's run on *Ultimate Spider-Man* was designed to be a modern reinterpretation of Spider-Man updating the character for newer and younger audiences while avoiding any continuity issues. Even with that reinterpretation, Bendis and Bagley were still having a discourse of some sort with Stan Lee and Steve Ditko. The original origin informed and, in essence, framed the work that was designed to reimagine the character all together.

Thus origin stories serve as Fixed Compositional Points for superheroes. No matter the reinterpretation, reimagining, reboot, relaunch, retcon, re-whatever, a superhero's origin remains fixed. This makes superhero literature one of the most unique compositional tasks in all of entertainment because there is never truly a "blank slate" when writing the story of a serialized character. There is always something informing future stories, plots, characters, reactions, and motives. Unless a completely new character is created, the Fixed Compositional Points need to be adhered to when writing serialized superhero stories.

WHAT DO FIXED COMPOSITIONAL POINTS MEAN FOR SUPERHERO LITERATURE?

Aside from making the genre of superheroes unique, recognizing the inherent precedents of superhero stories means recognizing a universe of stories that are intimately tied to certain sociohistorical, compositional, and multimodal aspects of the genre. Superhero stories can be read or experienced in singular and isolated spheres of continuity, but this is exceedingly rare. One example of a superhero storyline that is almost entirely insular is Christopher Nolan's Batman film series. In the comics, Batman is constantly influenced by and consistently influences other characters in the DC universe. In Nolan's films, there isn't even a hint of outside influence from other characters in the DC universe. For all anyone knows, the only superhero that exists in the Nolan world of Batman is Batman. However, there is still that dialogue between creators present as articulated by Peter Coogan's "resonant tropes." Martha Wayne still wears pearls that are torn from her neck by the man who kills Batman's parents in that dark alleyway, and Bruce Wayne is still left alone under a street light similar to David Mazzucchelli's cover of *Batman #404*.[34] Even with Christopher Nolan's emphasis on creating an insular continuity of Batman stories, those resonant tropes still inform the story and always will.

Creators honor and abide by the sanctity of the superhero origin stories because they are classic tales of power and heroism. In those origin tales are humanity's most admirable qualities projected through multimodal panels of action, adventure, and brightly colored suits. Origin stories are also familiar to most audiences as superhero stories have reached the cultural point where the characteristics and stories of superheroes are engrained in the minds of a wide range of people. Of course, some heroes' origins may not be as popular or as well known as others, but the basic premise of the superhero remains quite standardized. In almost every superhero origin story, an ordinary person gains special powers and chooses to use those powers to help mankind.

Creators work within the framework of the genre and its characteristics while honoring the past creators who came before them. Through that complicated compositional process, a discourse with other creators is played out in the adventures of the heroes who take to the comic pages, television screens, and movie theaters. And while what Stan Lee did with his fellow creators in the 1960s and 1970s with the Marvel Method has come into question in recent years through lawsuits, that model of collaboration did help create some of the most memorable stories in superhero history. All composition, no matter the medium, is predicated on the concepts of relating and understanding. Only through taking into account what has brought us, as a culture, to this point can we frame our future; superheroes do the same. The composition of superhero stories is all about connecting to our past and using that past to produce the future. Superhero stories engage us in a collaborative creation process because we readers are the ones who help bring them to life.

NOTES

1. Gerard Jones, *Men of Tomorrow: Geeks, Gangsters, and the Birth of the Comic Book* (New York: Basic Books, 2004), 289–91.
2. Daniel Whiston, David Russell, and Andy Fruish, "The Craft: An Interview with Alan Moore," in *Alan Moore Conversations*, ed. E. L. Berlatsky (Jackson: University Press of Mississippi, 2012), 130.
3. Whiston et al., "The Craft," 129–30.
4. Mark Evanier, *Kirby: King of Comics* (New York: Abrams, 2008), 112.
5. David Roach et al., "Garry Leach and Alan Moore," in *Alan Moore Conversations*, ed. E. L. Berlatsky (Jackson: University Press of Mississippi, 2012), 11.
6. Brian Cronin, *Was Superman a Spy? And Other Comic Book Legends . . . Revealed!* (New York: Plume Books, 2009), 160–61.
7. Joey Esposito, "Marvel Wins in Jack Kirby Lawsuit: Marvel Retains Rights to Kirby Icons," *IGN*, http://comics.ign.com/articles/118/1184787p1.html (accessed July 5, 2012).
8. Jill Pantozzi, "Kirby Estate Files Appeal in Marvel Lawsuit," *Newsarama*, http://blog.newsarama.com/2011/08/15/kirby-estate-files-appeal-in-marvel-lawsuit/ (accessed July 5, 2012).
9. Evanier, *Kirby: King of Comics*, 112.
10. Peter Elbow, "Closing My Eyes as I Speak: An Argument for Ignoring Audience," *College English* 49, no. 1 (January 1987): 50–69.
11. Ann E. Berthoff and James Stephens, *Forming, Thinking, Writing* (2nd ed.) (Portsmouth, NH: Heinemann, 1988), 167–68.
12. Scott McCloud, *Understanding Comics* (Allenspark, CO: Tundra Publications, 1993).
13. The New London Group, "A Pedagogy of Multiliteracies: Designing Social Features," *Harvard Educational Review* 66, no. 1 (Spring 1996): 60–92.
14. Gunther Kress, *Literacy in the New Media Age* (London: Routledge, 2003), 107.
15. Tasha Robinson, "Moore in *The Onion* Edits," in *Alan Moore Conversations*, ed. E. L. Berlatsky (Jackson: University Press of Mississippi, 2012), 98–100.
16. Alex Musson and Andrew O'Neill, "The *Mustard* Interview: Alan Moore," in *Alan Moore Conversations*, ed. E. L. Berlatsky (Jackson: University Press of Mississippi, 2012), 194.
17. Alan Moore and Eddie Campbell, *From Hell* (Marietta, GA: Top Shelf Production, 2000).
18. Alan Moore and David Lloyd, *V for Vendetta* (New York: DC Comics, 2008).

19. Alan Moore and Melinda Gebbie, *Lost Girls* (Marietta, GA: Top Shelf Production, 2009).

20. Lisa Ede and Andrea A. Lunsford, "Collaboration and Concepts for Authorship," *PMLA* 116, no. 2 (March 2001): 357.

21. Ede and Lunsford, "Collaboration and Concepts for Authorship," 361.

22. Peter Coogan, *Superhero: The Secret Origin of a Genre* (Austin, TX: Monkey Brain, 2006), 7.

23. Jeph Loeb and Tim Sale, *Batman: The Long Halloween* (New York: DC Comics, 2000).

24. "Gauntlet Thrown," *Batman: Two-Disc Special Edition*, directed by Tim Burton (1989; Warner Home Video, 2005), DVD.

25. "'Happening Again,'" *Batman Forever: Two-Disc Special Edition*, directed by Joel Schumacher (1995; Warner Home Video, 2005), DVD.

26. *Batman Begins*, directed by Christopher Nolan (2005; Warner Brothers).

27. Umberto Eco and Natalie Chilton, "The Myth of Superman," *Diacritics* 2, no. 1 (Spring 1972): 9.

28. C. W. Marshall, "The Furies, Wonder Woman, and Dream: Mythmaking in DC Comics," in *Classics and Comics*, ed. G. Kovacs and C. W. Marshall (Oxford: Oxford University Press, 2011), 90.

29. "Cold Blood," *Doctor Who*, directed by Ashley Way (2010; BBC Worldwide, 2010), DVD.

30. Coogan, *Superhero*, 7.

31. Coogan, *Superhero*, 8.

32. Brian Michael Bendis and Mark Bagley, "Powerless," *Ultimate Spider-Man* vol. 1, no. 1 (November 2000).

33. Stan Lee and Steve Ditko, "Spider-Man!" *Amazing Fantasy* vol. 1, no. 15 (August 1962).

34. Frank Miller and David Mazzucchelli, "Batman: Year One, Part 1: Who I Am and How I Came to Be," *Batman* vol. 1, no. 404 (February 1987), cover.

Chapter Seven

The Role Superheroes Play in Children's Learning

The original intention of comic books was to entertain children and adolescents with fanciful stories cheaply produced on flimsy paper and covered with a glossy front. Comic books did their job well, and children in the 1940s and 1950s reveled not only in the exploits of their favorite superheroes but also the adventures of Mickey Mouse, Archie, Betty Boop, Popeye, and many other humorous characters. There were also science fiction comics, western/cowboy comics, romance comics, and the precursor to Cliffs Notes and Spark Notes titled *Classics Illustrated*, where famous literary stories were brought to life in comic style. Never before had *Jane Eyre*, *Moby Dick*, and *The Count of Monte Cristo* been made so exciting.

Then came Dr. Frederick Wertham, whose crusade against comic books using his now infamous book *Seduction of the Innocent* nearly destroyed the industry.[1] The publication of Dr. Wertham's book eventually led to a Senate hearing, with the publishers of comic books including National (DC), EC (Entertainment Comics), Dell, Charlton, Atlas (Marvel), and others needing to defend their publication practices. While Dr. Wertham's attacks on comics primarily focused on the crime and horror genres (which were admittedly quite inappropriate for children), his attacks also included superheroes such as Batman, Wonder Woman, and Superman. Numerous authors have already detailed the events of these hearings, including Gerard Jones,[2] Bradford Wright,[3] and David Hajdu.[4] Most notably, Dr. Wertham attacked Batman's relationship with Robin saying that their relationship "is like a wish dream of two homosexuals living together."[5] Dr. Wertham attacked the texts that children of the period had grown up with, idolized, and even mimicked in their play. His critiques of horror and crime comics were aimed at the brutally violent nature of their stories and accompanying art, but his attacks on superheroes seemed to be a product of necessity as opposed to desire. Quite simply, Wertham's target was the crime and horror books, but he had to attack *all* comics in order to get a genuine response from congress, audiences, parents, and publishers. In order to force change, Wertham could leave no genre of the medium unquestioned.

Because of its historical importance, the influence of Dr. Wertham's seminal work on comics and juvenile delinquency needs to be included in any chapter on children and superheroes. And while one can raise many challenges to Wertham's arguments, his book did have one positive side effect: Wertham's work clearly demonstrated that superheroes, do, indeed, influence the children who read stories about them.

THE INFLUENCE OF SUPERHEROES ON CHILDREN

The importance of superheroes to children's lives is really a product of the fact that superheroes are, in the historical sense, intended for children. As was discussed earlier in this book, the morality of superheroes is socioculturally constructed and reflective of the culture from which they originate. For American audiences, superheroes are the ultimate bearers of what constitutes being morally just and righteous. For parents, having their children read superhero stories could be a way to help the children learn about values and morals they deem important. This was certainly true of early comic books. Today's more modern take on superheroes often examines the moral ambiguity of having powers, as seen in comic books like Mark Millar's *Ultimates*,[6] Frank Miller's *The Dark Knight Returns*,[7] and Brian Michael Bendis's *Daredevil*.[8] Yet even setting aside these exceptions, in the vast majority of stories, superheroes' moral compasses are always pointed at true north. Hopefully, children would not be exposed to those superhero texts whose more mature themes would only be suitable for adults.

So, assuming careful parents will keep copies of Alan Moore and Brian Bolland's *The Killing Joke* (which will be discussed later in this chapter) out of the hands of ten-year-olds, the beauty of the superhero genre is that it can have a positive influence on children. Children who are exposed to superhero characters learn that Superman always wins, Wonder Woman protects people, and the friendly neighborhood Spider-Man makes sure everyone is aware of his quest to defend the innocent. It's comforting to grow up with stories that share positive messages like this. As we grow older and we mature (again, hopefully), our lens through which we experience the world begins to get a bit grimy, and we start to question the role of the superhero and heroes in general. The realization that superheroes aren't real, various life experiences, changing interests, puberty, and many other natural progressions of life lead to challenging these representatives of both culture and our

childhood. But one fact remains even when we attempt to question the multicolored figures of childhood: superheroes remain the same, eternally reminding us of what is good, just, and what we believed in as children. For that
reason, superheroes play an important part in childhood and the moral development of many children.

One fact remains about superheroes, though, that instigates debate about
their potential influence on children. The superhero story has always been
one that incorporated violence into its narrative. No matter the decade and no
matter the audience, superheroes have always utilized their fists to resolve
problems. Most children are taught growing up to keep their hands to themselves, to respect each other, and to treat other people the way they'd want to
be treated. Most parents and teachers do not condone fighting or violence as
ways to solve problems. All of these are valuable life lessons, and they grace
nearly every elementary classroom's walls as rules to be followed. At the
same time, children who read superhero comics can end up idolizing a genre
that generally condones and even glorifies violence. This presents a cultural
paradox where the educational side of a child's life promotes civilized prob-
lem-solving skill development but the entertainment side presents the glory
of fighting in multicolored suits.

Umberto Eco addresses this very paradox in his 1972 article "The Myth
of Superman." As was discussed earlier in this book, Eco asserted that Superman's ability to remain a powerful cultural figure was rooted in his eternal
temporality. Since Superman never ages and his stories reflect a static world,
an audience is never able to reach what Eco calls "final consumption."[9] In
other words, a reader is never able to resolve Superman's exploits as a
complete story because the story literally never ends. Eco also addresses how
superheroes act as pedagogical tools for children:

> In this sense [heroes using powers for good] the pedagogic message of these
> stories would be, at least on the plane of children's literature, highly accept-
> able, and the same episodes of violence with which the various stories are
> interspersed would appear directed toward this final indictment of evil and the
> triumph of honest people.[10]

For Eco, superheroes using violence to defend the weak is justified because
superhero stories present that violence in a context that punishes what culture
considers to be wrong. Is it right for superheroes to use violence to stop
criminals? The answer is really dependent on an individual's value system.
While some audiences may not condone the violent actions of superheroes,
the intentions of these characters are undeniably noble. Again, when discussing the influence of superheroes on children, it needs to be made abundantly
clear that the contexts being discussed are those that are appropriate for child

audiences. Comics which portray violence for its own sake, like the series *Wanted*,[11] are absolutely inappropriate for children.

Most children today aren't exposed to superheroes through comic books, however. Comics have, in their historical development, become more of an adult-oriented medium, resulting in writers and artists drafting their stories to suit that audience. Again referencing Frank Miller, "In comics, in comic books, in superhero comics, people have wasted an awful lot of creative energy and hard work looking for kids who aren't there."[12] Therefore, most of the superhero comics that would be found on a shelf at a local comic book store today would not likely be appropriate for a child. Instead, children get most of their exposure to superheroes through television, movies, Internet sites, and other forms of media. Unlike superheroes' traditional platform of comic books, television and movies now serve as the premiere mode for superheroes when it comes to children.

Cartoons like *Super Hero Squad*, *The Brave and the Bold*, and *Young Justice* are only the latest in a long line of superhero cartoons aimed at children. *Super Hero Squad* in particular displays how superheroes are introduced to children. The show is animated with the heroes being depicted as big kids who work together to fight evil. Essentially, *Super Hero Squad* is the Avengers for children, and it features Iron Man, Thor, The Incredible Hulk, Wolverine, Captain America, and other Marvel characters.[13] Just how can a genre that has become so adult oriented return to its origins as a cartoon suitable for children to enjoy and learn from? The answer is by going back to superheroes' roots.

Super Hero Squad does this by incorporating life lessons into its stories such as the benefits of teamwork, being honest, and doing what is right. Mixed in with these lessons are the fantastic tales you'd expect from Marvel's flagship characters including battling the evil Doctor Doom and The Abomination. The show's value for children isn't just in its playful looking caricatures of Marvel superheroes. By watching *Super Hero Squad*, children also learn about communication between heroes who hold differing value systems. Captain America and Wolverine are two mainstays of the show, and their traditional ideologies clash on occasion.

Seasoned comic book readers who are aware of Wolverine's and Captain America's histories know that Captain America's disputes with Wolverine sometimes end in epic battles with major collateral damage. Captain America, having been a dutiful soldier who fought for America in World War II, clashes ideologically with Wolverine, whose life has been full of violent encounters including being experimented on by the Canadian government. For adult audiences, seeing these two heroes clash over ideological differences is hero deconstruction at its finest. For children watching a cartoon, a fight over ideological differences would send an extremely poor message to children: if you disagree with someone, it's OK to fight them over it. *Super*

Hero Squad will have the heroes disagree with each other from time to time, but the heroes in the show always settle their differences civilly, highlighting lessons about the value of cooperation and teamwork. Besides, in the comics, Wolverine has claws that he uses to brutally maim people. That would never be tolerated in a children's cartoon. So how does one event (ideological differences between heroes) reflect both adult audiences and child audiences in different ways?

For one, superheroes don't *need* to be violent in children's cartoons. In adult-oriented stories, there is a level of necessity to the violence as superheroes are purposefully putting themselves in situations that often require physical confrontations. Also, most adult audiences that enjoy superhero stories were exposed to the genre and the characters as children, so their original exposure to the characters was in a narrative structure that was more positive in nature. Children need the positive characteristics of superheroes to shine through, which can help teach life lessons of which even adults sometimes need to be reminded.

Secondly, if one takes away the violence of superheroes and strips them of the modern perception of their obsessive vigilantism and unwavering punishment of evildoers, what's left? What's left is a character that represents the best qualities of humanity: altruism, self-sacrifice, perseverance, and responsibility. Superheroes fight because they have to, but their messages still resound without the violence and without the hard-edged personas. Superheroes don't need to be "dark" to be a compelling genre. As was discussed in chapter 2 on the academicization of superheroes, a perception has arisen that equates "good" superhero stories with "dark" superhero stories. *Super Hero Squad* takes superheroes back to the stories of fun, friendship, and humor.

COMIC BOOKS FOR GROWNUP READERS

Only since the late 1980s have superhero stories become a genre that reflects adult-oriented value systems. Marv Wolfman, Frank Miller, Alan Moore, and other writers used the decade of the 1980s, which was characterized by its own excesses and glorification of moral ambiguity, as a setting to rethink the values of superheroes. For the first time in America's comic book history, writers questioned superhero's intentions. Denny O'Neil and Neal Adams had done something similar in the early 1970s with Green Lantern and Green Arrow addressing social ills as they traversed the United States,[14] but the decade of the 1980s was really a turning point for much of American culture in terms of values. Peter Coogan referred to this period of comics as the "Iron Age" of comics.[15] Movies became more violent, music was being redefined as a visual medium through the rise of MTV, and the world was experiencing significant political turmoil. Major comic titles in the 1980s such as *The*

Dark Knight Returns, Watchmen,[16] *The Killing Joke,*[17] Spider-Man's stories with Venom,[18] and *Teenage Mutant Ninja Turtles*[19] amped up the violence to unprecedented levels in superhero comics. Even the idea of tragic events happening to superheroes began in the 1980s. Jason Todd (the second Robin) dies brutally at the hands of the Joker,[20] Barbara Gordon is paralyzed by the Joker,[21] Jean Grey from the X-Men dies,[22] Elektra is killed by Bullseye,[23] Barry Allen (the Flash) dies,[24] Supergirl dies,[25] Captain Marvel dies of cancer,[26] and Spider-Man dresses in jet black for the first time.[27] Make no mistake, these are all excellent comic book stories and worthy of being read and experienced, but these are not stories for children. What happened? How did comics go from Batman using an oversized baseball bat to foil a museum robbery by the Joker to Batman struggling to try and talk sense into the Joker even after the Joker has brutally maimed Commissioner Gordon's daughter in *The Killing Joke*? The world of comics went from fun and care-free to intense and dark in the course of a single decade.

Part of the reason may have been the age of the creators in the 1980s. Many of these creators would have been children during the Silver Age of comics (1956–1970) when comics were primarily designed for children. Superman was still innocently flirting with Lois Lane, Batman was still working with Robin, Spider-Man was still caring for Aunt May while pining for Mary Jane, and Captain America was still excited to be working with the Avengers. It was an era of comics that acknowledged problems in the world, but the superheroes could definitely handle those problems. These are the types of stories creators in the 1980s grew up with. Nearly twenty years later, these creators were given the reins to all these iconic superheroes, and now they had the opportunity to really deconstruct and examine the characters of their childhoods. The issues of just how long Batman could work with Robin, Superman could only flirt with Lois, Spider-Man could wait to wed Mary Jane, and Captain America could remain happy being a man out of his own time were all questioned. The 1980s creators appeared to have had enough of the beauty and the majesty of the superheroes' perfect worlds.

Another reason for this phenomenon of superhero comics becoming more adult-oriented could also be attributed to the rise of comic book shops and the direct market. As was discussed in the chapter on fans battling creators, comics went from being a product that could be bought at any corner drugstore or supermarket to a specialty product that could mostly only be bought at designated shops. The theory behind doing this was to limit the costs of distribution and cater to audiences that specifically looked for comic books. A limited number of comics would still be sold at drug stores and supermarkets, but the newest issues would be sold at direct market comic book shops. This meant that the audience of children, who primarily bought comics with parents on trips to the drugstore or supermarket, became limited. Subsequently, the audience naturally shifted from one that needed a ride to the drugstore from mom or dad to a young adult with his/her own means of transportation for a trip intended to buy comics. Evolving with this change in distribution, publishers would begin to change the content of their comic books in order to meet this new audience's tastes and maintain their interests. This new audience, being older and more mature, wanted a product in their superhero stories that portrayed a world rife with injustice and brutality. Essentially, adult audiences wanted more "adult" stories.

Kids, inevitably, got left behind by this change. Comics were still at supermarkets and drugstores, but they gradually shifted from kid-friendly stories to ones fueled by adult situations due to the emergence of the direct market. Combining these two factors, creators growing up and comic book shops becoming the primary vendor of comics, created a scenario where children lost a major genre and medium in their lives.

WHERE DID KID-FRIENDLY SUPERHEROES GO?

The short answer to why kids quit reading comics was that over time most children gravitated toward television as their premiere form of entertainment. Superheroes had been on television since the 1950s when George Reeves first starred in *The Adventures of Superman*.[28] The next decade showcased the *Spider-Man* cartoon, which featured the now famous *Spider-Man* theme song.[29] The 1970s continued the trend with the *Super Friends*, which was a kid-friendly version of the Justice League of America.[30] All these shows predate the 1980s, which is really the point where comics split from their focus of a children's audience. The kid-friendly superhero cartoons from the 1960s and 1970s would have also been influences on the same creators who forever changed the face of superhero stories in the 1980s. Perhaps the 1960s and 1970s superhero cartoons and their undeniably jovial and cavalier content added to the exhaustion of the comic creators who, in the 1980s, took it upon themselves to deconstruct the superhero genre so brutally. In addition, even as comics were shifted toward an adult audience in the 1980s, television superheroes remained aimed squarely at children: *Transformers*,[31] *Thundercats*,[32] *G.I. Joe*,[33] and *He-Man and the Masters of the Universe*[34] became the new television superheroes for children born in the late 1970s and early 1980s. Add to this the popularity of *Star Wars*[35] at the time and the world of fantasy was set for children during the 1980s.

The feature films *Superman: The Movie*[36] and *Superman II*[37] were also major influences on children during this time period, but those films were in theaters necessitating that parents join in the fun. In all, these developments hastened the shift of superheroes for children from comic books to cartoons and films as the primary genres. Superheroes also remained important figures in the toy market. Both Marvel and DC influenced children through their lines of action figures, which were, in the early 1980s, quite a new concept.

As further evidence of this shift, in the 1980s Marvel and DC released four television cartoon series: *Spider-Man and His Amazing Friends* (1981–1983),[38] *The Incredible Hulk* (1982–1983),[39] various *Super Friends* continuations from 1980–1985, and a very short-lived Superman series in 1988.[40] It is very important here to mark the dates of these shows, as three of them were made before 1986, which marks the beginning of superhero stories becoming very dark in nature with the publications of *The Dark Knight Returns* and *Watchmen*. There were other superhero shows in the 1980s based on DC and Marvel comics, but they were simply one episode including one X-Men cartoon[41] and live-action shows such as *Superboy* which ran from 1988 to 1992[42] and *The Flash* which ran from 1990 to 1991.[43] Of these live-action shows, only *Superboy* had content that was consistently appropriate for children. *The Flash* was a somewhat more adult-oriented interpretation of the Scarlet Speedster. Additionally, *The Flash* was a prime-time show limiting the audience of children. Nevertheless, *The Flash* used lots of humor and choreographed fights which made it family friendly, too.

Though these kid-friendly superheroes did appear on television, their number was limited. And with comics leaving the supermarkets and drugstores and their content shifting rapidly to adult-oriented stories, children's exposure to superheroes became fairly limited from the early 1980s to the early 1990s. However, the 1990s saw a renaissance of sorts when it came to traditional superheroes. The only problem was that the content was no longer designed for children. Even the superhero cartoons of this period had evolved to more closely match the content of the comic trends from the 1980s. The *X-Men* cartoon reflected Chris Claremont's character-driven stories coupled with Jim Lee's art,[44] the *Spider-Man* cartoon incorporated the ultraviolent villains Venom and Carnage,[45] and *Batman: The Animated Series* was clearly created for adult audiences with its 1930s art-deco style.[46] Despite the brilliance of *Batman: The Animated Series*, which revolutionized animated storytelling, the series had very dark themes and imagery. The style and image of the superhero had changed for children and *Batman: The Animated Series*, along with its Marvel series counterparts, marked the beginning of this change.

No longer was Batman dressed in light blue with Mr. Freeze harmlessly robbing banks with an ice gun. Now, Mr. Freeze was a tragic hero with deep psychological stresses that, in a superhero context, explained his psychotic breakdown and subsequent need to terrorize his victims with a gun that froze them. In *Batman: The Animated Series*, Mr. Freeze's wife, Nora, was stricken with an illness that had no cure. In order to save her, Mr. Freeze cryogenically preserved her so that she could be reanimated at a future date when a cure was found. During his experiment, an accident occurred that caused

Victor Freeze to not be able to survive in temperatures above freezing. In order to finance his experiments to cure his wife, Mr. Freeze had to begin committing robberies.[47]

Character development, even in cartoons, was taken to new levels as the trend moved toward giving superheroes more substance and depth than ever before. Children's superhero stories before the 1980s were characterized by their binary interpretations of good and evil. Unlike the modern interpretation of Mr. Freeze, Silver Age stories featuring that supervillain were filled with bombastic plans for freezing city hall or stealing artifacts from the ice age: rather laughable goals and motivations. Of course, Stan Lee's Marvel stories in the 1960s began to challenge the typical superhero formula as he introduced flawed characters who self-analyzed their own motivations. Likewise, Denny O'Neil and Neal Adams's stories in the 1970s rethought many of DC's characters, giving them more realistic situations to address. The difference between those stories and the 1980s stories was in their level of severity, however. The Silver Age was the beginning of superhero stories becoming multidimensional and meta-textual in their relevance and character deconstructions. As much as Marvel's characters are credited with this (as they should be), the stories were, at their cores, still for children. There are recorded instances of college students in the 1960s citing Spider-Man and The Incredible Hulk as being significant literary and socially relevant characters,[48] but children were still quite protected in terms of content when it came to comic books. This was especially due to the use of the Comics Code which had been developed in the wake of Congress's investigation of comics publishing. The Comics Code Authority had been developed by the industry to self-regulate publishing standards in order to ensure that comics did not get published with overly offensive content. Most comics published from 1954 onward carried a bright white and black stamp with a stylized letter "A" and the proclamation, "Approved by the Comics Code Authority."[49]

What eventually led to comic publishers' abandonment of the comics code was the turn toward serious-themed comics in the 1980s. As adult-oriented stories became the norm and publishers shifted their focus toward selling to adult readers, the comics code ceased to be relevant. Since the code had been self-imposed by the industry, it was easy for the industry to ignore it. The fact that no one, including Congress, took note of the Authority's stamp of approval losing significance in comics further indicates that the readership of comics had clearly moved from children to adults.

This trend highlights the cultural significance that the 1980s writers had on superhero comics and children's changing interactions with them. Whereas the 1960s and the Silver Age of comic books redefined the characteristics of the superhero, the 1980s blew up superheroes into tiny pieces and exposed their inner workings as being fatally flawed and often unrelentingly violent. In other words, most parents would allow their children to read an issue of

The Amazing Spider-Man from 1968 where Spider-Man fought a super villain and still got home in time to join Aunt May for supper. Most parents would not allow their children to read *The Killing Joke* in 1988 where the Joker paralyzes Barbara Gordon and forces Commissioner Gordon to look at naked pictures of his daughter while she's writhing in pain. *The Killing Joke* clearly would not get the Comics Code Authority's stamp of approval, but by the time *The Killing Joke* was published, most children had stopped reading comics.

WHAT SUPERHERO STORIES MEAN FOR CHILDREN TODAY

There is a brutal brilliance to Moore and Bolland's *The Killing Joke* that causes uneasiness on the part of the reader. It is almost as if the reader asks him- or herself, "Should I be reading this?" It is difficult to believe that the characters from that particular graphic novel are the same ones who fought over trinkets in oversized environments only two decades earlier.

This creates a phenomenon where a character can have multiple personalities given specific contexts, audiences, and temporality. Batman in 1995 is extremely different from his 1955 counterpart, but the literal character remains the same. Superheroes become what society needs them to be, catering to audiences of all kinds. And while the 1980s saw the end of the superhero as being a concept strictly designed and marketed for children, that didn't mean the characters were gone entirely for children.

For modern children, superheroes are still powerful constructs through which to learn life lessons. Given the demotion of superhero comic books in children's lives, the bulk of experience with this genre is, as was discussed earlier, primarily in the films and the television shows/cartoons. What also gets lost in this discussion is how adults view superheroes as they relate to children. The attacks by Fredric Wertham on comic books notwithstanding, adults should have a say in how children experience the genre and its messages.

In 1975, Harris Leonard published an article about using superhero literature in college classrooms for the prestigious academic journal *College English*. In the article, Leonard made the following observation regarding superheroes and children:

> American children are a comic book generation; that is, their heroes are comic book heroes, their ideas of justice and morality are comic book ideas, and their gods are comic book gods. Superman is more real to many children than are their parents. Superman's world works. Their parents' world doesn't. It is not surprising, then, to find many adults who retain this comic book view of the world; at least, the uneducated ones do. [50]

There is a two-fold point in Leonard's observation. First, children learn about morality and justice from superheroes. On the surface, that point is reasonable, and this chapter has echoed that sentiment. Second, in Leonard's opinion, people who retain this simplified view of justice and morality are "uneducated" adults. As is so often the case, academics like Leonard choose to denigrate superhero literature. While the 1975 publication date of this article needs to be taken into account, this view that superhero literature is a sophomoric and trivial form of entertainment still persists to this day. Leonard's claim is really a wild exaggeration, as it somehow assumes that people don't mature as they grow older. But the kids who as children thrilled to Batman's black and white battles for justice grew up to become the masterful comic creators like Bolland and Moore who captured Batman's struggle to not kill the Joker despite all the hideous crimes he had committed. Rather than be limited to simplistic understandings of justice, kids raised on comic books usually end up having highly sophisticated ideas about morality.

Fortunately, more recent literature on the subject of children and superheroes highlights the value of these characters and their messages about values. For instance, Justin Martin looked at children's self-perception of themselves in a study that involved children referencing superheroes' moralities. Specifically, Martin's study involved forty-two fourth-grade students completing Likert scales (scales of 1–10) comparing their own morality to that of certain superheroes: Batman, Superman, Spider-Man, the X-Men, and the Fantastic Four. These children rated themselves in similar ways as superheroes on identical questions. For Martin, "superheroes' commitment to justice and its relationship to a belief in a just world may potentially serve an educational function for children's moral development."[51] The children in Martin's study were asked to reflect not only about themselves, but also the fictional characters. Through that reflection, the children made informed decisions about themselves as morally just people. One limitation of this study was the admission by the researcher that "Results indicate that males may identify with superheroes more than their female peers."[52] Nearly all discussions of superheroes with both children and adults alike are subject to this traditional gender bias. Nonetheless, Martin's study shows that learning about superheroes can enhance children's moral development, and this offers good support for the argument that superhero literature holds value. Since superheroes generally embody what a culture regards as the transcendent and desirable qualities of humanity, children can certainly benefit from using superheroes and their exploits as reference points for developing their own moral codes.

GIRLS AND SUPERHEROES

The trend of girls not having the same connection to superheroes as boys is reflected in the literature on superheroes and children as well. The overwhelmingly male presence in superhero literature has ramifications not only for children and superheroes, but culture in general. The chapter on diversity in superhero literature, chapter 8, addresses the role of women in the genre, but young girls experience superhero literature in a unique way.

Sociocultural stereotypes have always held that girls play with dolls and enjoy much calmer theaters of play while boys favor more "rough and tumble" play scenarios. Penny Holland has written about what she calls "zero tolerance" when it comes to children's play. Zero tolerance is an "approach that means that children are not allowed to bring toy weapons into settings, are not allowed to construct or present them with found materials, and are not allowed to enact war play or superhero scenarios."[53] While Holland's opinions regarding zero tolerance are not explicit one way or the other, she says that in her view, "no harm could be done by acting on that assumption."[54] Part of her findings during her study included how girls reacted to superhero play. She found that, girls' "participation in these scenarios [gun, war, and superheroes] was active and enthusiastic and girls often revealed a high level of knowledge about the character themes being drawn on, which gives the lie to the assumption that girls are simply not interested in this area of play."[55] How the girls knew about the character details of the superheroes is unknown, but it seems logical to assume that they learned it from other children or from exposure to superhero entertainment genres.

Penny Holland also noted another interesting aspect of girls and rough play: "girls were rarely seen to show an interest in weapon construction: their interest seemed to rest more squarely with the chase and vanquishing of foes themes underlying much of the dramatic play that emerged."[56] While girls may experience superheroes in a way different than young boys, the "themes" that Holland references are what matters. Even though boys, at least according to Holland, enjoy creating weapons, the theme of vanquishing evil and participating in a scenario that reinforces the tenets of justice and morality was what was most enjoyed by both boys and girls.

Gerard Jones echoes similar sentiments in his book *Killing Monsters: Why Children Need Fantasy, Super Heroes, and Make Believe Violence.* Jones finds similarities in boys' fascinations with superheroes to girls' fascinations with pop stars:

> Enter Britney Spears, every inch the living Barbie doll, but pumping her fists, strutting the stage, blasting out her pop-powered lyrics about hitting and strength, dominating videos full of leaping bodies and flashing explosions by the sheer force of her physical, sexual, cartoony presence.[57]

The link for Jones here is empowerment, which is the primary reason for children finding value in superheroes. Jones's description of Britney Spears as powerful mirrors the image of the powerful superhero. What Jones is arguing is that boys and girls both admire figures, whether real or fictional, who help them imagine themselves as strong and in control. Jones says that adult women tell him that when they were growing up "they identified less with Princess Leia or any of Indy's female friends than with Luke Skywalker, Han Solo, and [Indiana] Jones himself."[58] Those male characters exude strength while their female counterparts represent a narrative trope that relies on age-old representations of women as weaker supporting characters. This refers more to adult women, but the roots of this preference are constructed in the younger years.

Eric Hoffman's *Magic Capes, Amazing Powers: Transforming Superhero Play in the Classroom* also found value in girls participating in superhero play, but there was a distinction made that "Witches, princesses, magic potions, and fairies are common in the fantasy play of young girls. While many people don't think of this as superhero play, I include it in this book because girls use it to explore many of the same issues boys do when they are shooting monsters."[59] Again, although Hoffman notes some distinctions between the actual content of the scenarios boys and girls enact, the underlying purpose to that play remains exploring how to gain power over one's environment. The games may be different for boys and girls, but the goals end up being the same. In their play both boys and girls explore themes of finding strength, utilizing power, and constructing fictional worlds through interactions.

Of course one can't turn a blind eye to the poor job superhero stories generally do in promoting gender equality; most superhero stories are notoriously male-dominated. As Grant Morrison notes of the superhero genre, "Superhero stories were written to be universal and inclusive, but often they've been aimed, it must be said, at boys and young men."[60] Nevertheless, girls do get involved in superhero play as evidenced by the aforementioned books on superhero play in general, but a distinction is always made by the researcher verifying the contexts in which boys and girls learn lessons concerning power, strength, bravery, and morality.

AFFORDANCES AND CONSTRAINTS OF SUPERHEROES FOR CHILDREN

Superheroes can help children develop perceptions of right and wrong. That development occurs not only through schooling and parenting, but also through play, which becomes the one context in children's lives that allows for some autonomy: "While they have limited control in many areas of their real lives, assuming the role of a superhero provides an opportunity to be strong, powerful, and able to control any situation."[61] Karen Bauer and Ernest Dettore assert in an article from *Early Childhood Education Journal* that despite parents perceiving superhero play as "bizarre" and teachers perceiving that same play as "disruptive," there is a benefit for children from superhero play. In particular, Bauer and Dettore say that children playing and imitating superheroes can help with social-emotional development, aesthetic development (putting thoughts into drawn/created images), and cognitive development. The morals and values that are inherent in superheroes as a concept are personified in the children who use superheroes as a vehicle for play. Whether they are interacting with the toys and action figures or simply saying to a friend, "I'm Green Lantern!" makes no difference. Children take on the personas of the figures they emulate while they play. Thus, when a child pretends to be an intergalactic policeman who was chosen from among all the humans on Earth to wield a ring of unimaginable power because he was the most morally just and worthy (Green Lantern), this play helps a child think about the values he wants to have as part of his world.

There are some concerns when it comes to superhero play, however. Penny Holland's commentary and analysis on zero tolerance includes preschool-age children playing with make-believe guns, participating in war situations, and playing as superheroes. Most of her book deals with children and play guns, but the limiting of superhero play was met with trepidation by Holland. In regard to superhero play, she said, "The most significant overall support to children's war, weapon, and superhero play was probably the day-to-day validation of children's interests and creative endeavors."[62] In addition to superhero play validating children's interests, it supported "the intrinsic struggle between good and evil that seems to hold such powerful attraction for young children, particularly boys."[63] Through superheroes, children explore some of the most important aspects of culture and society.

Children can create their own, unique understanding of how the world works through superhero play. Gerard Jones echoed this sentiment saying, "Superhero play has unstated but inherent structure and rules that can keep the aggression from flying out of control."[64] Gerard Jones attributes children's fascination with superheroes to their positions in life: "Of all the challenges children face, one of the biggest is their own powerlessness."[65] Jones, whose career as a writer has included superhero comics, shared his own exploration of superhero literature as a child and how rediscovering those characters in adolescence helped him through the understandably stormy years of middle school. Specifically, "The Hulk smashed through the walls of fear I'd been carrying inside me and freed me to feel everything I had been repressing: rage and pride and the hunger for power over my own life."[66] The Incredible Hulk is a particularly telling character for a young man to favor given the ambiguous nature of the creature. The Hulk, whose stories have dealt with the conflict between man and monster, is not always considered a superhero. Instead, many of the Hulk's stories have dealt with encounters with other characters that fail to understand Bruce Banner and his predicament in life. For a young man struggling with self-identity, idolizing a character that has an alter ego he can't control makes perfect sense; both the fictional character and the young man struggle with how the world perceives them and how to react to those perceptions. In this way, Jones was able to examine some of his own struggles with adolescence by exploring similar struggles when he read about the man/monster the Hulk.

Ironically, many superheroes experience a loss of childhood that directly results from their origins: Batman, Daredevil, Dick Grayson (Robin/Nightwing), and Wolverine are just a few of the heroes whose childhoods are prematurely shattered. These are the same fictional characters who often inspire children to achieve greatness, to never give up, and to seek out the best that humanity has to offer. Perhaps that is the best characteristic these tragic heroes have to offer: a valuing of childhood that comes from heroes who often pine for their own lost innocence. The irony of children wanting to be fictional characters whose reasons for fighting stem from tragic childhoods is perhaps lost on very young children, but that is also a blessing for those same children. When very young, children often only recognize and explore the polarity of a superhero's mission. For example, Batman remains an extremely popular superhero that children try to emulate. Batman's loss of his parents is well chronicled in DC Comics in multiple ways, and the exploration of that split second of brutal violence in an alleyway is one of the golden moments in superhero literature. Yet young children never play out that scene from Batman's life. It wouldn't make sense for them to do so given the horrible situation in which the young Bruce Wayne found himself. Instead, children play out Batman foiling a bank robbery or stopping a bad guy from stealing diamonds. The essence of Batman, which has been constructed over seventy years of continuity, is encapsulated in a brief scenario that highlights his most elemental character trait: the fighter of crime. Not all components of a superhero's essence need to be displayed in every incarnation.

It is essential when discussing superhero play and children that the perception of superheroes as being overly violent is an adult construction. Adults write superhero comic stories, adults are responsible for their distribution, and adults are the ones who crave the tragedies that sometimes come packaged with the superheroes. There is nothing wrong with this at all, and creators are the first to admit that tragedy in superhero literature is one of the aspects that makes it an appealing genre to study. But children who play superheroes, who imagine superheroes as their role models, do so in regard to their own experiences with the characters, experiences that, for the better, generally do not include the super-violent and/or tragic elements of the superheroes' mythologies. When kids pretend to be Wolverine, they imagine themselves as the Wolverine from the *Super Hero Squad*, not the dark hero of the film *X-Men Origins: Wolverine*.[67]

Unfortunately, for all the importance superheroes can have for children, when a child reaches the front door of the school, they usually have to leave their superheroes behind. Too often, fictional characters that children grow up with are demeaned in traditional schooling in favor of literature that reflects a more standardized vision of what is worthy of being read. From elementary school all the way through graduate school, the characters that children grew up with are rarely honored despite their influences on childhood. Yet for educators to ignore superheroes is to miss the power for learning embedded in these characters. In her book *Writing Superheroes: Contemporary Childhood, Popular Culture, and Classroom Literacy*, literacy educator Anne Haas Dyson documents the rich learning that occurred in an urban classroom of seven- to nine-year-olds who not only played in the roles of superheroes but also wrote their own simple superhero stories as part of their school work. What Dyson found supports the argument this chapter has been making, that superheroes provide fertile grounds for children to explore a wide range of issues that concern them. Even more importantly, Dyson learned that when children play as superheroes, this play transforms them into heroes themselves:

> In truth, these children were sometimes superheroes, in two senses. In their creation of imaginary worlds on paper and playground, the children often imagined themselves heroes with powers rooted in accident of nature or science. Their actions were responses to impending physical doom—most often the destruction of the world by evil others. But in their own social worlds, children sometimes become superheroes of another sort, ones with powers rooted in social circumstance. Their actions were responses to verbal constraints—they were not intent on saving the adult world, but on engaging in child imagined ones.[68]

What we ought to take from Dyson's research and the other scholars mentioned in this chapter, is that superheroes can play powerful roles in children's development. It is vital to acknowledge the significant influence superheroes have on people growing up and not ignore them when these same people become teenagers and adults. Superheroes will always have lessons to teach us no matter how old we are, and those lessons will also encompass what we, as a culture, value.

NOTES

1. Fredric Wertham, *Seduction of the Innocent* (New York: Reinhart and Company, Inc., 1954).

2. Gerard Jones, *Men of Tomorrow: Geeks, Gangsters, and the Birth of the Comic Book* (New York: Basic Books, 2004), 274–77.

3. Bradford Wright, *Comic Book Nation: The Transformation of Youth Culture in America* (Baltimore: Johns Hopkins University Press, 2003), 154–79.

4. David Hajdu, *The Ten-Cent Plague: The Great Comic-Book Scare and How It Changed America* (New York: Farrar, Straus and Giroux, 2008).

5. Wertham, *Seduction of the Innocent*, 190.

6. Mark Millar and Bryan Hitch, *The Ultimates: Ultimate Collection* (New York: Marvel Comics, 2010).

7. Frank Miller and Klaus Janson, *The Dark Knight Returns* (New York: DC Comics, 1986).

8. Brian Michael Bendis and Alex Maleev, *Daredevil: Ultimate Collection,* vol. 1 (New York: Marvel Comics, 2010).

9. Umberto Eco and Natalie Chilton, "The Myth of Superman," *Diacritics* 2, no. 1 (Spring 1972): 22.

10. Eco and Chilton, "The Myth of Superman," 22.

11. Mark Millar, J. G. Jones, and Paul Mount, *Wanted* (New York: Top Cow Productions/Image Comics, 2007).

12. "The Men Without Fear: Creating Daredevil," *Daredevil*, directed by Mark Stephen Johnson (2003; 20th Century Fox, 2003), DVD. Documentary on DVD Extras.

13. *The Super Hero Squad: Volume 1*, directed by Michael Gerard (Shout! Factory, 2010), DVD.

14. Dennis O'Neil and Neal Adams, *Green Lantern/Green Arrow Collection: Volume 1* (New York: DC Comics, 2004).

15. Peter Coogan, *Superhero: The Secret Origin of a Genre* (Austin, TX: Monkey Brain, 2006), 214–18.

16. Alan Moore and Dave Gibbons, *Watchmen* (New York: DC Comics, 1986).

17. Alan Moore and Brian Bolland, *Batman: The Killing Joke* (New York: DC Comics, 1988).

18. David Michelinie and Todd McFarlane, *Spider-Man Visionaries: Todd McFarlane* (New York: Marvel Comics, 2003).

19. Kevin Eastman and Peter Laird, *Teenage Mutant Ninja Turtles: The Ultimate Collection*, vol. 1 (San Diego, CA: IDW Publishing, 2012).

20. Jim Starlin and Jim Aparo, "A Death in the Family, Book 2," *Batman* vol. 1, no. 427 (December 1988).

21. Moore and Bolland, *The Killing Joke*.

22. Chris Claremont and John Byrne, "The Fate of the Phoenix!" *Uncanny X-Men* vol. 1, no. 137 (September 1980).

23. Frank Miller, "Last Hand," *Daredevil* vol. 1, no. 181 (April 1982).

24. Marv Wolfman and George Pérez, "A Flash of the Lightning!" *Crisis on Infinite Earths* vol. 1, no. 8 (November 1985).

25. Marv Wolfman and George Pérez, "Beyond the Silent Night," *Crisis on Infinite Earths* vol. 1, no. 7 (October 1985).

26. Jim Starlin, *The Death of Captain Marvel* (New York: Marvel Comics, 1982).

27. Jim Shooter and Mike Zeck, "Secret Wars—Invasion," *Marvel Super Heroes Secret Wars* vol. 1, no. 8 (December 1984).

28. *The Adventures of Superman: The Complete First Season* (1952; Warner Home Video, 2005), DVD.

29. *Spider-Man: The '67 Collection* (1967; Walt Disney Video, 2004), DVD.

30. *Super Friends! Season 1, Volume 1* (1973; Warner Home Video, 2010), DVD.

31. *Transformers: The Complete First Season* (1984; Shout! Factory, 2009), DVD.

32. *Thundercats: Season 1, Part 1* (1984; Warner Home Video, 2011), DVD.

33. *G.I. Joe: A Real American Hero: Season 1.1* (1985; Shout! Factory, 2005), DVD.

34. *He-Man and the Masters of the Universe: Season One, Volume 1* (1983; BCI/Eclipse, 2005), DVD.

35. *Star Wars*, directed by George Lucas (20th Century Fox, 1977).

36. *Superman: The Movie*, directed by Richard Donner (Warner Brothers, 1978).

37. *Superman II*, directed by Richard Lester (Warner Brothers, 1981).

38. *Spider-Man and His Amazing Friends*, currently unavailable on DVD. Originally aired on NBC 1981–1983.

39. *The Incredible Hulk*, currently unavailable in North America Region DVD format. Originally aired on NBC in 1982.

40. *Ruby-Spears Superman* (1988; Warner Home Video, 2009), DVD.

41. *X-Men: Pryde of the X-Men* (1989; Best Film & Video Corp., 1992), VHS.

42. *Superboy: The Complete First Season* (1988; Warner Home Video, 2006), DVD.

43. *The Flash: The Complete Series* (1990–1991; Warner Home Video, 2006), DVD.

44. *X-Men: Volume 1* (1992–1993; Walt Disney Video, 2009), DVD.

45. *Spider-Man*, currently unavailable as complete seasons on DVD. Originally aired on Fox 1994–1998.

46. *Batman: The Animated Series, Volume One* (1992; Warner Home Video, 2004), DVD.

47. "Heart of Ice," *Batman: The Animated Series, Volume One*, directed by Bruce Timm (1992, Warner Home Video, 2004), DVD.

48. "As Barry Jenkins, Ohio '69, Says: 'A Person Has to Have Intelligence to Read Them,'" *Esquire* vol. 66, no. 3 (September 1966): 117.

49. Wright, *Comic Book Nation*, 172–73.

50. Harris K. Leonard, "The Classics—Alive and Well with Superman," *College English* 37, no. 4 (December 1975): 406.

51. Justin Martin, "Children's Attitudes toward Super Heroes as a Potential Indicator of Their Moral Understanding," *Journal of Moral Education* vol. 36, no. 2 (June 2007): 241.

52. Martin, " Children's Attitudes toward Super Heroes," 248.

53. Penny Holland, *We Don't Play with Guns Here: War, Weapon and Superhero Play in the Early Years* (Maidenhead, UK: Open University Press, 2003), 2.

54. Holland, *We Don't Play with Guns Here*, 10.

55. Holland, *We Don't Play with Guns Here*, 55.

56. Holland, *We Don't Play with Guns Here*, 56.

57. Gerard Jones, *Killing Monsters: Why Children Need Fantasy, Super Heroes, and Make-Believe Violence* (New York: Basic Books, 2002), 94.

58. Jones, *Killing Monsters*, 82.

59. Eric Hoffman, *Magic Capes, Amazing Powers: Transforming Superhero Play in the Classroom* (St. Paul, MN: Redleaf Press, 2004), 10.

60. Grant Morrison, *Supergods: What Masked Vigilantes, Miraculous Mutants, and a Sun God from Smallville Can Teach Us about Being Human* (New York: Spiegel & Grau, 2011), 40.

61. Karen L. Bauer and Ernest Dettore, "Superhero Play: What's a Teacher to Do?" *Early Childhood Education Journal* 25, no. 1 (September 1997): 17.

62. Holland, *We Don't Play with Guns Here*, 55.

63. Holland, *We Don't Play with Guns Here*, 34.

64. Jones, *Killing Monsters*, 72.

65. Jones, *Killing Monsters*, 65.

66. Jones, *Killing Monsters*, 15.

67. *X-Men Origins: Wolverine*, directed by Gavin Hood (2009, 20th Century Fox).

68. Anne Haas Dyson, *Writing Superheroes: Contemporary Childhood, Popular Culture, and Classroom Literacy* (New York: Teachers College Press, 1997), 1–2.

Chapter Eight

Diversity in Superheroes

Superhero stories are all grounded in the exploration and deconstruction of themes. Since none of these characters is real and the possibility of them ever existing is basically nil, superheroes become representations of human ideals, emotions, tragedies, evils, and conflicts. At face value, Superman fighting Lex Luthor is a brightly clad man tangling with a man in a business suit. Thematically, however, Superman's dispute with Luthor goes much deeper encompassing issues of human ingenuity, the messiah complex, alienation, and jealousy. In the hands of skilled writers, the simple action stories of superheroes often are transformed into socioculturally loaded narratives ripe with complex emotions and deep character deconstruction.

These themes of difference, alienation, and mutantism make superhero stories an excellent genre for exploring the concept of "the other," the person who is different and never quite gets accepted by society. When it comes to superhero literature, issues of otherness are also complicated by a nonfictional history that reflects monoculturalism among most of the comic creators. To a great extent, comic writers, artists, inkers, editors, and other members of the many creative teams are predominantly white males. This traditional homogeneity among the genre's creators affects both racial diversity and gender equality with the comics' stories themselves. The hypersexualized presentation of superheroines and female characters in general in superhero literature presents problems for new and old readers alike. The obvious lack of racial diversity in the superhero world is also highly problematic.

Of course these problems are not new, and many others have discussed them. In his blog *40 Acres and a Cubicle: The Official Blog of Post-Racial America*, O. K. Kai makes this observation about the ongoing problem of the lack of diversity in the superhero genre:

This Summer's movies have been packed with action and super powers. The three most anticipated movies of this summer were based on superheroes. *The Avengers* surpassed my expectations, I didn't bother to see the *Spider-Man* reboot, and *The Dark Knight Rises* was just as epic and dramatic as I hoped it would be. . . . These movies remind me of my childhood, when I used to pretend that I was a superhero and ran around outside with my friends. But I had to make up superheroes back then, you know, because I'm Black. Black boys these days are in the exact same predicament, even when there are movies like *The Avengers* that are packed with characters. Come to think of it, there are no Black superhero movies. Decades of cinema and no one has trusted the fate of the world solely in the hands of a superbrotha. [1]

Kai does discuss the films *Blankman*, *Blade*, and *Spawn*, which all starred black superheroes, but he questions whether this is real progress: "Hellspawns and vampires almost act as analogies for the Black male struggle, trying to do good while the world fears your kind and wants to kill you."[2] In Kai's and other's views, superheroes still have a long way to go to create a sense of equality. Fortunately, some recent superhero storylines have helped bring even more attention to these concerns and show that comics publishers are perhaps finally trying to more fully acknowledge the need to tell superhero stories using a broader view of humanity.

A MATTER OF CASE STUDIES

The lack of diversity in superhero comics is an extremely large issue, and discussing all of its implications in one chapter of a book dedicated to the academicization and canonization of superhero literature is impossible. Therefore, this chapter is not intended to be a comprehensive examination of the issue of superhero diversity. Instead, the overarching concerns of the lack of diversity in superhero literature will be explored through two major and contemporary comic book stories: The introduction of Miles Morales, a half-black and half-Hispanic teenager, as the new Ultimate Spider-Man and the hypersexualized depiction of Starfire and Catwoman in DC's New 52 reboot. While this limits the scope of this chapter, it does provide a useful starting point for discussing the issue of superhero diversity at the present moment.

A NEW SPIDER-MAN

Marvel Comics has a limited number of black superheroes: Black Panther, Storm, Blade, Falcon, Dagger, Bishop, Luke Cage, and recently Nick Fury and Spider-Man, to name some of them. All of these characters are important in the continuity of the universe, but for the most part their name recognition is not nearly as high as for white superheroes. Many readers may not even know who some of the characters mentioned above are, and even seasoned readers may have a difficult time referencing specific stories where the characters have had feature roles.

One name on that list may come as a surprise: Spider-Man. We'll take up that issue in a moment, but other than Spider-Man, among the other black superheroes listed, only Storm from the X-Men is very well known. As a black woman, Storm became a major player in the Marvel Universe when she debuted with the X-Men in *Giant Size X-Men #1*,[3] and Halle Berry's depiction of the character in the X-Men films made Storm one of the most popular superheroines ever. However, even Storm with her now strong name recognition is nowhere near as popular as Spider-Man.

Recently, the Spider-Man character in the Ultimate Comics continuity has had his racial identity changed. Marvel Comics made an editorial decision to have Miles Morales, a "half-black, half-Hispanic"[4] teenager assume the vaunted role of everyone's favorite wall crawler. In this section we will examine this important change to *Ultimate Spider-Man* to see how this editorial change is currently affecting current comic books and superhero literature.

Marvel's Ultimate line of comic books was discussed in detail in chapter 4, as it was a reboot Marvel initiated in order to update its stories and distance some of its new stories from their previous convoluted continuities. As it is an alternative line of comic books, Ultimate Comics are *not* what Marvel calls the 616 universe. The 616 universe is what is considered to be the universe where all of Marvel's main stories and continuity occur, similar to DC's Earth 1. Therefore, from Marvel's perspective, it is the 616 universe that is considered its primary universe in terms of continuity, and it is the 616 universe whose stories most readers are familiar with from their past. So, for the sake of clarity, it's important to note that Marvel has two Spider-Man characters, one in the 616 universe and one in the Ultimate universe. The Spider-Man in the 616 universe is still Peter Parker, a Caucasian male. But in the Ultimate universe, Spider-Man is now Miles Morales, who was classified by *USA Today* as of "half-black, half-Hispanic" ethnicity.

The Ultimate Comics version of Peter Parker died in *Ultimate Comics Spider-Man #160* at the hands of the Green Goblin.[5] After Parker's death, Miles Morales, who also gains his spider powers from a radioactive spider, takes up Peter Parker's job as Spider-Man and carries on the webslinger's legacy in the Ultimate universe. Reaction to this from the fan community was mixed, but many fans did not approve of this move. Axel Alonso, the current editor in chief of Marvel Comics, defended the move saying, "What you have is a Spider-Man for the 21st century who's reflective of our culture and diversity. We think that readers will fall in love with Miles Morales the same way they fell in love with Peter Parker."[6] This quote comes from *USA*

Today's online article from August 1, 2011, which revealed who the new Ultimate Spider-Man was going to be.

At the bottom of the *USA Today* article's webpage, fan posts reacting to the news were intense. There were 462 posts made (as of May 13, 2012), and the following 4 sample posts give some flavor for the range of reactions fans had:

PMF
I'm sorry but I find this to be idiotic. I grew up in the Projects of NYC. I was born here, my parents came from Cuba in the 40s. My favorite comic book character was Captain America—a blonde haired, blue eyed, white guy and I never felt anything negative about having to look like him or anything like that. Reinventing existing characters, parallel universe or not, is an easy out in terms of creativity. Sure, create culturally diverse characters but note the key word . . . CREATE. Don't reinvent, create. Marvel, you guys were a big part of this 49 year olds youth and the positive images of heroes like Cap helped. Enough with reinventing please.

barreljumper.com
SPIDER-MAN IS PETER PARKER.

techguy74
Why do all Super Heroes, Princesses, TV shows have to be PREDOMINANT-LY WHITE??
Most of you don't even realize how vanilla the entertainment in our society really is. . . . You rarely see a minority super hero. You almost never see a minority save the day in the movies. . . . Most TV programming is predominately of the vanilla flavor. . . . Most of the sports team I am on are vanilla. Face it—minorities want and need super heroes as well.

JoeinLA
I'm more interested in this than seeing Peter Parker go through the motions for another 40+ years. I actually read comics and haven't bought a Spider-Man book for years.[7]

The majority of the comments posted were negative in nature, berating Marvel Comics for changing a favorite childhood character. Nevertheless, a limited number of fans did make posts that supported the character change. As noted above, the responder named "techguy74" cited the overabundance of white superheroes in superhero literature as one reason why he supported Miles Morales becoming Ultimate Spider-Man. Even without providing specific statistics, it seems clear that this poster's claim is accurate about the vast majority of superheroes being white. This is obviously true of the most famous superheroes, such as Superman, Batman, Wonder Woman, and Captain America. It is hard to ignore the sociocultural implications of this lack of diversity among superheroes. In light of this observation, it seems very significant that Marvel Comics was willing to change the race of a character who had been white for close to fifty years. This is, without a doubt, one of the more unique and socially relevant editorial moves Marvel has ever made.

One of the important aspects of superhero literature as a genre is that this genre evolves. Evolution can be good and it can be bad, but certainly there seems great potential good for Marvel trying to take a prominent step forward in making a major superhero more representative of society as a whole. Of course, change is not easy for everyone, and fans often resist these kinds of major evolutions. The sometimes static nature of superhero comic fandom, as was discussed in chapter 3, very often does not want superheroes to change very much, if at all. If fans can become irate just because DC put pants on Wonder Woman, it's not surprising that many fans would react negatively to the changing of a major superhero's ethnicity.

One major difference in the Miles Morales and Peter Parker Spider-Man characters is their costumes. Whereas Peter Parker wore (and still wears in 616 continuity) his traditional red and blue suit, Miles Morales wears an all-black suit with stylized red webbing on it. Changing the character's attire is a significant strategy by Marvel to distinguish the new Spider-Man from the original Spider-Man. The connection between characters and their costume is very strong, as evidenced by the uproar that attire changes can cause. When Miles Morales first becomes Spider-Man, he wears Peter Parker's original-style suit, but he is told that wearing the suit may not be respectful to the recently deceased Peter Parker. This leads Miles to say to himself, "Maybe the costume is in bad taste."[8] Since comparisons were and will continue to be made between Miles Morales and Peter Parker, differentiating their attire appears to be a practical move by Marvel to help separate the two characters. This change allows Miles to make the mantle of Spider-Man his own going forward.

Marvel has changed the ethnicity of its characters before. For today's fans of Marvel Comics, Nick Fury, the eye patch–wearing head of S.H.I.E.L.D., is African American. But for the first forty years of his existence as a character, Fury was a white man characterized by graying sideburns, similar in appearance to Reed Richards from the Fantastic Four. Changing Fury's race was a move made by Mark Millar and Brian Hitch in the *Ultimates* comic series which reenvisioned Marvel's Avengers superhero team. In the comic Nick Fury himself even states that if someone were to play him in a movie, it would have to be Samuel L. Jackson.[9]

This issue of race being changeable is discussed by Adilifu Nama in his book *Super Black*:

> These racially remixed superheroes offer audiences familiar points of reference that, as black superheroes, suggest a range of ideas, cultural points of interests, compelling themes, and multiple meanings that were not previously

present. Frequently, the black versions are more chic, politically provocative, and ideologically dynamic than the established white superheroes they were modeled after. [10]

Nick Fury's character changed from that of a Cold War spy whose ruthlessness was necessary and understandable in a Cold War setting, to a man whose leadership and ability to deal with major problems was of paramount importance.

The villain Kingpin was also changed in the film adaptation of *Daredevil*. [11] Traditionally the Kingpin was a rotund and bald white man who controlled all of the crime in New York City. As Frank Miller put it, "He was the Jackie Gleason of supervillains." [12] Michael Clarke Duncan, an African American actor, was cast in the role for the feature film because of his undeniable presence in both a physical and emotional sense. Both Nick Fury and Kingpin are major mainstays in the Marvel Universe, but both of their traditional characteristics were reinterpreted for modern contexts and audiences. While the Kingpin's character never maintained the transition from the *Daredevil* film to the comic books (probably due to the film's negative reception), Nick Fury's transition seems to have more legs going forward. The recent Marvel Studios films have featured Samuel L. Jackson as Nick Fury (just as Nick himself wanted!), and the 2012 film *The Avengers* has become one of the most successful motion pictures of all time. [13] This has essentially cemented Nick Fury's continued existence as an African American character in the Marvel universe. Additionally, Marvel has recently written Nick Fury's change in ethnicity into the continuity of the 616 Marvel Universe (original continuity) in a story that showcases the original Nick Fury having a son who is of African American descent. [14]

Although these are important moves to diversify its heroes, Marvel's changing the race of Nick Fury and the Kingpin doesn't represent nearly the cultural significance of changing Spider-Man's race. Spider-Man is a major popular and American culture icon and he reaches much more broadly into public cultural consciousness than Nick Fury or the Kingpin ever will. So when Marvel Comics radically changes the character of Spider-Man, the reaction is bound to be passionate both for and against this editorial decision.

And there needs to be a distinction made here when it comes to the discussion of Miles Morales becoming Ultimate Spider-Man. Marvel did not alter "Peter Parker"; instead, a second character who is of a different ethnicity took up the identity of Spider-Man. For all intents and purposes, Peter Parker is deceased in the Ultimate Marvel Universe. The boy who replaced Spider-Man has taken up the cause that Peter Parker left behind. This boy, Miles Morales, also happens to be of black and Hispanic descent, but it is not Morales's race that drives him. Instead, he is trying to fight the same injustices and evils that Peter Parker always fought. Morales's value system still reflects that of the traditional superhero.

That distinction in superhero literature, separating the man from the costume, is a major theme that has been deconstructed in many stories including *Daredevil: Born Again*,[15] *Smallville*,[16] and *Batman: Knightfall*.[17] That separation usually leads to the character reclaiming or attaining his or her position as the costumed superhero. An unbreakable link between hero and alter ego is always celebrated in these stories, and for Miles Morales as Ultimate Spider-Man, this creates a conundrum. Peter Parker gained super powers after being bitten by a radioactive spider, but that event didn't actually make him into a superhero. In order for Parker to truly become Spider-Man, he needed to experience the tragedy of his uncle being murdered. Miles Morales possesses one-half of this equation (the spider powers), but the unique tragedy that Peter Parker experienced isn't there for Miles Morales. Thus while Morales gained the powers and mantle of Spider-Man, he did not also have the seminal experience by which Parker gained his lesson about great power coming with great responsibility. It remains to be seen how Morales will fare as Spider-Man without that catalyst, one that remains perhaps the most important catalysts in all of superhero history.

The truest answer, though, about whether the new Ultimate Spider-Man is a success has to do with how well his comic book is selling. Diamond Distributors is a major comic book distributor in the United States, and it keeps track of how comic books sell, focusing on both units sold (how many literal comic books were bought) and how much money a book made. This is an important distinction to make, since some comic books cost more than others. Here is how *Ultimate Comics: Spider-Man* sold in its first few months of publication. In its first month of publication (September 2011), *Ultimate Comics: Spider-Man #1* (first solo title of Miles Morales as Spider-Man) ranked ninth in overall sales. That's impressive, although it is also typical for an issue #1 of a title to sell well since fans are often excited about #1 events. In addition, there is also usually extra buying of issue #1s by people who are hoping the title may gain in collectible value. This sort of speculative buying also pushes up the total number of sales for many issue #1s in comics. That same month, Marvel released *Ultimate Comics: Spider-Man #2*. Sales for issue #2 of the comic ranked only thirty-fifth. That is a drop of twenty-six positions between issues 1 and 2 in the same month. This rank is where the title has remained over its first few months of publication: thirty-seventh in October, thirty-seventh in November, thirtieth in December, thirtieth in January 2012, and so on. Somewhat more telling, perhaps, is that *The Amazing Spider-Man*, the original Spider-Man title in the 616 continuity, currently sells better than *Ultimate Comics: Spider-Man*.[18]

Marvel has a trick up its sleeve, though. In the summer of 2012, they are having an "event series" where the two Spider-Man characters will cross over into each others' books in a series called *Spider-Men*. Trying to appeal to as many Spider-Man fans as possible makes sense for both titles.

Going back to why this matters, Miles Morales becoming Spider-Man is a gamble on the part of Marvel and its editorial board. While sales for *Ultimate Comics: Spider-Man* may not be exactly where Marvel wants them to be, the fact that the book is in the upper third of all comic book sales every month is a good indication that the character is working.

Interestingly, despite Spider-Man's race changing, stories in *Ultimate Comics: Spider-Man* do not focus on social injustice issues or any other subliminal societal concerns. Instead, the comic is simply about Spider-Man with all the charm and wit that one would expect from the traditional web-slinger. Nevertheless, Adilifu Nama makes one last assertion regarding black superheroes who take on the role(s) of traditionally white superheroes: "Black superheroes should never be just a colorized version of the original because that would affirm notions that African Americans are at best a passive reflection and at worst a pathological reaction to white America."[19] From Nama's perspective, and that of many other people, Morales still has a lot to accomplish in his role as Spider-Man.

Only time will truly tell whether making Miles Morales into Spider-Man will be a move that superhero comic book fans can get behind. On the positive side, though, having the young Morales become Spider-Man does affirm that the superhero genre is open to racial diversification. Miles Morales is representative of a new style of superhero narratives where traditional and archaic perceptions of superhero mythology and lore are challenged. That new style reflects changing social landscapes and evolving identities of who our superheroes are. Not everyone may be happy with the decisions that comic book editors make, but as the United States' population grows ever more diverse, there is something very important about the idea that anyone can take up the mantle of Superhero, no matter what his or her race is.

STARFIRE'S SEXUAL PROPOSAL

Unlike the famous wall crawler, Starfire is a DC Comics character with whom few casual fans are likely to be familiar. As a member of the Teen Titans, Starfire is an alien from the planet Tamaran with reddish/orange skin and dark red hair. Physically, Starfire is proportioned like most superheroines. She is an exaggerated Barbie doll with long legs, a thin waist, and a large bust. When the character first premiered in 1980,[20] she was physically sexualized, but time and different creators have evolved the character into someone who is physically unrealistic and hypersexualized. Not only is the character's body often sexually depicted using suggestive poses, her clothing is really nothing more than a purple swimsuit. In the issue *Red Hood and the*

Outlaws #1,[21] which will become the focus of this analysis, Starfire wears a literal purple swimsuit that even the most cavalier of Victoria's Secret models might raise an eyebrow at.

The history of Starfire's character is also quite minimal in that she has always been a supporting member of the superhero team The Teen Titans. Starfire has been romantically involved with Dick Grayson, the original Robin, and now Nightwing, and her powers are quite standard for a superhero: flight, enhanced strength, and the ability to shoot lasers from her hands. Simply put, only the most devoted of fans would consider her anything more than a Grade B character.

Whereas Marvel Comics pushed the envelope with Miles Morales in a socioculturally positive way, one might claim that DC Comics actually regressed in its New 52 relaunch in regard to Starfire and many other superheroines. As a character in the comic series *Red Hood and the Outlaws*, Starfire's appearance and demeanor in the premiere issue of the series left many readers and critics disappointed and confused. "The Outlaws" that the title refers to are a group of disgruntled "heroes" who take it upon themselves to operate independently. The outlaws include the Red Hood (Jason Todd, the second Robin, who had previously died at the hands of the Joker and was resurrected), Roy Harper (Green Arrow's former partner who had a falling out with the emerald archer), and Starfire. Together, they operate as a group that fights for its own purposes.

Because Starfire is an alien from another world, her perceptions of human social mores and cultural customs are limited. In the first issue of *Red Hood and the Outlaws* by Scott Lobdell and Kenneth Rocafort, Starfire is characterized as a highly sexual being. While Starfire and Roy Harper are lounging on the beach together, Starfire offers a proposal:

Starfire: "Do you want to have sex with me?"

Roy: "KAK! Um, but—uh—aren't you—um, sorta—Jason's girl?"

Starfire: "Absurd. I am free to do **what** I want **when** I want. If you are not interested I can probably—"

Roy: "No. No—happy to oblige. So, is there anything I need to know about making love to a Tamaranean?"

Starfire: "Just that love has nothing to do with it."[22]

In this rather unusual exchange, the writers work in Starfire's background as an alien, a Tamaranean, as a way to justify her brazen proposal. The writers are asking us to believe that Starfire can act outside human moral codes since she's an alien. What becomes problematic, however, is the way the character is physically portrayed. Yes, Starfire is an alien, but she is drawn to look exactly like a human. Her face and body are human. Her skin is orange and her eyes are pure green and lack pupils, but otherwise everything about her looks human. She has no claws, no tentacles, no scales. She looks like every other perfectly proportioned human superheroine. Starfire may be "Tamaranean," but her appearance is so humanlike that a closer analysis of her alien code of sexuality is warranted.

DC's New 52 reboot/relaunch was designed to be a new beginning where the old ways of reading and interacting with superhero literature and comic books in general was supposed to be challenged, updated, and altogether changed in a positive way. In the months leading up to DC's New 52 relaunch, Laura Hudson, a columnist who writes about comic culture from the website Comics Alliance,[23] wrote an article that highlighted issues of women creators in comic books. She reported on an incident at a comic book convention panel where the co-publisher of DC Comics, Dan DiDio, was asked by a fan why only 1 percent of the comic creators at DC were females. According to Hudson, DiDio answered the question in a very defensive manner: "'What do those numbers mean to you? What do they mean to you? Who should we be hiring? Tell me right now. Who should we be hiring right now? Tell me.'"[24]

It's hard to read DiDio's response as anything but defensive. After all, DiDio is a leading figure in a major comics publishing house. Comics have traditionally been a very male-dominated medium. The few female comic creators in the field have received much less publicity than their male counterparts. In analyzing this issue, Laura Hudson points out that DC's track record with issues of diversity is not very strong in general. She observes that in DC's reboot transition series, *Flashpoint*, the postapocalyptic world in which the story takes place includes a reference to the continent of Africa as being "ape-controlled,"[25] a very problematic and poorly worded statement. Hudson asserts that this lack of cultural sensitivity "didn't come from any sort of prejudice, but simply from this sort of lack of awareness."[26] However, these instances, the "ape-controlled" story point and the 1 percent question from the fan, were part of the build-up to the huge reboot/relaunch DC had planned. Dan DiDio himself even praised the creative direction of the New 52 from a diversity perspective, saying in an interview with the *Washington Post*, "One of the things we looked at was that we wanted the DC Universe to be reflective of our reading audience, and by doing so it was important for us to look at characters like Batwing."[27] Batwing is a black superhero in the Batman stories, and he primarily operates out of Africa. One of the stated goals of DC's publication team, then, was for the New 52 to diversify the DC Universe beyond its traditional limitations.

The comic book news site comicbook.com even published a short news story detailing "Five Things We Love about DC Comics Relaunch."[28]

Among those five things were "More Ethnic Diversity" and "More Women." Interestingly enough, this short news story was published on August 30, 2011. That was one day before *Justice League #1* was released, a date that marks the beginning of the New 52. That means the list was made before Starfire made her unprompted sexual proposal in *Red Hood and the Outlaws #1*.

The point remains that the New 52 was supposed to revolutionize superhero literature, which for the past seventy years has been quite standardized from both a narrative and sociocultural perspective. It is very disappointing, then, that rather than getting more realistic portrayals of women, readers are instead given a sexualized Starfire who offers to have no-strings-attached sex just because she's an alien. Yes, she's an alien, but her offer seems a lot more like male wish fulfillment than a well-thought-out alien code of conduct. Even if a reader accepts that Tamaraneans really are pretty radically different from humans, Starfire's portrayal still seems highly regressive and damaging, a very poor way to usher in a new era of cultural diversity and gender equity in the superhero universe.

One of the main problems with Starfire's characterization is where her power is derived as a superhero. Yes, she can fly and shoot lasers, but those powers are never really the crux of any superhero's value. Superman's value comes in the form of his morality and his duality, both as a human in disguise and an alien. Navigating those identities becomes Superman's appeal, while the flashy aesthetics of flight and strength become the vehicle through which that identity navigation occurs. For Starfire, there is no underlying structure of self-identity, and the identity navigation that Lobdell and Rocafort assert in *Red Hood and the Outlaws* is that of pure sexuality: on my planet it's OK to have sex with as many people as I want, so the same code will apply to my actions on Earth. Maybe readers could accept this in the 1960s, but today free love doesn't seem like much of a base from which to build a complex personal identity.

And if comparing Starfire to Superman seems a bit dissonant, since Superman is a male and Starfire is a female, then consider Starfire when placed up against the seminal superheroine Wonder Woman. Just as both Superman and Starfire are isolated because they are aliens, Wonder Woman also experiences problems with being an outsider. Although Wonder Woman is not an extraterrestrial alien, she does come from the island of Themyscira where no men are allowed. When Wonder Woman comes to the United States, or "Man's World," as she calls it, she experiences the same identity navigation challenges as Starfire and Superman. Wonder Woman must define her place in a new world whose beliefs and value systems do not perfectly match her own. Yet Wonder Woman doesn't go around proposing sexual acts with her acquaintances out of the blue. Instead, Wonder Woman actively questions the world in which she finds herself, where men hold more power than women. There are few blatantly sexual scenes in Wonder Woman's history and iconography. Her attire and appearance are undoubtedly sexual, but acts of sexuality are quite rare in Wonder Woman stories. Perhaps the most infamous sexual depiction of Wonder Woman occurred in Frank Miller's sequel *The Dark Knight Strikes Again* where Miller has several splash pages of Superman having intercourse with Wonder Woman while in flight.[29] In the context of Wonder Woman's mythology, that scene revealed a side of Wonder Woman that had not been previously explored. For the most part, however, Wonder Woman's mythology has been rooted in being a strong woman who believes in what she stands for and so her sexual characteristics are linked to the sociocultural foundations of her character. It's not that a character like Starfire can't have sex; it's just that the writers offer no character development on which to justify the act, leaving us forced to view it as primarily lurid and exploitive.

Finally, Wonder Woman's attire brings another issue to this discussion. The functionality and design of Wonder Woman's suit was addressed in chapter 5 on superhero iconography, but as revealing as Wonder Woman's costume is, it is nowhere near as revealing as Starfire's. Additionally, Wonder Woman's costume has a backstory in which her attire represents the cultural norms of Themyscira. Since Wonder Woman was created in 1941, her costume also clearly is linked to the patriotic focus of America during World War II. Starfire's superhero costume lacks all of these groundings. Instead, it's just a thin purple bikini that shows off her body.

Given all of this, where does Starfire's power, as both a woman and a superhero, derive? The short answer is that Starfire's power is rooted in her sexuality. Superheroines have always been depicted as hypersexualized going back to Wonder Woman in the 1940s, Susan Storm in the 1960s, and Phoenix/Jean Grey in the 1980s. This is, unfortunately, nothing new. However, none of these characters relied heavily on their sexuality, almost as if that sexuality were itself a super power. This is where Starfire breaks troubling ground. If *Red Hood and the Outlaws* is supposed to be one of DC's New 52 Comics, meant to rethink the superhero genre, it seems less than effective. It's laudable that DC wanted to feature more female superheroes in its relaunch, but in Starfire's case, maybe more isn't so great after all. Or, recalling the issue of only 1 percent of comics creators being female, maybe it would have helped if a woman had been part of the creative team for *Red Hood and the Outlaws*. Or consider what George Gene Gustines and Adam Kepler from the *New York Times* have to say on the subject: Starfire, they say, has changed "from a buxom free spirit into a lobotomized bimbo."[30] For that reason, Gustines and Kepler ranked *Red Hood and the Outlaws* as one of "Our Worst" of DC's New 52 reboot.

WHAT STARFIRE'S DEPICTION MEANS

All of the criticism and all of the analysis of Starfire's depiction in *Red Hood and the Outlaws* is truly about the state of superhero literature at this point in time. Superhero literature has, and always has had, a male-dominated readership, and that demographic is accommodated in such titles as *Grimm's Fairy Tales* and *Red Sonja*. Those titles are not "superhero" titles, but they are still sold alongside titles such as *Superman*, *The Amazing Spider-Man*, and *The Avengers* on comic shop shelves. Beautiful faces, large busts, and slim waists have always been the standard physique of female characters in comics, whether those females had super powers or not. Just perusing an issue of *The Amazing Spider-Man* drawn by Todd McFarlane from the late 1980s will give insight into this. Mary Jane Watson was originally written as a homely and pretty girl in the 1960s, but she was hypersexualized by McFarlane in the 1980s and 1990s.

Essentially, Starfire's depiction is nothing new in the history of superhero literature and comic books. What made this a topic worthy of discussion was its placement in the New 52, which aimed to reinvent superhero literature. Starfire also wasn't alone in terms of controversy regarding the reboot's presentation of female characters. Catwoman, whose characteristics thus far have been praised as being progressive for female superheroes, also experienced a shocking reintroduction in the New 52.

In *Catwoman #1*,[31] Catwoman is shown in full costume having sex with Batman on the final page of the first issue. No veteran reader of Batman stories is gullible enough to believe that Batman and Catwoman never engaged in sexual relations, but it is the actual depiction of the event that left some readers stunned. Again, citing Laura Hudson: "I know why Catwoman and Batman would have sex; there's nothing wrong with the idea."[32] Hudson's concern is the reasoning behind the creative decision to show the event: "They [creators] just wanted to see Catwoman and Batman bang on a roof. And that is the whole problem with this false notion of 'sexually liberated' female characters: These aren't those women. They're how dudes want to imagine those women would be."[33] This takes the discussion full-circle to Dan DiDio's defensive answering when the question about female creators was asked at the comic convention panel. The overwhelming number of male creators in a genre that has been traditionally criticized for gender inequity is only bound to create problems, both narrative and sociocultural. Alex Zalben, a writer for MTV Geek, gave a similar review of the first issue of *Catwoman*, saying, "This is not a mature take on Catwoman, a progression we've seen on the series for about eighty issues before this. Like with *Batgirl*, this is a regression of Selina Kyle into a male sex fantasy."[34] In DC's New 52, both Starfire and Catwoman are depicted as products of male sexual fantasy wish fulfillments, undercutting their potential to offer any true value as strong female role models.

The sociocultural significance of both Starfire's and Catwoman's depictions in their respective first issues is not grounded in the actual, textual content. For ages there have been problematic depictions of women in the worlds of comics, music, television, movies, books, and every other medium one can find. Instead, the significance of these depictions lies in the reactions they invoke. What would have been truly disheartening would have been if there had been no uproar at all over these comic books.

The same can be said for Miles Morales and Ultimate Spider-Man. Changing Spider-Man's race is a good development, but only if people read the story. Audiences react to changes because they care about what happens in the stories. The death of Peter Parker, in any continuity, is a major storyline. This fictional loss is one that supremely affects the universe of superhero literature. Marvel's decision to then have a young man who is half-black and half-Hispanic take up the mantle of one of the most beloved superheroes in history is bound to cause reaction, and therein lies the controversy: Do publishers plan major story events because they feel this is the creative direction the story needs to go in, or do they plan events only to sell more issues?

In the chapter on reboots and relaunches, it was asserted that events happen in superhero literature for both of those reasons: story progression and publicity. Both of these justifications make sense, but one is strictly for sales while the other is about exploring uncharted territory. Sometimes, the two go hand-in-hand. Historically, some of the most significant events in superhero literature are linked to controversy or increased press, including the death of Superman, the death of Captain America, and Spider-Man's revealing his identity to the world in *Civil War*.

The events in *Ultimate Spider-Man*, *Red Hood and the Outlaws*, and *Catwoman* are all part of the ongoing culture and discourse of the superhero genre. These events may instigate discussions about diversity and gender inequality in superhero comic books, but they are also catalysts that keep the genre growing in both a narrative and sociocultural context. If superhero stories remained forever "safe" in their content, the product would become stagnant.

If nothing else, the significance of these events can be attributed, once again, to the passion and the influence of superhero readership. Ultimately, it is the readers who decide what is controversial, what is acceptable, and what is not. Jeffrey Brown stated in his book *Black Superheroes, Milestone Comics, and Their Fans* that "texts can and do influence readers, producers can and do socially manipulate consumers both intentionally and unintentionally, and audiences can and do interpret texts in a variety of ways, including resistance and playful cooption."[35] The fact that these characters (Miles Morales, Starfire, and Catwoman) elicit such strong responses emphasizes the continuing discourse between fans and creators. The passion inherent in fans' and critics' responses to changes in characters' directions reflects a readership that genuinely cares about its heroes. Additionally, the uproar over Starfire and Catwoman solidifies the presence of a strong and significant female readership in an otherwise male-dominated sphere of entertainment.

The changes to superhero comics discussed here are only part of the ongoing evolution of the superhero genre. At the time this book is being written, Marvel has had a same-sex marriage in the pages of *Astonishing X-Men*[36] and DC has revealed that the Golden Age Green Lantern, Alan Scott, is a gay man as a further element in the New 52 reboot.[37] These new developments are part of what the superhero genre is all about: exploring the world in different and unique ways that reflect ever-changing sociocultural landscapes.

NOTES

1. O. K. Kai, "A Dark Night for Black Superheroes," *40 Acres and a Cubicle*, http://40acresandacubicle.com/2012/07/25/a-dark-night-for-black-superheroes/ (accessed January 12, 2013).
2. Kai, "A Dark Night for Black Superheroes."
3. Len Wein and Dave Cockrum, "Second Genesis," *Giant Size X-Men* vol. 1, no. 1 (August 1975).
4. Brian Truitt, "Half-Black, Half-Hispanic Spider-Man Revealed," *USA Today*, www.usatoday.com/life/comics/2011-08-01-black-spider-man_n.htm (accessed May 13, 2012).
5. Brian Michael Bendis and Mark Bagley, "Death of Spider-Man—Part 5," *Ultimate Comics Spider-Man* vol. 1, no. 160 (August 2011).
6. Truitt, "Half-Black, Half-Hispanic Spider-Man Revealed."
7. Truitt, "Half-Black, Half-Hispanic Spider-Man Revealed."
8. Jonathan Hickman et al., "Ultimate Fallout, Chapter Four," *Ultimate Fallout* vol. 1, no. 4 (October 2011), 8.
9. Mark Millar and Bryan Hitch, *The Ultimates: Ultimate Collection* (New York: Marvel Comics, 2010).
10. Adilifu Nama, *Super Black: American Pop Culture and Black Superheroes* (Austin, TX: University of Texas Press, 2011), 92.
11. *Daredevil*, directed by Mark Steven Johnson (20th Century Fox, 2003).
12. "The Men Without Fear: Creating Daredevil," *Daredevil*, directed by Mark Stephen Johnson (2003; 20th Century Fox, 2003), DVD. Documentary on DVD Extras.
13. Agence France-Presse, "'Avengers' Third Highest Grossing Film of All Time," *Yahoo! News*, http://news.yahoo.com/avengers-third-highest-grossing-film-time-232528940.html (accessed July 8, 2012).
14. Christopher Yost et al., *Battle Scars* (New York: Marvel Comics, 2012).
15. Frank Miller and David Mazzucchelli, *Daredevil: Born Again* (New York: Marvel Comics, 2010).
16. *Smallville: The Complete Series* (2001–2011; Warner Home Video, 2011), DVD.
17. Chuck Dixon and Doug Moench, *Batman: Knightfall*, vol. 1 (New York: DC Comics, 2012).
18. Diamond Comic Distributors, Inc., "Industry Statistics: Top Comics Archives," Diamond Comic Distributors, www.diamondcomics.com/Home/1/1/3/237?articleID=96607 (accessed July 8, 2012).

19. Nama, *Super Black*, 125.

20. Marv Wolfman and Jim Starlin, "Where Nightmares Begin!" *DC Comics Presents* vol. 1, no. 26 (October 1980).

21. Scott Lobdell and Kenneth Rocafort, "I Fought the Law and Kicked Its Butt!" *Red Hood and the Outlaws* vol. 1, no. 1 (November 2011).

22. Lobdell and Rocafort, "I Fought the Law and Kicked Its Butt!" 13.

23. www.comicsalliance.com

24. Laura Hudson, "Answering Dan DiDio: The Problem with Having Only 1% Female Creators at DC Comics," *Comics Alliance*, www.comicsalliance.com/2011/07/28/dc-dan-didio-female-creators/ (accessed July 8, 2012).

25. Geoff Johns and Andy Kubert, "Flashpoint, Chapter One of Five," *Flashpoint* vol. 2, no. 1 (July 2011).

26. Hudson, "Answering Dan DiDio" (accessed July 8, 2012).

27. Michael Cavna, "The New 52: DC's Dan DiDio Shares His Take on Wednesday's Hotly Anticipated Relaunch," *Washington Post*, www.washingtonpost.com/blogs/comic-riffs/post/the-new-52-dcs-dan-didio-shares-his-take-on-wednesdays-hotly-anticipated-relaunch/2011/08/30/gIQAoSKwqJ_blog.html (accessed July 2012).

28. Scott Johnson, "Five Things We love About DC Comics Relaunch," *Comic Book*, http://comicbook.com/blog/2011/08/30/five-things-we-love-about-dc-comics-relaunch/ (accessed July 8, 2012).

29. Frank Miller and Lynn Varley, *Batman: The Dark Knight Strikes Again* vol. 1, no. 2 (2001), 25 – 31.

30. George G. Gustines and Adam W. Kepler, " Not All Superheroes Are Equal (At Least the Second Time Around), *New York Times*, www.nytimes.com/2011/10/01/books/for-new-dc-comics-whats-working-and-whats-not.html (accessed July 9, 2012).

31. Judd Winick and Guillem March, "And Most of the Costumes Stay On," *Catwoman* vol. 4, no. 1 (November 2011).

32. Laura Hudson, "The Big Sexy Problem with Superheroines and Their 'Liberated Sexuality,'" *Comics Alliance*, www.comicsalliance.com/2011/09/22/starfire-catwoman-sex-superheroine (accessed July 9, 2012).

33. Hudson, "The Big Sexy Problem with Superheroines and Their 'Liberated Sexuality," (9 July 2012).

34. Alex Zalben, "New 52 Review: Catwoman," *MTV Geek*, http://geek-news.mtv.com/2011/09/22/new-52-review-catwoman/ (accessed July 9, 2012).

35. Jeffrey A. Brown, *Black Superheroes, Milestone Comics, and Their Fans* (Jackson: University Press of Mississippi, 2001), 11.

36. Marjorie Lie and Mike Perkins, *Astonishing X-Men* vol. 3, no. 51 (August 2012).

37. James Robinson and Nicola Scott, *Earth 2* vol. 1, no. 2 (August 2012).

Chapter Nine

Why Superheroes Never Die

Let's just get this straight: If there's any mother%@#$er out there that can overcome being set upon by a villain pretending to be his dad leading a club of villains in a prolonged assault on his sanity, forcing him into going insane under the cover of a separate identity based on a Silver Age story in order to overcome his enemy and escape a chopper crash in order to join the other heroes for a final crisis wherein he shoots the God of Evil who also manages to blast him and kill him, only he lived and actually got sent back in time where he skipped forward through various lives until he defeated said Evil God's ultimate weapon that has come to resemble the bat demon and is also the guy pretending to be his dad . . . it's BATMAN. [1]

Even for hardcore fans of comic books, Batman's "death" story, which started in Grant Morrison's *Batman: R.I.P.* [2] and ended in *Final Crisis*, [3] pushed the boundary of the superhero death to new extremes. As the former writer/editor at DC Comics Denny O'Neil once said, "I mean, it's the biggest cliché in comic books that no one ever stays dead."[4] Superheroes can be drowned, stabbed, blown up, thrown into the sun, or shot with a ray gun and still not die. As ridiculous as that sounds, the "deaths" (or lack thereof) of superheroes are actually significant characteristics of a genre that prides itself on the power of its characters and the indomitable spirits those characters possess.

Like Umberto Eco's commentary on Superman being a significant character because of his temporal ambiguity,[5] superheroes' experiences of time are much different than characters in other genres. Since superhero stories never end (because there's always a next issue), an ending that involves a death can create confusion. Death is a concept that people fear to embrace because of its finality. Like Hamlet said, no one has ever returned to tell humanity about what is beyond this life; once death happens, there's no going back. We all want to live forever, or at the very least, pass into a world where we do live forever with all the people we love. This romantic idea is embodied by our superheroes, whom we love as cultural icons. Since we can't live forever, superheroes have to live forever for us.

DEATH AS A NEW BEGINNING

Perhaps the most famous death in comic book history was Superman's death in 1992. Part of the Man of Steel's appeal is his invulnerability, which has been established and glorified in his multiple incarnations. Superman could stop bullets with his chest, fly over buildings, and bend steel with his bare hands, and all of this resonated with audiences young and old for over fifty years (which was when his "death" occurred). More importantly, nothing, except for Kryptonite, could kill Superman. That was what readers had always thought until Superman's creative team outlined the death of the world's premiere superhero early in 1992.

Every year the creative teams on superhero comics meet to discuss where their stories are going. Since major characters such as Superman, Batman, Spider-Man, and the X-Men have multiple titles, it becomes necessary to map out where the different writers, artists, and editors are going so that the stories meld together; continuity needs to be maintained. For the creative team on Superman, every meeting at the beginning of the year started with one of the creators, Jerry Ordway, joking, "Let's just kill him!" with everyone giving a hardy laugh at such a notion. However, in 1992, everyone took his joking as a serious storyline.[6] What if Superman was killed? What if the hero no one thought could be killed finally met his end?

In *Superman #75*, the unthinkable occurred. Superman was killed by the then unknown villain named Doomsday. Appropriately named, Doomsday literally beat Superman to death: no kryptonite, no elaborate plan, no capturing Lois Lane and luring Superman to his doom while saving her. Doomsday just beat the living hell out of America's premier superhero. The comic sold millions of copies. It was also one of the first comics to feature a "polybag" where the comic was packaged with extra items including a poster of Superman's funeral and a fictional *Daily Planet* news article. The comic also featured splash page after splash page of Superman fighting to the death. His signature costume, which had been a symbol of truth, justice, and the American way was ripped to shreds as the comic progressed and the fight became more intense. By the end of the story, Superman was clad only in his signature red and blue pants with Lois Lane crying over his lifeless body as his cape made a makeshift flag that blew in the wind.[7]

Seeing Superman laid out on a pile of rubble with other heroes crying, Lois Lane sobbing, Jimmy Olsen morbidly taking pictures, and the tattered cape blowing in the wind brought the finality of Superman's fight to a startling halt. To boot, the page opened up into a two-page spread that declared, "For this is the day—that a **Superman** died."[8]

Superman #75 was a huge commercial success, and it was met with major press attention ranging from CNN covering the sale of the comic at various comic shops around the country to the *New York Times* questioning the place of Superman in modern culture. Why did people accept having one of the greatest heroes of all time die? The answer was rather disheartening: America had grown bored with its heroes. In the *New York Times* piece about Superman's death, a commentator wrote that Superman's "invulnerability became a bore. It bored the writers and editors at D.C. Comics."[9] Granted, Superman was over fifty years old at the time the story was published, so it seems reasonable comics creators had done as much as they could with the character by that point. A character whose sociocultural value was rooted in his everlasting nature was made to adapt to an evolving culture that demanded its heroes experience pain, suffering, and all the unfortunate ills that humanity has to endure. Simply put, by having Superman die, he was made to be more human than he ever had been before.

Superman's death was more than just a story, though. The manner in which Superman met his demise is particularly telling. Given his long history, fans would likely expect Superman to die from Kryptonite poisoning at the hands of his arch enemy Lex Luthor. Instead, Superman's death came at the hands of a brutal unknown enemy. In fact, that brutality was quite shocking in 1992 when the comic first appeared. Generations of fans had grown up with Superman being able to withstand trips through the burning sun, being punched into orbit by killer robots, and surviving captures and tortures by countless mad scientists' machines. Doomsday, a genetically altered killing machine who had bones protruding out of his body that acted as body armor, was all violence with no finesse. Perhaps Doomsday's appearance and the manner in which Superman died was indicative of the style that comic audiences demanded in the early to mid-1990s. Grant Morrison addressed this very topic in his book *Supergods* saying, "Was the superhero truly a man of Tomorrow—a progressive image of futurity—or a nostalgic fantasy with nothing to offer beyond a sad, tired muscle show?"[10] Echoing the sentiments of other critics from the early 1990s, Morrison said the death of Superman epitomized that era's questioning of the role of superheroes in a changing cultural landscape.

America had just emerged from the 1980s, a decade that had been highlighted by its excess and its promotion of "greed being good" by Gordon Gecko in *Wall Street*.[11] A great reanalysis of what constituted success, being a hero, and nobility was occurring in America at this time, and that social conversation had to be addressed in the comics as well. Superman's death was the first major moral question for superheroes as a genre since the publication of Fredric Wertham's *Seduction of the Innocent* in 1954.[12] Other superheroes had died throughout the course of superhero comics history, but Superman, being the premier superhero, elicited a cultural response that transcended the pages of comic books. If Superman could actually die, what did that mean for other superheroes and for America itself?

While it's nice to think that people learned some lessons from Gecko's story of unbridled greed, it seems more likely that DC Comics learned a lot about generating huge sales from having a splashy event. So it didn't take the company long to follow Superman's death with a major trauma for Batman. Although they didn't kill the caped crusader, Batman was paralyzed by the villain Bane in *Batman #497*,[13] an event with major ramifications for the Batman mythology. Thus, within one year's time, the top two characters in DC were killed and paralyzed. A genre that had for years aimed at inspiring hope in its readers had been degenerated by a publishing culture of one-upmanship where tragic events were used to sell more issues regardless of whether those events helped progress the character's mythology. As much as comic deaths are story-telling vehicles, they are also publicity stunts that encourage both frequent comic readers and casual comic readers to take notice for one glorious issue.

The early 1990s were also highlighted by the rise of Image as a major publisher in comics. Made up of former creators from DC and Marvel, Image produced comics that presented hard-edged superheroes more in line with what audiences from the late 1980s and early 1990s had craved. These super-heroes were violent and unforgiving. They often killed evil-doers, and didn't care what others thought. Despite the nontraditional style of comics that Image Comics produced, its stories were tight and well written. Creators such as Todd McFarlane, Jim Lee, and Rob Liefeld spoke in interviews about the empowerment they felt as they broke free of the creative stagnation they said they had experienced earlier in their careers.

While some of these claims may have been true and others likely were exaggerated, in a way it seemed as if America had lost its soul when it came to comic books in the 1990s. It's perhaps not surprising to note that comic collecting also experienced a major bubble burst in the late 1990s. The saturation of the market coupled with a nauseating number of "collectors' items" and innumerable "issue #1's" had driven readers away from both the genre and the medium.[14]

Superman wasn't the first major superhero to die, though. Supergirl died in 1986's *Crisis on Infinite Earths #7*[15] and Barry Allen (The Flash) died one issue later in the same series.[16] Captain Marvel also met his demise due to cancer in what is now considered to be one of the first superhero graphic novels ever created, *The Death of Captain Marvel* in 1982.[17] But Superman's death set a precedent that was more reflective of the changing cultural per-ceptions of superheroes than simply superheroes literally dying. Characters die in stories all the time, but Superman was different. Superman wasn't supposed to die. Superman *couldn't* die. The power of the superhero, which had to extend beyond the scope of human understanding, was meta-textually brought back down to Earth and reevaluated by the very same people who created those super powers. In the death of Superman story, the grandeur and the majesty of Superman was replaced by, what Umberto Eco called, "final consumption."[18]

Audiences need their traditional heroes though. Without them, a culture loses track of what it holds dear. Without heroes, a culture has no guiding light to follow. The everlasting quality of superheroes needs to be maintained in order to link succeeding generations to a core set of values and beliefs. Times change, cultures change, and environments change, but superheroes maintain the best that humanity has to offer. If superheroes die, then what a culture values most may be lost forever in the winds of time and change.

SUPERMAN AS A CHRISTLIKE FIGURE

Superman returned from the dead a little less than one year after his much publicized death. In an overarching storyline encompassing multiple titles, it was revealed that Superman had put his body into what equates to a Kryptonian coma in order to save himself. It was always clear that Superman would return, however. If thought about rationally, DC would never allow its flagship character to disappear forever. DC's very identity as a publisher is too intimately connected to the Man of Steel.

Yet there is a more important reason for Superman returning from the dead than mere financial gain on the part of his publisher. Superman's mythology is ripe with Judeo-Christian symbolism and imagery including the parallels between Superman and Moses's origins[19] and Superman and Jesus both being symbols of peace and hope for humanity. There is no exact parallel in comparing Superman and Jesus Christ, but the themes of their stories have significant similarities.

Even before Superman's "death" in 1992, Frank Miller had hinted at Superman being reborn in his seminal work *The Dark Knight Returns* in 1986. After Superman saves Gotham City from a nuclear attack, he is caught up in the blast of the nuclear weapon. As the mushroom cloud blots out the sky and its sunlight, Superman quickly begins to shrivel up and nearly dies. Only after begging the Earth to help him heal does Superman find the strength to persevere.[20] Miller's panels in that section are powerful, as they put the Man of Steel against a multicolored sky with lightning bolts seeming to go right through him. And as readers of comics had been exposed to Superman as the most omnipotent being in superhero literature for his then almost fifty-year existence, seeing him shrivel up like an old man on his death bed would have been shocking and scary. Lou Anders wrote about this scene in an article comparing the mythologies of Superman and Batman saying, "This is nothing short of the death and resurrection of Christ, thematically necessary to establish the Man of Steel as the Son of God."[21] In order to make Superman stronger, he first needed to experience death, or at the very least, experience a situation where death was imminent.

Superman #75 was a bit more blatant with Superman's death, as already discussed. Where the strong parallels between Christ and Superman appear is after Superman dies. Superman's tomb is found to be empty,[22] mirroring the scene in the Bible where Christ's body is found to be missing when Mary and other mourners go to Christ's tomb to grieve. This is not meant to be a religious argument that Superman is somehow comparable to Christ. Instead, this similarity is highlighted to draw attention to the sense of hope that remains even when humanity loses a great hero, whether that hero is real, fictional, religious, mythological, or otherwise. Even Bryan Singer's motion picture *Superman Returns* featured a scene similar to a resurrection of Superman when he falls from the sky after pushing a giant mountain of kryptonite into space. After being rushed to the hospital, it is implied that Superman is dead or nearly dead. However, just as happened after Superman's death in the comics, Superman's hospital suite is found to be empty later on.[23] These incidents are not merely coincidences in storytelling, nor are they dismissible as blatantly copying Christian dogma. Instead, these are deep-seated themes that have lasted over many ages, across countless stories and evolving cultures.

Superman is just the latest in a long line of heroes who have returned from death: Odysseus returned from Hades, Sherlock Holmes was brought back by Sir Arthur Conan Doyle after fans' complaints about Holmes's death, and King Arthur's epitaph is "The Once and Future King," implying that he will return again. It gives humanity hope that its greatest heroes will return because "Superman has always been there, a strong, comforting presence, and the idea that he could die is horrifying."[24] Superman returned from the dead because humanity, both the fictional humanity of Superman's world and the real humanity of our world, needed him to return. The world needs Superman. As Larry Tye notes in his book, *Superman: The High-Flying History of America's Most Enduring Hero*:

> What could be more U.S.A. than an orphaned outsider who arrives in this land of immigrants, reinvents himself, and reminds us that we can reach for the sky? Yet today this flying Uncle Sam is global in his reach, having written himself into the national folklore from Beirut to Buenos Aires. It is that constancy and purity—knowing that he is not merely the oldest of our superheroes but the most transcendent—that has reeled back aging devotees [and new ones alike]. It is what makes the Man of Tomorrow timeless as well as ageless.[25]

Superman is a mythological guiding light. We need to know that somewhere, even if it is only in our imagination, he is flying ahead of us to lead the way to better days.

NOBODY DIES FOREVER

No one ever thought that Superman would remain dead. It was almost a forgone conclusion that Superman would return, just as Batman would beat the paralysis Bane had inflicted on him. Superheroes never remain dead, so it's almost a joke to hear about a superhero being fatally wounded or killed. Comic book deaths are subject to a different set of physics, temporality, and emotionality because, for one thing, they're fictional. However, that fictionality only goes so far. Marvel and DC are both guilty of killing their heroes in order to gain publicity and new readers. Like the concept of the reboot that was explored earlier in this book, superheroes can only die so many times.

In February of 2011, David Gabriel, Marvel's vice president of sales, stated at the ComicsPro retailer summit, "'As a result of the *Fantastic Four* sales and media coverage, Marvel is going to kill a main character every quarter.'" He then made sure to say, "'This is not a joke.'"[26] The statement about "the *Fantastic Four* sales and media coverage" refers to *Fantastic Four #587*[27] where Johnny Storm was killed. The comic originally didn't initially have much press coverage, but then news outlets began carrying the story even though Marvel had not been actively pushing for coverage. This is unlike Marvel's death of Captain America story where the "death" was heavily publicized. The emphasis on death stories generating revenue may be disheartening from an audience standpoint, but it also seems understandable from a business point of view. Comic publishers' goals are to sell as many issues as possible: no ifs, ands, or buts. If killing a major character from the Fantastic Four is necessary to increase sales, then that's what the publisher will do. However, it seems troubling to imagine this phenomenon being actively built into Marvel's creative decisions, publishing strategy, marketing plans, and even public image.

It seems that Marvel has lived up to its word, though. The year 2011 saw the death of the Ultimate version of Peter Parker in *Ultimate Comics: Spider-Man #160*,[28] the Ultimate version of Doctor Octopus in *Ultimate Comics: Spider-Man #157*,[29] and Thor in the seventh issue of the *Fear Itself* miniseries.[30] There were also other "deaths" throughout 2011, but one would be hard pressed to consider these deaths of "major" characters. However, in 2012, the event mini-series *Avengers vs. X-Men* saw the death of Professor Charles Xavier at the hands of his former student, Scott Summers (Cyclops).[31]

DC is guilty of adopting a similar publishing strategy. While 2011 was not a significant year for DC in terms of "death" stories, the company did completely revamp its entire universe when it released the New 52 (discussed in depth in chapter 5). However, 2010 saw DC revisit much of its publishing history as it relates to "death" stories in the miniseries *Blackest Night* where all of the major characters who had died were resurrected as zombies. In *Blackest Night #1* the recently returned Flash, Barry Allen, asks Hal Jordan, "Who else died while I was gone? I want to know, Hal." Hal Jordan responds by using his ring to project the image of all the heroes who had died. [32] The morbidity of the situation aside, the number of characters in the image is astounding, and it stands as an example of how fleeting character deaths in comic books are. Not surprisingly, perhaps, *Blackest Night* ends with the resurrection of twelve DC characters who had all died, including Aquaman, Hawkman, Hawkgirl, and even the longtime ghost Deadman.

In contrast to other genres, though, the genre of superhero stories is deeply entwined with this phenomenon of life after death. No other genre in literature or entertainment treats death in such a cavalier fashion, yet that triviality is also a strength that makes superhero stories unique. Because superhero stories have always been serialized tales featuring ongoing stories where the heroes nearly always win, deaths only serve to amplify the resilient nature of superheroes. And as a genre that is uniquely American, it only makes sense for the superheroes to be as strong as the people who created them.

THE INEVITABLE RETURN

As superheroes are such a socioculturally significant part of the American cultural and media landscape, their "death" stories are indicative of what America values. The indomitable American spirit is largely about never giving up, and so neither do America's superheroes. Death is only another villain who needs to be defeated in order to continue the never-ending battle they've all selflessly enlisted in. Since death can be defeated in fiction, superheroes should (and are) able to defeat it.

This phenomenon isn't limited to just superheroes, of course. *The Lord of the Rings* saw Gandalf return from the dead; Harry Potter returns at the end of Rowling's final book as well. Both characters lived in worlds where magic made this possible, and superheroes are no exception to that. Like Gandalf and Harry Potter, the superheroes experience death only to return wiser, stronger, and more prepared to meet the challenges that await them.

Batman's death story was mentioned at the beginning of this chapter, and as usual, his return was no surprise when it was announced. In Bruce Wayne's absence, Dick Grayson (the original Robin) had taken over as Batman and remained the caped crusader for over a year in the comic books. As Batman, Dick Grayson's storylines made for great analyses as to what constitutes being Batman, and it was tacitly implied that Commissioner Gordon and the villains knew that the Batman they were interacting with was not the original Batman.

Bruce Wayne's return was a mind-bending trip through time. Wayne was thrown back in time by the villain Darkseid in *Final Crisis #6*[33] and had to fight his way forward in order to return. Troy Brownfield's humorous quote at the beginning of this chapter actually does the Batman death story more justice than would be possible in a full summary anyway. And as funny as Brownfield's account of the story may seem, it is also fairly accurate. The convoluted details aren't really that important, anyway. What really mattered were the directions the stories took when the hero was gone. That is where the value in "death" stories comes into play. Even though everyone knows the hero will eventually return, it's the way the story works while the character is gone that is often the most interesting part of the superhero's tale.

COPING WITH SUPERHERO DEATHS

Batman's supporting cast is huge, encompassing Robin, Nightwing, Commissioner Gordon, Catwoman, Alfred, and a plethora of other characters. The story immediately after the "death" of Batman was a miniseries titled *Battle for the Cowl.*[34] The title refers to Batman's signature mask. What happens to Gotham when Batman isn't there to protect it? What do the villains who have tried for years to kill Batman do once the Caped Crusader is gone? Does Alfred remain at Wayne Manor? All of these are interesting storylines for readers, and the Batman comics of that period, 2009–2011, reflect the inherent confusion that a missing main character can incur.

More than anything else, though, the value of a character who has "died" is emphasized in the actions, or inactions, of the character's friends once he or she is gone. It's similar to the idea in the film *It's a Wonderful Life*[35] in that people cannot know the difference they truly make in the world until they see what the world would be like without them.

Captain America's death was addressed earlier in this book in chapter 3 as it pertained to the battle between fans and creators. When Captain America was killed in *Captain America #25*,[36] the issues of *Captain America* that followed featured the fictional news coverage of the event, Tony Stark (Iron Man) coping with the death of his friend, James "Bucky" Barnes (Captain America's former sidekick from the Golden Age of comics) searching for Captain America's signature shield in order to preserve the sanctity of the shield as a symbol of freedom, and finally the process of searching for someone to replace Steve Rogers as Captain America. Just as Batman's absence in his universe advanced the mythology of his own nobility, Captain

America's absence did something similar. Both characters affected the lives of everyone around them even after their deaths.

What undercuts these interesting post-death narratives, though, is the fact that readers know the dead character will inevitably return. Leaving aside the obvious implausibility of returning from the dead, the fact that dead superheroes always end up returning weakens the set of narratives that occur immediately following their deaths. Superman, Batman, and Captain America all featured extensive comic book issues after their death stories, chronicling funerals, wakes, grieving heroes, and many other understandable reactions to death. These issues are powerful and evoke strong emotions because it's not just the fictional universe that has lost a hero: when a superhero dies in comics, the real world also suffers a cultural loss.

Superhero deaths are also unique in the realm of storytelling because, as opposed to other genres that use death as an ultimate end, superhero stories use dying as a vehicle for advancing a story. It is almost like deciding to take one step backward and then two steps forward. The hero dies in order to solidify his or her position or power in a given universe. Superman's absence made audiences yearn for the return of the Man of Steel because the DC universe needed the figurehead of Superman to be there.

Superhero death stories are significant from a sociocultural perspective in that we, as a culture, know the hero will come back. The inevitable return, despite its undercutting of grieving tales, nevertheless makes audiences giddy. Superman, Batman, Captain America, Spider-Man, and the rest will never truly die because they're too culturally significant to be eliminated. And even though it's a kind of game, readers are still happy to see their heroes return. Aside from the financial reason for publishers to never truly kill off a superhero, superheroes inspire hope and are examples of what society deems to be noble ways to act. If superheroes truly died, a part of culture might die with them since there would no longer be the same kind of models to uphold those sets of values. And perhaps, for that long year in 1993 while Superman lay dead, America did lose a part of its collective conscience. Could it be that we all share a bit of the blame in allowing Superman to become subject to the horrors of humanity, horrors that he, as our collective superhero, was never meant to experience?

ARE THERE ANY "TRUE" DEATHS?

Here is an abbreviated rundown of superheroes who have died. It is also important to note that this list of deaths does not include "Else-World" stories, Marvel's Ultimate line, or "out of continuity" stories:

- Superman
- Batman
- Captain America
- Flash (Barry Allen)
- Green Lantern (Hal Jordan)
- Spider-Man
- Supergirl
- Jean Grey
- Wonder Woman
- The Human Torch (Johnny Storm)
- Hawkeye
- Aquaman
- Thor
- Martian Manhunter
- Robin (Jason Todd)
- Green Arrow

Every single one of these characters returned from the dead at one point or another. The amount of time between returns varies from a few issues to a couple of decades, but they all returned nonetheless. Also, the inherent confusion of having to announce that the deaths listed do *not* include certain types of stories is indicative of the nature of comic book deaths. This prompts the following question: does anyone in comics ever truly die?

The answer is yes, but it is a conditional yes. Yes, if they affect a major character's mythology so significantly that bringing him or her back from the dead would irreparably alter the mythology of a character. If the narrative value of the character as a deceased entity is greater than the character's value as a living entity, then the character will remain dead. Spider-Man's mythology is a perfect example of this.

Spider-Man has been drastically affected by two major deaths in his mythology: Uncle Ben and Gwen Stacy. Uncle Ben is the reason Spider-Man exists, and Gwen Stacy was Peter Parker's first love. In Spider-Man's premier issue, *Amazing Fantasy #15*,[37] Peter selfishly steps aside and lets a robber run past him because he feels the robber doesn't concern him. Upon returning home that night, Peter finds that his uncle has been murdered by the same robber that Peter allowed to pass by unhindered. This leads Peter to learn that "With great power comes great responsibility." Uncle Ben exists as the catalyst for Peter Parker to become the superhero Spider-Man. Therefore, Uncle Ben must remain dead despite the fact that in Spider-Man's universe Ben's resurrection would be extremely easy to accomplish. Sure, Spider-Man could go to Doctor Strange and try to get Strange to resurrect Peter's long-dead uncle; he could even make another deal with Mephisto to bring Uncle Ben back (see "One More Day" storyline). Peter Parker's life would never be the same if this happened, though, so Uncle Ben remains dead because his death is forever destined to be the driving force behind Spider-Man's purpose in comics. Every action that Spider-Man ever takes ultimately relates back to his uncle's death in *Amazing Fantasy #15*.

Gwen Stacy's death is a bit more open to issues of possible resurrection, but no writer has dared to tackle that issue, at least in a direct way. A story revealing that Norman Osborn, the Green Goblin, had fathered twins with Gwen Stacy was published in 2004–2005.[38] However, Gwen Stacy herself never returned.

Gwen Stacy was killed by the Green Goblin in *Amazing Spider-Man #121*, which featured a fantastic cover warning the reader that one of these characters (all of Spider-Man's supporting cast was on the cover) would die inside the pages of the comic. In the climax to Spider-Man's rivalry with the Goblin, Gwen Stacy is dangled over a bridge and is dropped forcing Spider-Man to save his love before her imminent demise. As one would expect, Spider-Man shoots his web at her feet and saves her before she hits the water. However, after pulling Gwen Stacy back up, he finds that she has died from the force of the fall. What makes this death even more poignant is the tacit implication that Spider-Man inadvertently killed Gwen even as he was trying to save her because he caused her neck to break from the jolt of his webbing catching her. The story ultimately ends the next issue with Spider-Man defeating his nemesis in battle while mourning the death of his first love.[39]

A break from the traditional formula of a superhero saving a major character in the mythology created a moralistic reflection on the part of Spider-Man. Instead of swinging away with Gwen Stacy under his arm and kissing the girl, Spider-Man begins to question his actions as a vigilante. Even though Stacy's death didn't affect the other characters in Marvel's universe directly, it created a precedent in superhero literature that characters could actually die. There is a distinction between Uncle Ben and Gwen Stacy, though. Uncle Ben died only a few pages into Spider-Man's mythology, effectively creating Spider-Man as a superhero. Gwen Stacy arrives, becomes a major character, takes part in many stories, and affects Spider-Man's mythology, all before she dies. This causes Stacy to create connections not only to the superhero in the story but also to the readers following the stories. For the genre of superheroes, this was the first death that legitimately challenged the cavalier attitudes of the characters in regard to their sometimes reckless actions. Did Gwen Stacy die because of Spider-Man's actions? Was Gwen already dead when the Green Goblin dropped her from the bridge? In reality, it doesn't necessarily matter. In fiction, as in life, what really happened matters less than what people think happens. If Spider-Man blames himself for Gwen's death, he has to live with that guilt the way so many people live with guilt, both for their real and imagined failings. It is the way in which the superhero, or the real person, copes with the death that impacts his actions going forward. Uncle Ben's death may have created Spider-Man's moral conscience, but Gwen Stacy's death was the one that forced Spider-Man to face that conscience head on. That Spider-Man has remained a hero, despite facing all this guilt, is a testament to him as a character and to the idea that superheroes exist to uphold the values of society we hold most dear.

BATMAN'S LOST PARENTS

Bruce Wayne's parents, Thomas and Martha, are the ultimate deaths in comics. With the utmost certainty, it can be guaranteed that these two characters will never come back from the dead. Batman exists because they were murdered in front of Bruce's eyes when he was a child. Even more so than Spider-Man's Uncle Ben, the Waynes represent unfathomable loss that no one should have to endure, and Bruce Wayne's obsession with fighting crime is emblematic of that loss and of its resulting impact on his life and sense of direction. Bruce Wayne's life is more self-determined than any other fictional character's, yet despite this it always seems as if Bruce Wayne never ceases floundering in the tragedy of his childhood loss.

Being the heir to a billionaire family's fortune is no comfort to Bruce, and this speaks volumes to the power of both parentage and mother/father figures. Bruce never stops utilizing his vast fortune to fund his vigilantism as he tirelessly researches newer and better technologies to construct his superhero's self-identity. Batman fights crime because he genuinely feels he needs to, not because he wants to. Most superheroes experience loss, though. In fact, going back to chapter 1, loss is one of the critical characteristics of the superhero. Superman lost his biological parents as well, but he never truly knew them. Daredevil lost his father to mob violence, but his mother was still alive and living in a convent. Even Wonder Woman lost her home when she selflessly left Themyscira for "Man's World," but Batman established a connection with his parents, had an expectation of living a wonderful normal life, and then had that life ripped away at gunpoint. As Batman himself laments this loss in Frank Miller and David Mazzucchelli's *Batman: Year One*: "Since the walk. That night. And the man with frightened, hollow eyes and a voice like glass being crushed . . . since all sense left my life."[40]

As a comic book death, Batman's parents represent the loss that he needed to become a superhero: the vacuum in life that needs to be filled with the vigilantism that superheroes thrive on. If the Waynes were brought back to life, it would nullify and disrespect everything that Bruce Wayne had built his life on since that day. Additionally, Batman's influence on the DC universe is so profound that altering his presence would undoubtedly reverberate through all of the other DC characters. Even Batman's characteristics as a crime fighter, which embody darkness, mystery, and ruthlessness, developed because he saw his parents being murdered before his eyes.

David Mazzucchelli's image of Bruce Wayne under a streetlight with his dead parents next to him in *Batman: Year One*[41] probably best presents the despair of that tragic situation and exudes an unmistakable understanding as to why this young man with tears rolling down his face eventually subjects himself to a self-imposed purgatory of crime fighting for which there can never truly be an end. Batman lives in purgatory every day through his commitment to fighting crime and simultaneous self-sacrifice of a normal life. The power of the character comes from that passion and despair. By temporarily putting Bruce Wayne's psychological issues on the conscious backburner, Batman's drive for vengeance is what we all believe we might do if we had the motivation, drive, and resources that Bruce Wayne possesses. All of this is rooted in the death of Batman's parents when he was a little boy. For that very reason, the Waynes are the most important deaths in superhero literature.

SUPERHERO DEATHS AS UNIQUE LITERARY EVENTS

The front cover of the *New York Daily News* on May 7, 2007, featured the death of Captain America. There in all of his glory was the quintessential American soldier laid out with a gunshot wound to his chest. *Captain America #25* featured the tragic death of the hero, but the graphic novel of the story featured a short section in the back where the writer Ed Brubaker held up a copy of the newspaper marveling at how a fictional literary event had gained such mainstream news coverage. The *New York Daily News* was not alone in covering the event; the *New York Times*, the *New York Post*, *Time*, and *Newsweek* all featured stories about Marvel's star-spangled hero meeting his demise on the steps of a courthouse.

Of course, this event never *actually* happened. Captain America is not real, the story *Civil War* which led to Captain America's demise never happened, and there was never going to be an actual court case where Steve Rogers (Captain America) was going to be tried for rebelling against the U.S. government's Superhero Registration Act. Yet legitimate news outlets took precious space (some of them on their covers) and devoted time and energy to covering this fictional event the same way they might cover any other news story. The question is "why?" Why would news outlets cover an event that has little to no bearing on real life? Why cover an event that took place in a marginalized literary genre, a genre that openly celebrates fantastical narratives?

The reason is because superheroes are more real than we think they are. They're not literally real, but superheroes' lives have an impact on the world's psyche. Captain America's death was an event that drastically affected the Marvel Universe and provided some of the most riveting storytelling in the character's long and storied history. For the world of comic books, Captain America's demise resulted in a rethinking of the hero's place in America. The same thing also occurred in reality. In a meta-textual way, Captain America's fictional death led to a real-world rethinking of America's relationship with a hero who wore his country's flag so proudly and embodied the spirit of America both physically and emotionally. If Captain America, the superhero who had fought for his country so valiantly in World War II, could die, then did this mean that American comic readers had reached a point where their own faith in America's ideals had begun to crumble?

It is important to note that the story of Captain America's death was told over sixty years after the end of World War II, the point where Captain America's modern mythology begins and a historical moment also strongly rooted in real-world history. The end of World War II marked the rise of the United States as a world superpower, and in the Marvel universe the end of World War II marked the time when Captain America is frozen in ice and, via suspended animation, winds up in our present-day world. Yet the creators who told Captain America stories in the 1940s are gone. Instead, a new generation of comic creators has been given the task of telling Cap's story, a generation that lives in a world where the United States remains a world power, but whose military power is as likely to be called into question as to be celebrated. Perhaps, the reenvisioning of Captain America's story was the logical next step, so that the fictional legend's demise could mirror what might be the slow decline of a nation as well. Or maybe Captain America's death story was just a good way for Marvel to sell some extra comic books that month. It might never be clear what the exact reason for Captain America's death was, but that is less important than the fact that the event itself occurred.

Superhero deaths are unique in their scope because comic culture is quite insular. Outside of major "death" stories, mainstream audiences usually don't have extensive working knowledge of superhero stories. Fans of comics might well have been aware of the why, the how, the where, and the when of Captain America's death as it happened, a death intimately linked to Marvel's *Civil War* series as well as Captain America's arch enemy the Red Skull. Audiences outside of comics, though, had little, if any, idea of why the character had been killed. All that was known by audiences outside of comics was that the character who wears the star-spangled costume and carries a shield had finally died. This is significant because even without any prior information or storyline to reference, news of Captain America's death still spread far and wide.

The same thing happened when Superman died in 1992. News outlets went wild over the news. Upon hearing that The Man of Steel would die, news coverage of his fictional demise was made available to a general public that might otherwise not have been familiar with Superman beyond casual watching of one or two feature films. Nevertheless, the death of the fictional hero was treated like a genuine news event.

The sociocultural value of the superhero is reinforced by death stories and their subsequent coverage in real news. If no one cared about these characters, there would be no reason to announce their deaths to the world.

WHY "DEATH" STORIES ARE NECESSARY IN SUPERHERO MYTHOLOGY

In comics, there will always be a next issue. Superheroes are truly never-ending stories with most of the major characters having the number of their exploits reaching into the high hundreds or low thousands mark. Superman and Batman alone have over three thousand individual issues to their names, and this is quite common for comic book superheroes. The same thing is true for Sunday newspaper comic strip characters. Charlie Brown, Garfield, Blondie, and Prince Valiant, to name only a few, have had thousands of stories told about them. Part of this is the culture of early comics where the goal was to be a weekly strip in a newspaper, which made the most money. Comic books were new fads when they first appeared in the 1930s, so syndication of comic book characters was where the real money was. Therefore, it became the responsibility of the publishers (and the burden of the creators) to pump out as many stories as possible in order to gain new audiences. At the same time, creators needed to keep their stories fresh and new in order to maintain seasoned readers of a given character. This culture of pumping out stories at an incredible pace has not necessarily subsided in recent years.

Comic books still come out every month, and creators are still expected to keep the stories original and engaging. The publishing culture of the early 1900s is still alive and well in comic books. It is easy to compare this style of publishing to that of news magazines such as *Time*, where new issues come out every week. However, the difference between those publications and comic book publishing is the isolation inherent in each book's production. Only a few creators will work on one comic book in a given month. For weekly news magazines, the whole of the group puts all of its collective effort into one issue. This is not meant to imply that comics are more difficult to produce than news magazines: far from it. Publication of any kind is grueling and requires a mentality that often values quality of content over quality of personal life. Comic publishers have had to face this challenge on a monthly basis since the early 1930s, and they have rarely been able to make use of real-life situations. Yet just like news magazines, all of the stories released by comic book publishers need to be original stories of high quality every month.

This pressure to publish leads back to the emergence of death stories. The culture of comic book publishing necessitates the creation of stories that challenge and engage readers no matter what. This pressure is built into the genre's DNA, and it is probably the reason for its longevity. The expediency of the issues' releases results in stories that are rooted primarily in creator's passions at the time the stories are needed, and those stories can never be exactly the same. Granted, the formulas for superhero stories are often predictable, and the amount of stories where Superman stops a plot by Lex Luthor are uncountable. But, those stories can never be *exactly* the same. How can stories that are designed to never end maintain appeal and simultaneously invigorate audiences both old and new? The answer is the "death" story.

Death is an unavoidable part of life, so perhaps it was inevitable that it would make its way even into the lives of seemingly invincible superheroes like Superman. While fans may not be happy when "death" stories occur, their passions are nevertheless reflected in the surge in sales for the superhero "death" issues. And everyone knows the superhero will come back at one point or another. For creators, a death story allows for a thoughtful analysis of not only the individual hero, but also the world in which that hero makes an impact. The most powerful comic book images ever created include Superman lying in a pile of rubble with his suit tattered, Captain America sprawled out with a bullet wound in his chest, Batman's burnt body being carried by Superman, and the Flash's body disintegrating before our eyes as he races to save all of existence. The stories behind these moments may be convoluted and polluted by continuity, but the cores of these heroes are kept intact even in their moments of death. The superheroes die for their audiences and then return to them rejuvenated and ready to continue their neverending battle. Just as death is inevitable in real life, it is equally inescapable for superheroes. It is their death and their life, then, that make superheroes all the more valuable as sociocultural icons.

NOTES

1. Troy Brownfield, "The REBORN Identity: 10 Comics Deaths That Didn't Stick," *Newsarama*, www.newsarama.com/comics/reborn-identity-10-deaths-that-didnt-stick-110711-1. html (accessed July 11, 2012).

2. Grant Morrison, Tony Daniel, and Lee Garbett, *Batman: R.I.P.* (New York: DC Comics, 2010).

3. Grant Morrison, J. G. Jones, and Doug Mahnke, *Final Crisis* (New York: DC Comics, 2010).

4. "Robin's Requiem: The Tale of Jason Todd," *Batman: Under The Red Hood*, directed by Brandon Viettei (Warner Home Video, 2010), Blu-Ray. Blu-Ray exclusive Documentary on Extras.

5. Umberto Eco and Natalie Chilton, "The Myth of Superman," *Diacritics* 2, no. 1 (Spring 1972).

6. "Requiem and Rebirth: Superman Lives!" *Superman: Doomsday*, directed by Bruce Timm (Warner Home Video, 2007), Documentary on DVD Extras.

7. Dan Jurgens and Brett Breeding, "Doomsday!" *Superman* vol. 2, no. 75 (January 1993).

8. Jurgens and Breeding, "Doomsday!" 26–28.

9. Maitland McDonagh et al. "Look! It's a Bird! It's a Plane! It's Curtains for the Man of Steel," *New York Times*, November 15, 1993, Arts & Leisure, H25.

10. Grant Morrison, *Supergods: What Masked Vigilantes, Miraculous Mutants, and a Sun God from Smallville Can Teach Us about Being Human* (New York: Spiegel & Grau, 2011), 294.

11. *Wall Street*, directed by Oliver Stone (20th Century Fox, 1987).

12. Fredric Wertham, *Seduction of the Innocent* (New York: Reinhart and Company, Inc., 1954).

13. Doug Moench and Jim Aparo, "Knightfall—Part 11: The Broken Bat," *Batman* vol. 1, no. 497 (July 1993).

14. Bradford Wright, *Comic Book Nation: The Transformation of Youth Culture in America* (Baltimore: Johns Hopkins University Press, 2003), 283.

15. Marv Wolfman and George Pérez, "Beyond the Silent Night," *Crisis on Infinite Earths* vol. 1, no. 7 (October 1985).

16. Marv Wolfman and George Pérez, "A Flash of the Lightning!" *Crisis on Infinite Earths* vol. 1, no. 8 (November 1985).

17. Jim Starlin, *The Death of Captain Marvel* (New York: Marvel Comics, 1982).

18. Umberto Eco and Natalie Chilton, "The Myth of Superman," *Diacritics* 2, no. 1 (Spring 1972): 22.

19. Anton Karl Kozlovic, "The Unholy Biblical Subtexts and Other Religion Elements Built into *Superman: The Movie* (1978) and *Superman II* (1981)," *The Journal of Religion and Faith* vol. 7, no. 1 (2003).

20. Frank Miller and Klaus Janson, *Batman: The Dark Knight Returns* (New York: DC Comics, 1986), 176–79.

21. Lou Anders, "A Tale of Two Orphans: The Man of Steel vs. The Caped Crusader," in *The Man From Krypton*, ed. G. Yeffeth (Dallas, TX: BenBella Books, Inc., 2005), 75.

22. Jerry Ordway and Tom Grummett, "Funeral for a Friend—Part 5: Grave Obsession," *Adventures of Superman* vol. 1, no. 499 (February 1993).

23. "Not Alone," *Superman Returns*, directed by Bryan Singer (2006; Warner Home Video, 2007), DVD.

24. Steven Harper, "Supermyth!" in *The Man from Krypton*, ed. G. Yeffeth (Dallas, TX: BenBella Books, Inc., 2005), 99.

25. Larry Tye, Preface to *Superman: The High-Flying History of America's Most Enduring Hero* (New York: Random House, 2012), xiv.

26. Jill Pantozzi, "Hey, That's My Cape! Marvel Killing Characters for Money?" *Newsarama*, www.newsarama.com/comics/hey-thats-my-cape-marvel-deaths-for-sales-110216.html (accessed July 11, 2012).

27. Jonathan Hickman and Steve Epting, "Three, Part Five: The Last Stand!" *Fantastic Four* vol. 3, no. 587 (January 2011).

28. Brian Michael Bendis and Mark Bagley, "Death of Spider-Man—Part 5," *Ultimate Comics Spider-Man* vol. 1, no. 160 (August 2011).

29. Brian Michael Bendis and Mark Bagley, "Death of Spider-Man—Part 2," *Ultimate Comics Spider-Man* vol. 1, no. 157 (June 2011).

30. Matt Fraction and Stuart Immonen, "Thor's Day," *Fear Itself* vol. 1, no. 7 (December 2011).

31. Brian Michael Bendis and Oliver Coipel, *Avengers vs. X-Men*, vol. 1, no. 11 (November 2012).

32. Geoff Johns and Ivan Reis, "Blackest Night, Part 1," *Blackest Night* vol. 1, no. 1 (September 2009): 15–17.

33. Grant Morrison, Doug Mahnke, Carlos Pacheco, and J. G. Jones, "Final Crisis: How to Murder the Earth," *Final Crisis* vol. 1, no. 6 (January 2009).

34. Tony Daniel and Fabian Nicieza, *Batman: Battle for the Cowl* (New York: DC Comics, 2009).

35. *It's a Wonderful Life*, directed by Frank Capra (RKO Radio Pictures, 1946).

36. Ed Brubaker and Steve Epting, "Civil War: The Death of a Dream, Part One," *Captain America* vol. 5, no. 25 (April 2007).

37. Stan Lee and Steve Ditko, "Spider-Man!" *Amazing Fantasy* vol. 1, no. 15 (August 1962): 1–11.

38. J. Michael Straczynski and Mike Deodato Jr., *Amazing Spider-Man Volume 8: Sins Past* (New York: Marvel Comics, 2005).

39. Gerry Conway and Gil Kane, "The Night Gwen Stacy Died," *Amazing Spider-Man* vol. 1, no. 121 (June 1973); Gerry Conway and Gil Kane, "The Goblin's Last Stand!" *Amazing Spider-Man* vol. 1, no. 122 (July 1973).

40. Frank Miller and David Mazzucchelli, *Batman: Year One* (New York: DC Comics, 2005), 21.

41. Miller and Mazzucchelli, *Batman: Year One*, 21.

Chapter Ten

Technology and the Superhero

In the summer of 2010, *The Dark Knight*[1] became a runaway success. Not merely a blockbuster summer movie, the film would be viewed again and again by crowds that would make it the second-highest grossing film at the time (and still one of the highest grossing films of all time).[2] Director Christopher Nolan had created a masterpiece, from the poignant and troubled final performance of Heath Ledger as a truly terrifying Joker to a relentless pace that kept audiences enthralled. Yet for all its brilliance, *The Dark Knight* is, well, a bleak and depressing film. As one watches Batman race against time through a city whose every inhabitant is imperiled by the Joker's twisted desires, one is quickly struck by the idea of how horrible it would be to live in a world of superheroes and the supervillains they seem to attract. Walking out of the film, it's a pleasure to find oneself *not* living in Gotham City and, for all his glory and saving the day in the end, to also be able to say with some relief I am *not* Batman.

Though unable to match Batman's might at the box office that year, another highly successful superhero film did premier that same summer: *Iron Man*.[3] *Iron Man* was everything *The Dark Knight Returns* was not: lighthearted, fun, humorous, bright, and colorful. Iron Man of course had his own problems and a supervillain to defeat, but even when he was down, you knew nothing could wipe the grin off Tony Stark's face, as perfectly played by Robert Downey Jr. In fact, being Iron Man is so thrilling that the film ends with Stark actually saying, "I am Iron Man." Stark enjoys being the hero and, as we watch him revel in that role, as viewers we also find ourselves thinking that wearing Iron Man's armored suit would be pretty cool.

That is the true brilliance of the Iron Man concept. Because, ultimately, it's just a special suit, meaning anyone can put it on and gain the powers of Iron Man. As Christian Bale and writers of Batman for many years now have tried to show us, you have to be a little demented to be Batman; it is exactly what we might expect of a man whose parents were gunned down before his eyes. But Iron Man is different. Downey helps us see that being Iron Man would be fun. It's like being in a video game because all we need is the technology. This, then, is *Iron Man*'s impact on the concept of the superhero. Iron Man makes the superhero a technological construct, and in the twenty-first-century world of technology in which we live, this brings the possibility of being a superhero almost within reach. For we live in an iWorld of technology in which more and more equipment is tailored for us. Why would we not, then, expect technology to eventually deliver us the superpowers readers of comic books have always craved?

TECHNOLOGICAL ORIGINS

The first superhero, or, at least, the first super-powered comic book character is considered to be Doctor Occult, the Ghost Detective, who first appeared in issue number 6 of *New Fun*.[4] But of course, the first major superhero who truly stood the test of time is Superman. As most everyone knows, when he was still just a baby, Superman was sent in a rocket ship, from his doomed home world of Krypton to Earth. The contemporary explanation for how Superman got his powers is that the radiation from Earth's yellow sun imbued him with his great strength and other powers because the yellow sun's radiation is different from the radiation given off by the red sun of Krypton. However, early on it was gravity, rather than radiation, which writers Jerry Siegel and Joel Shuster used to explain the development of Superman's powers. In June 1949 in *Superman #58*, the writers claimed:

> Everyone knows that Superman is a being from another Planet, unburdened by the vastly weaker gravity of Earth. But not everyone understands how gravity affects strength! If you were on a world smaller than ours, you could jump over high buildings, lift enormous weights . . . and thus duplicate some of the feats of the Man of Steel![5]

In this early story, Siegel and Shuster offer readers a way to gain the powers of Superman. All one has to do is travel to another world where the gravity is weaker than Earth's. In this way we can see the linkage of superpower to technology. All one really needs to become a superhero is the right kind of technology: a space ship powerful enough to carry one to a planet where the gravity is weak. Not only do the writers suggest this idea, more importantly they assume that is what any reader would want: to be able to get Superman's mighty powers. So in this way, right from the starting days of the superhero, technology is offered as a means for turning the ordinary individual into a superhero.

In fact, the idea that one could gain powers by traveling to another planet actually predates Superman. In the 1917 novel *A Princess of Mars*, Edgar Rice Burroughs tells the story of Confederate American Civil War hero John Carter traveling to Mars. Like Superman, John Carter gains super strength and the ability to leap huge distances because, as Burroughs describes it, Mars's gravity is weaker than Earth's:

> Springing to my feet I received my first Martian surprise, for the effort, which on Earth would have brought me standing upright, carried me into the Martian air to the height of about three yards. I alighted softly upon the ground, however, without appreciable shock or jar. Now commenced a series of evolutions which even then seemed ludicrous in the extreme. I found that I must learn to walk all over again, as the muscular exertion which carried me easily and safely upon Earth played strange antics with me upon Mars. [6]

Burroughs sends his hero to Mars without the aid of a rocket. Instead, John Carter enters a cave where he is exposed to a mysterious smoke that enables him later to reach his hand out toward Mars and somehow beam his body to the planet. While Burroughs's explanation for John Carter's trip lacks any technological specificity, the implication is the same as that of the Superman story. To gain superpowers, the key is to find a way to travel to another world.

Unfortunately, for those of us hoping to someday make one of these journeys to a world with weaker gravity, there's a big problem: few such worlds exist. In *The Science of Superheroes*, Gresh and Weinberg explain that "a human who could lift 100 kg on Earth could lift 600 kg on the Moon, which has one-sixth the gravity of earth."[7] But the reverse is much more difficult. For Superman to be a thousand times stronger on Earth than he is on Krypton, Krypton would need to be a thousand times more massive than Earth, but "a planet with even fifty times the gravity of earth 'is essentially impossible to construct, given the physics of solid matter as we understand it.'"[8] Even getting to a planet with a different sun won't help, Gresh and Weinberg tell us, because red light and yellow light are both the same.

So while science seems to rule out journeys to worlds where we can become superpowered, these early stories nevertheless help establish the idea that technology and science can be the basis for gaining superpowers. They also set up that idea of gaining superpowers as something desirable. From very early on, Superman's stories weren't just about a hero, they were about a character readers wished they could be. One key to gaining that power is technology.

BATMAN'S UTILITY BELT

While it was the technology of a spaceship that brought Superman to a world where he could gain superpowers, technology was even more important in the Golden Age days of Batman. Right from his first appearance, in *Detective Comics #27*,[9] Batman wore a utility belt. However, Les Daniels notes in *Batman: The Complete History* that it wasn't until *Detective Comics #29* that Batman first used an item from the belt.[10] In that story, "The Batman Meets Doctor Death," Batman is wounded by a henchman named Jabah. To save himself, Batman reaches into his utility belt and pulls out a small glass vile that releases a choking gas when Batman throws it on the ground. The gas stops Jabah, and Batman, who was holding his breath against the gas, leaps to safety through a window.[11] Two issues after that, in *Detective Comics #31*, Batman adds two more pieces of technology to his arsenal, a helicopter he calls his batgyro and a batarang.[12] From here begins the long line of Batman's bat-gadgets, as he uses his fortune as millionaire heir Bruce Wayne to assemble an arsenal of crime-fighting technology.

Technology then becomes one of the central keys to Batman's success. Lacking superpowers, he must rely on technology to help him succeed against the odds. And it is this use of technology that links the fictional Batman to the real reader. The technology makes it appear that anyone could be Batman if he were to put on the utility belt and start fighting crime. Of course, we don't really think it's quite that simple, but the technology does help us as readers imagine ourselves in Batman's shoes. We know we don't have Superman's powers, but we certainly could throw a batarang or drive the batmobile.

That link between hero and reader was even further strengthened with the introduction of Robin, The Boy Wonder, in *Detective Comics #38*.[13] Robin perfectly fit with the age of the young boys buying Batman comic books at the time, and sales reportedly doubled as a result of his introduction.[14] Although Robin's utility belt didn't match the look of Batman's, even in his first appearance he made use of it, pulling out a stone and slingshot in order to take down one gangster he was fighting. This helped cement the idea that, even if they couldn't be Batman, comic book readers could imagine themselves as a kid sidekick, and comic books quickly filled with them. Sidekicks certainly relate to the idea of readers imagining themselves to be superheroes, but often these sidekicks had the same powers of their mentors, like Kid Flash or Toro. Robin, though, was significant in that he lacked superpowers, just like Batman. He was acrobatic, strong, and could fight well. He often needed to use the same bat-weapons Batman used to succeed. This helped cement this connection between Batman and Robin and technology. Their lack of super powers made technology key to their role of superheroes.

As time has passed, some of this link to technology has been diminished. Frank Miller's *The Dark Knight Returns*[15] focused much more attention on the grim nature of Batman. Though he remains a force for justice, it's clear that Batman has many psychological wounds stemming from watching the murder of his parents. The smiling Batman who introduced Robin to readers on the cover of *Detective Comics #38* seems long gone from the grim-faced vigilante of modern times. Today's reader might still think it would be interesting to be Batman, but that reader is also keenly aware that wearing the bat cowl comes at a high price. Thus, as the world moves closer to having the technology needed to create superheroes, readers find themselves faced more and more with questions about what possessing such technology might do to a person.

BE CAREFUL WHAT YOU WISH FOR

When Stan Lee began writing the Marvel stories of the 1960s, he was quick to show that technologically generated superpowers were not always a good thing. Lee used the space race of the time as the backdrop for the origin of the Fantastic Four. Reed Richards convinces his friend Ben Grimm, along with his fiancé Susan Storm and her brother Johnny, to sneak onto a military base and steal a rocket Reed has been working on. Reed needs Grimm to pilot the rocket. The group does manage to get into space, but their exposure to gamma rays during the trip turns them into the Fantastic Four. Reed, Sue, and Johnny all gain powers that enhance their lives, but Ben turns into a monstrous pile of walking rocks. Although he gains super strength, Ben is horrified by his new appearance.[16]

Early Fantastic Four stories often focused on Ben's unhappiness about being the Thing and Reed's various efforts to try to reverse the effects of the gamma rays. In *Fantastic Four #8*,[17] Reed actually manages to create a formula that turns Ben into a normal human again. Unfortunately, the effects are very temporary and Ben quickly transforms back into the Thing. This upsets Ben, as one would expect. The Thing turning back into Ben Grimm happens a few more times throughout the course of the early issues, and the Thing's transformations back and forth become a trope of the series.

As the years passed, Ben Grimm seemed to become much more comfortable as the Thing, particularly thanks to meeting and falling in love with the blind Alicia Masters.[18] Alicia was able to see the caring person that Ben was since she wasn't repulsed by his outward appearance. So although his trip into space cost Grimm his human form, this technology did not take his humanity.

The Fantastic Four also enjoyed many other benefits from technology. As a scientific super genius, there seemed to be no end to the amazing gadgets that Reed Richards could invent. Early Fantastic Four stories often included sketches of the Baxter Building that was home to the team. These sketches showed all of the high-tech machinery Reed had built. In addition, the team would often fly off on missions using their fantasti-car, though making this bathtub-shaped object fly seemed to stretch believability even for a technological genius like Reed. Again, technology played a central role in Fantastic Four stories both in how the team got their powers and how they won many of their battles.

Lee further explored the perils of technology with the Incredible Hulk. In this case, he tied into the world's fears about nuclear weapons. When a young boy named Rick Jones accidentally wanders into a gamma bomb test zone, the bomb's inventor, Bruce Banner, has to throw Jones out of the way of the radiation, but is unable to dodge it himself. This exposure turns Banner into the Hulk.[19] With the Hulk, Lee was able to fully explore the man versus monster themes that he first raised with the Thing. Where the Thing quickly became regarded by the public as a hero, the Hulk was feared and hunted. The Hulk still was a hero, saving Rick many times and even joining the Avengers briefly, but his anger combined with other peoples' misunderstandings continually forced the Hulk to flee humanity.

As time passed, the Hulk came to symbolize the potential for anger we all have inside us. Writers regularly had Banner trying to find a cure, but always failing to be able to control the raging beast that was the Hulk. Just as important, the Hulk's origin remains linked to the development of military weapons. In the film *Fat Man and Little Boy*,[20] director Roland Joffe tells the story of the real-life development of the first atomic bombs. During the film, one physicist has to grab a radioactive component to protect the rest of his team. This exposure quickly leads to a painful death for him. In reality, many of the scientists who worked on the first bomb died of radiation sickness, since the dangers of radiation were not understood very well at the time. The Hulk is a reminder that man's efforts to harness some technologies, especially technologies of mass destruction, are fraught with peril.

Finally, a discussion of the downsides of technology certainly needs to include mention of the Amazing Spider-Man. Like so many other superheroes, Spider-Man's origin is linked to a scientific accident. The bite of a radioactive spider gives Peter Parker superhuman powers. In perhaps the most brilliant story he ever wrote, in *Amazing Fantasy #15*,[21] Lee had Peter do what most of us might really do if we got superpowers, not fight crime but use the powers to get rich. After appearing on a TV special, Peter walks down a hallway where a man runs past him while being chased by a cop who yells "stop him." Peter does nothing to intervene and, when the cop criticizes him for not even sticking out his foot, Peter callously replies, "From now on I just look out for number one."[22] Of course in the cruelest of ironies, the fleeing crook later shoots Peter's Uncle Ben, and Spider-Man learns that "with great power there must also come . . . great responsibility."[23]

All three of these origin stories (Spider-Man's, the Hulk's, and the Fantastic Four's) are similar in that the heroes gain their powers due to exposure to radiation. Spider-Man's is not as direct as the others, but it's clear that the radiation is what causes Peter's transformation. The underlying theme here is that science could be used to give a person superpowers. The idea extends much further back of course, to the creation of Captain America in the U.S. military's Super-Soldier Project.[24] Yet the significant change Lee introduced was to make that scientific change double-edged. As science and technology evolved, it created circumstances in which superheroes could emerge. Yet Spider-Man, the Thing, and especially the Hulk all found that the powers they were given came at a very high price. In many stories, these characters wished only to be turned back into normal people who could live ordinary lives. Yet this is the very essence of technological advances: the clock can never be turned back. For all a reader might wish to have superpowers, these stories offer a warning about the perils such wishes can bring.

RINGS, SHIELDS, AND OTHER TECHNOLOGICAL GADGETS

Hopefully, most comic book readers are steering clear of radioactive hazard areas, so it's unlikely anyone will turn into the Hulk. So if a person wants to become a superhero, their best bet is to get their hands on a superhero gadget. The superhero universe is awash in technological gadgetry: power rings, weapons, armor, and all sorts of other devices. There are far too many to discuss them all, of course, but a few can help illustrate the importance of the technological gadget.

Superhero gadgets offer a unique perspective on the nature of many heroes' powers. On the one hand, these technology items certainly make the heroes more effective at fighting the bad guys. Daredevil's billy club is a good example. The club started as a cane for Matt Murdock to use because he is blind. However, he doesn't actually need the cane since he has radar that lets him "see." The cane of course complements Murdock's disguise as a blind person, but then converts into the billy club he uses both as a weapon to hit villains with and as a kind of rope for swinging through New York City. In some ways, the club would seem to be a poor choice, since it could connect Daredevil with his alter ego. After all, some blind people do own walking sticks that collapse the way Daredevil's does. In a way, Daredevil's disguise might be better if he were to shed the club entirely. Why carry an item that risks, even slightly, revealing one's true identity, particularly when other potential risks already exist, like Murdock and Daredevil often being in the same place at roughly the same time? Some questions, of course, are better not asked when reading comics.

Yet leaving that issue aside, the true value of Daredevil's billy club is that it allows him to incorporate an essential item of the blind person into his superhero persona. The billy club becomes a symbol for rising above one's limitations. This is what we come to expect of technology in the twenty-first century: that it can work miracles. We want devices that help us to navigate our world. Perhaps not a billy club that can let a blind person swing through the air, but certainly digital maps on cell phones that we can call upon when we are lost. Even better, there is research now being conducted that hopes to use nanotechnology to send visual stimuli from a microchip implant directly to a person's brain, bypassing nonfunctioning eye nerves.[25] It's not Daredevil's radar, but it is a technological advance of amazing potential nevertheless.

Perhaps even more tricky than Daredevil's billy club are the technological gadgets that don't work like technological gadgets. Green Lantern's power ring runs on willpower. It uses an energy source, a lantern, and is able to project rays and create all manner of objects. The ring comes to Hal Jordan from a dying alien.[26] This technology is controlled by one's willpower making the concept rather absurd. For one thing, if the device is controlled by thought, it seems problematic that Jordan could control the ring, since he thinks in a language different from that of the alien Abin Sur, who gave the ring to him. Then again, much of our thinking is done through imagery. Therefore, the idea of conjuring a physical object would probably cut across intergalactic species, which is a very good thing given the size of the Lantern Corps.

More importantly, what the power ring does perfectly is link Green Lantern's imagination to the reader's own. It's very easy to imagine wearing a power ring and dreaming up items to defeat bad guys. And many young readers of *Green Lantern* would don real rings to help heighten this imagining (this even works for older readers wearing wedding bands). The ring also manages to capture another aspect of peoples' relationships with technology. Willing technology to do what is required of it is a dream of many people: that a computer will do what they want, that a web page will load faster, that an application will come unfrozen, or that a lost document will rematerialize on the desktop. The contemporary computer user often finds him- or herself staring at the screen trying to direct willpower at the machine to fix a problem. If only the Guardians of Oa made our computers.

The symbolic importance of this superhero technology should not be underestimated. Even if readers can't get the powers, they can get the gadgets. Spider-Man is an excellent example of this. Much of Spider-Man's early draw for readers was the way he struggled with real-world problems. Yes, he had been bitten by that radioactive spider, but he had a real life with girl problems and money worries. In addition, although his powers were great, his most interesting power, his ability to shoot webs, didn't come from the spider's bite. Instead, Peter simply built the web shooter he used because he was a science prodigy. Peter needed to develop his own technology to round out the spider skills he was given, and if Peter could do it, then perhaps other smart readers who had girl troubles of their own could.

Unfortunately, as good as Sam Raimi's movie *Spider-Man*[27] was, this is one aspect he got wrong. Rather than have Tobey Maguire's Peter Parker build a web shooter, Raimi had webbing come right out of Peter's arm in the film. In addition to being somewhat disgusting, this actually removes a link between Peter and the audience. We've also already discussed how problematic that radioactive spider bite is, so by making all of Spider-Man's powers be linked to the bite including his web-shooting ability, the filmmakers block the audience from being able to imagine building their own web shooter or, more practically, buying one at Walmart. This contradiction didn't stop the sale of toy web shooters following the movie's release. Fortunately, the 2012 release of *The Amazing Spider-Man*[28] restored the technology of the web shooter to the Spider-Man story, reestablishing an important technology to the list of devices would-be superheroes would like to get their hands on.

Finally, this section on technological gadgets would not seem complete without a few words about Captain America's shield. Even better than Daredevil's billy club, Cap's shield is the perfect wedding of form and function. The shield is the perfect symbol of all the patriotism Captain America is meant to embody. Every time Cap lifts that shield high, he's waving the American flag for the whole world to see. But it also helps that the shield is made of nearly indestructible vibranium. Captain America first began using his circular shield in *Captain America Comics #2*,[29] and despite hundreds of battles, he has almost always been able to use it to deflect every bullet fired his way. The special composition of the shield also makes it perfect for absorbing powerful enemy blows and also for ricocheting back to Cap when he bounces it off an enemy's head.

As with other superhero gadgets, it's very easy for readers to imagine themselves holding Cap's shield. And this idea was explored quite powerfully in the issues of *Captain America* following the tragic assassination of Steve Rogers, the first Captain America, in *Captain America #25*.[30] After Cap's death, in the story arc *Fallen Son*, Shield Director Tony Stark asks Hawkeye to take up the shield to assume Captain America's mantle. Stark explains that none of his shield operatives could manage to use the shield without injuring themselves. Hawkeye, the perfect marksman, has the timing needed to wield the shield, but he eventually declines Stark's offer to become Captain America, feeling he is unworthy to assume the mantle.[31] Sometime after that, when the shield disappears, Cap's old partner Bucky Barnes begins a search for it.[32] Bucky had long been thought to have died during World

War II but had finally returned as the Winter Soldier: first an agent of the Soviet Union and then as an independent hero. When Bucky eventually locates the shield again, he is able to wield it thanks to having one arm which is robotic. Like Hawkeye, Bucky also feels unworthy to take up the role of Captain America. However, he eventually changes his mind deciding that the world needs the symbolism of good that Captain America and his shield represent.

Although this fine story arc by Ed Brubaker hinges on the moral challenge of wielding the shield, it's safe to say that most Captain America readers could imagine themselves being able to hold that red, white, and blue shield up high (at least until the bullets started flying).

FROM STAR TREK TO SIRI

As technology has continued to develop, the real world has moved closer to the worlds of fiction. In both comics and film, computers remain a key element of this evolution. One of Superman's greatest foes was the sentient computer Braniac, and when the Justice League was turned into the weekly Saturday morning kids' show *The Superfriends*,[33] the League's headquarters in the Hall of Justice contained a talking computer that issued Trouble Alerts whenever a major crisis threatened. Many other intelligent androids and robots also exist in comics, from the original Human Torch, to the Red Tornado, to the villainous Ultron.

Central to most of these conceptions is the idea of the intelligent computer. This idea was perhaps best developed in the original *Star Trek* series in the 1960s. The series was not a superhero show, but rather a science fiction. Despite this difference, the colorful uniforms of the cast, the hand-to-hand combat scenes, and the noble heroism of the crew's missions all dovetail well into superhero tropes. More importantly, in terms of a technology discussion, the *Enterprise* had a super computer. The crew of the *Enterprise* regularly spoke to the computer, which processed their questions, and offered help. This intelligent computer could be accessed both on board the *Enterprise* and through the communicators that the crew carried with them whenever they teleported to the surface of an alien planet.

The *Star Trek* crew's reliance on its ship's computer foretold the kind of interdependence that we have begun to develop with our own technology in the twenty-first century. Most everyone walks around with communicators glued to their ears, as the smart phone has become the ubiquitous technology of the day. When Apple released the iPhone 4S, that communicator even came with its own talking computer: Siri. From a practical perspective, Siri actually has fairly good functionality. If you speak to the phone slowly and enunciate clearly, you can get the computer (which has a woman's voice) to send a short message to your spouse to pick up some milk on the way home from work. Siri is also great for helping you find directions to the nearest comic book shop. People have even asked Siri more esoteric questions, such as "Are you human?" Her reply to this one is sometimes "Close enough, I'd say."[34] The Siri technology is still evolving, and Siri is, fortunately, not nearly as intelligent as Braniac or Ultron. Nevertheless, the idea of the talking computer, which once seemed only science fiction, now is available from a cellular phone.

The superhero who probably best represents this is Oracle. Oracle was really Barbara Gordon, who had been the superheroine Batgirl until the Joker broke her back in *The Killing Joke*.[35] At this point, Gordon faced a crisis. Unable to walk, she might have had to live a normal life. Instead, she turned to technology to enable her to remain a superhero. Having lost her ability to walk, Gordon dedicated herself to building the world's most powerful computer system and used that computer to gather information. She then used this computer system to fight evil. The computer is the perfect superhero gadget for today's world. It gives us access to a nearly unlimited wealth of information. And now, thanks to Siri, we share in that world of limitless information. Although most of us use the computer to check our e-mail and Facebook pages rather than fight crime, today's computers still empower us in ways that once seemed out of reach.

TODAY'S TECHNOLOGICAL SUPERHERO: YOU

In issue #8 from the comic book series *2001: A Space Odyssey*,[36] which was based on the infamous film, Aaron Stack is playing in a live-action game called Hero World. The game allows people to wear real costumes, battle real villains, and have real adventures. But Stack drops out in frustration because, in the end, it is still only a game. As he quits, another player chides him saying, "If you can't make it in Hero World, you can't make it anywhere."[37] Soon after, Stack encounters an alien monolith that turns him into a living robot called Machine Man. He becomes a real superhero, fighting villains in the Marvel universe.

Machine Man represents one possible evolution of superhero technology, the fusion of the human body with the computer. If computers and human brains could be directly linked, we would gain instant access to information and the ability to control computer machinery. Such linkages have been the realm of one area of science fiction for many years now, cyberpunk, whose ideas have been explored in such seminal books as William Gibson's *Neuromancer*[38] and Neal Stephenson's *Snow Crash*.[39] Yet current research has begun to move these linkages out of the realm of science fiction and into the real world. In 1998, MIT cybernetics researcher Kevin Warwick had a computer chip implanted in his skin that he used to remotely control a computer:

> Warwick played the part of guinea pig in what was then touted as the first nonmedical implant experiment. With a tiny glass capsule full of transponders under the skin of his arm, Warwick essentially became a human remote control: Every time he walked through the door of his building at the University of Reading, sensors in the doorways would immediately register the presence of the transponders in his implant. The lights would come on, his computer would boot up and connect to his Web site, doors would open, and his office would greet him with a "Hello, Professor Warwick!" In a very Big Brother touch, his computer could also track his comings and goings and his exact location within the building.[40]

Warwick's computer implant is still a long way from turning him into Machine Man, but it does mark the start of explorations for linking us directly to our computers. Even if we can't find a way to plug in our brains, it's not hard to imagine how we might enclose ourselves with a computer body like Iron Man's. In some ways, this almost seems preferable. Iron Man can take his armor off. Unlike Machine Man, Tony Stark hasn't had to give up his humanity to become one with the computer. Instead, his armor is removable, except for the part that keeps a piece of shrapnel from entering his heart and killing him. Iron Man's armor makes him powerful, enables him to fly, and gives him direct access to the armor's onboard computer system. Over time, Stark built many suits of armor, improving on his original design and making himself more powerful. Eventually these suits became stand-alone items that anyone could wear. One such suit was the green armor worn by Stark's friend Kevin O'Brien who used it to become the Guardsman.[41] Unfortunately a malfunction in that armor's cybernetic circuitry ended up turning O'Brien into a supervillain. Stark later fixed that flaw and the suit was used by O'Brien's brother Michael to become a superhero.[42] More disturbing than this storyline was the *Dark Avengers*[43] series in which Norman Osborn was able to gain access to some of Stark's suits of armor and used them to become the Iron Patriot. The Iron Patriot acted outwardly as a hero but remained evil at his core.

For good or bad, then, anyone can put on a suit of Iron Man's armor and blast off into adventure. And therein lies the power of Iron Man as a character. In many ways, Iron Man is the perfect superhero because anyone, good or bad, can become him. The real Iron Man, Tony Stark, also helped develop this vision of Iron Man. While Stark was a hero, he also was a real bad boy. He would flirt with women, get into arguments with other heroes, and party hard. In fact, Stark's overindulgences eventually led him to problems with alcoholism, a storyline powerfully explored in the nine-issue "Demon in a Bottle" story arc by David Michelinie and Bob Layton.[44] In the story, Iron

Man attends an awards ceremony where his armor malfunctions, accidentally causing it to fire a repulsor ray blast that kills a foreign ambassador. Depressed by the incident, which not only lands Iron Man in trouble with the police but also causes the value of his company, Stark International, to plunge, Tony begins drinking heavily. Stark encounters a number of other problems, and is soon drinking constantly, to the point where he can't even control his armor. Finally, Stark is confronted about his drinking by a friend named Bethany Cabe, who gets him to admit to his problem and to enter a withdrawal program.

"Demon in a Bottle" is a gripping Iron Man story because it not only captures the high-flying adventure of being the armor-clad superhero, but it also highlights how even the most advanced technology in the world can't save us from our own failings. This brings the idea of the technological superhero to its fullest fruition. As we make technology more and more a part of our daily lives, we gain abilities that people only dreamed of in the past: unlimited access to information, instant contact with our friends 24/7, and the opportunity to entertain ourselves even while standing in the grocery line. The more marvelous and ubiquitous technology becomes, the more it seems like our opportunity to get our hands on a piece of superhero technology is just around the corner. Maybe we can't imagine getting Iron Man's armor just yet, but it certainly seems like Batman's utility belt can't be that far from the assembly line.

In fiction, superheroes represent many of our hopes and dreams for a better world. In real life, we place those hopes and dreams in technology. We consistently look to technology to make life better, from speeding up our computers to making our phones lighter and clearer. But even more than that, we also hope, if maybe more wistfully, that advances in technology will someday cure cancer, end climate change, and eliminate pollution. On some level, technology has become the world's real superhero. When we have a problem, we turn to technology to solve it. Trying to lose weight? Download a weight loss app. Need to find date? Sign up for an Internet dating site. Want to end world hunger? Just go to a nonprofit site where you can donate. We want to believe that technology can help us with everything we want, and perhaps it can.

It's not hard to end up believing that with all the other amazing things technology can do, it's possible for technology to someday turn us into superheroes. The trick, though, is whether we'll be ready for that technology when it arrives. In "The Trial of the Super-Friends" television show,[45] directors Ray Patterson and Carl Urbano provide an entertaining look at whether the gadgets make the hero. In a diabolical plot, supervillains from the Legion of Doom steal Green Lantern's Power Ring, Wonder Woman's lasso, and Batman and Robin's utility belts. The supervillains then capture these four heroes and put them on trial. Presiding over the trial, Lex Luthor quickly finds the four guilty of having upheld the law and stopped many of the villains' evil schemes. The sentence for the heroes' crimes is to be teleported to an alien planet where they must fight android replicas of themselves. The androids have been created by Braniac and given the real heroes' power devices. To the stunned outrage of the supervillains, however, the real superheroes are able to defeat their android counterparts even without their technological devices. The moral of the story, of course, is that it takes more than fancy gadgets to make a superhero. To become a superhero, a person has to be courageous, resourceful, wise, and, above all else, dedicated to doing good. Let's hope, then, that if technology is someday able to give us superpowers, we'll remember that vital part about using those powers to do good.

NOTES

1. *The Dark Knight*, directed by Christopher Nolan (2008, Warner Brothers).

2. "*The Dark Knight* Box Office Statistics," *Box Office Mojo*, http://boxofficemojo.com/movies/?id=darkknight.htm (accessed January 12, 2013).

3. *Iron Man*, directed by Jon Favreau (2008, Paramount Pictures).

4. Douglas Wolk, "75 Years of the First Comic Book Superhero (It's Not Who You Think)," *Time: Techland*, http://techland.time.com/2010/07/05/75-years-of-the-first-comic-book-superhero-its-not-who-you-think/ (accessed January 12, 2013).

5. Jerry Siegel and Joe Shuster as quoted in Louis Gresh and Robert Weinberg, *The Science of Superheroes* (Hoboken, NJ: Wiley, 2002), 16.

6. Edgar Rice Burroughs, *John Carter of Mars: The Collection* (Purple Rose Publishing, 2010), 10.

7. Gresh and Weinberg, *The Science of Superheroes*, 17.

8. Gresh and Weinberg, *The Science of Superheroes*, 17.

9. Bob Kane and Bill Finger, *Detective Comics* vol. 1, no. 27 (May 1939).

10. Les Daniels, *Batman: The Complete History* (San Francisco: Chronicle Books, 1999), 29.

11. Bob Kane and Bill Finger, *Detective Comics* vol. 1, no. 29 (July 1939).

12. Bob Kane and Bill Finger, *Detective Comics* vol. 1, no. 31 (September 1939).

13. Bob Kane and Bill Finger, *Detective Comics* vol. 1, no. 27 (April 1940).

14. Daniels, *Batman: The Complete History*, 37.

15. Frank Miller and Klaus Janson, *The Dark Knight Returns* (New York: DC Comics, 1986).

16. Stan Lee and Jack Kirby, *Fantastic Four* vol. 1, no. 1 (November 1961).

17. Stan Lee and Jack Kirby, *Fantastic Four* vol. 1, no. 8 (November 1962).

18. Lee and Kirby, *Fantastic Four* vol. 1, no. 8.

19. Stan Lee and Jack Kirby, *The Incredible Hulk* vol. 1, no. 1 (May 1962).

20. *Fat Man and Little Boy*, directed by Roland Joffé (Paramount Pictures, 1989).

21. Stan Lee and Jack Kirby, *Amazing Fantasy* vol. 1, no. 15 (August 1962).

22. Lee and Kirby, *Amazing Fantasy* vol. 1, no. 15, 8.

23. Lee and Kirby, *Amazing Fantasy* vol. 1, no. 15, 11.

24. Joe Simon and Jack Kirby, *Captain America Comics* vol. 1, no. 1 (March 1941).

25. Rebecca Boyle, "Tiny Fractal-Shaped Eye Implants Could Mimic Neurons, Allowing Blind Patients to See," *Popsci*, www.popsci.com/technology/article/2011-05/tiny-fractal-shaped-eye-implants-could-mimic-neurons-allowing-blind-patients-see (accessed January 13, 2013).

26. John Broome and Gil Kane, *Showcase Comics* vol. 1, no. 22 (October 1959).

27. *Spider-Man*, directed by Sam Raimi (Sony Pictures, 2002).

28. *The Amazing Spider-Man*, directed by Marc Webb (Columbia Pictures, 2012).

29. Joe Simon and Jack Kirby, *Captain America Comics* vol. 1, no. 2 (April 1941).

30. Ed Brubaker and Steve Epting, "Civil War: The Death of a Dream, Part One," *Captain America* vol. 5, no. 25 (April 2007).

31. Jeph Loeb and John Romita Jr., *Fallen Son: The Death of Captain America* vol. 1, no. 3 (July 2007).

32. Ed Brubaker and Steve Epting, "The Initiative: The Death of the Dream, Part Two," *Captain America* vol. 5, no. 26 (July 2007).

33. *Super Friends! Season 1, Volume 1* (1973; Warner Home Video, 2010), DVD.

34. Elena, "Siri Answers 20 Hilarious Questions," www.freemake.com/blog/siri-answers-20-hilarious-questions/ (accessed May 24, 2012).

35. Alan Moore and Brian Bolland, *Batman: The Killing Joke* (New York: DC Comics, 1988).

36. Jack Kirby, "The Capture of X-51!" *2001: A Space Odyssey* vol. 1, no. 8 (July 1977).

37. Kirby, "The Capture of X-51!" 1.

38. William Gibson, *Neuromancer* (New York: Ace Books, 1984).

39. Neal Stephenson, *Snow Crash* (New York: Bantam Books, 1992).

40. Janelle Brown, "Professor Cyborg: Programming Humans" excerpt, *Mark of the Beast*, www.countdown.org/end/mark_of_the_beast_06.htm (accessed January 12, 2013).

41. Allyn Brodsky and Don Heck, "Anything—for the Cause!" *The Invincible Iron Man* vol. 1, no. 31 (November 1970).

42. Gerry Conway, Bill Mantlo, and George Tuska, "Showdown with the Guardsman!" *The Invincible Iron Man* vol. 1, no. 97 (April 1977).

43. Brian Michael Bendis, Mike Deodato, Greg Horn, and Chris Bachalo, *Dark Avengers* (New York: Marvel Comics, 2011).

44. David Michelinie, Bob Layton, John Romita Jr., and Carmine Infantino, *Iron Man: Demon in a Bottle* (New York: Marvel Comics, 2006).

45. "Trial of the Superfriends," directed by Ray Patterson and Carl Urbano. In *Challenge of the Superfriends: Attack of the Legion of Doom* (Warner Home Video, 2004), DVD.

Chapter Eleven

Reflections on Creating a Canon

The preceding chapters have presented some of the profound and unique characteristics of superhero literature. This genre is responsible for producing definitions of heroism that evolve with audiences and that reaffirm what is important to the collective, cultural consciousness. The heroes in these stories have conquered death, censorship, relegation, and creative strife only to come out stronger and more socioculturally relevant than ever.

On its surface, it would seem like the superhero genre should have never been able to do this. The genre's origins are as humble as they can get, coming from cheap, pulp magazine publishers who only cared about the amount of money that could be made on a single issue being sold to children. The plethora of unpopular heroes during the Golden Age of comics is proof of this mentality, and the survivors of this age are the names of literary legend: Superman, Batman, Wonder Woman, Green Lantern, the Flash, and Captain America. These characters survived for complex reasons, and those reasons have been subjects of the preceding chapters of this volume.

Marvel Comics' rise in the 1960s only reaffirmed the importance of superheroes to American culture through Marvel's creation of socially relevant superheroes that tapped into the humanistic aspects of superheroes and their struggles with power. And in the continued evolution of superheroes through the 1980s, 1990s, and 2000s heroes were redefined to better match what society needed them to represent.

The discussions in this book have brought us to a point where superheroes' legitimacy as culturally relevant texts needs to be cemented in both the cultural and academic landscapes. Culturally, these texts have already achieved a certain level of respect, as evidenced by major motion pictures about superheroes becoming wildly successful. At the time this is being written, *The Avengers* has become the third-most-successful motion picture in history,[1] and *The Amazing Spider-Man* and *The Dark Knight Rises* have rounded out a summer where superhero films reigned supreme. The public has a desire to interact with these characters, and the box office numbers are proof of this.

Yet while there is public desire to celebrate superheroes, these characters remain largely excluded from discussions in academic contexts. Chapter 2 explored this problem in depth. Yet the absence of these texts from academic consideration eliminates major components of culture, history, and literature from the overall discourse of academia. Like the traditional canon of graphic novels that was presented in chapter 2, this chapter presents a canon that honors and privileges these superhero texts in various media. From comic books to graphic novels to television shows to motion pictures, superhero literature deserves to be recognized within the framework of a literary and academic construct.

Part of the significance of superhero literature is the unique nature of its composition and its continuity. Superheroes are not bound by author ownership or stories that have specific beginnings and ends. Instead, superhero narratives exist in an ever-evolving world of changing writers, artists, editors, sociocultural landscapes, and diverse audiences. The uniqueness of superhero literature necessitates the development of its own canon not because it doesn't deserve to be included in traditional canons, but because superhero literature has created a new and powerful world of storytelling.

THE IDEA OF THE CANON

Canon refers to standards in any field of study. There is a canon of central works in the social sciences, natural sciences, political sciences, philosophy, religion, literature, and so on. Generally, these are the standard texts, ideas, theories, concepts, laws, and otherwise integral aspects of knowledge in a given field. While this book has been mainly discussing the sociocultural aspects of superheroes and how those aspects make the study of this particular genre in academic contexts worthy, traditional literary canon represents a strong place to begin this discussion.

Literary canon is what most American schoolchildren/adolescents/teens are exposed to in their English classes. It is the canon of great literature that, for all accounts and purposes, makes up the contents of literature survey courses. There are of course variations on which texts are read from state to state and from region to region, but there are some texts that almost every student will have been exposed to by the time they go to college or start working. The famous literary critic Harold Bloom wrote the book *The Western Canon* in 1994 which set about establishing and defending classic works of literature and helping to produce a set library of what Bloom felt were the works most worthy of study. Bloom's canon reflects works from Ancient Greece all the way up through the twentieth century, and it has become a seminal work in the field of literature and discussions of canon.[2]

Bloom's canon is, in terms of literary studies, quite traditional. *The Western Canon* has been debated and critiqued, particularly for its overreliance on the works of mostly white authors. The book *Debating the Canon: A Reader from Addison to Nafisi* by editor Lee Morrissey is a useful examination of the debates that have arisen over the canon.[3]

Our goal is not to engage actively in the complicated debate over the canon's validity or its contents. Instead, it's enough to point out that there are no superheroes on Bloom's list. In fact, Bloom's book does not even discuss any graphic novels: No *Maus*,[4] no *Contract with God*,[5] no *Watchmen*,[6] and definitely no cartoon characters. Most schools and academic institutions still honor this aging perception of what literature is despite the advances of technology, the rise of graphic literature, and theories such as "multiliteracies"[7] and "multiple intelligences"[8] becoming more prevalent in education. Bloom's canon reflects a very traditional definition of literature, and that tradition is still holding strong despite the monomodality of the texts on Bloom's list. It needs to be said that there is nothing wrong with these traditional texts either. The literary works Bloom favors certainly have sound merit. This critique is not to meant to discount the classics by any means. From Homer to Dickens and from Aristotle to Hemingway, traditional literature certainly has value because the authors that make up the canon of traditional literature have established themselves as standards, and their views and commentaries on history, the human condition, and the universe are brilliant.

Though Bloom's views regarding what should be placed in the literary canon may be very traditional, he does offer an excellent argument about the basic value of establishing a canon:

> If we were literally immortal, or even if our span were doubled to seven score of years, say, we could give up all argument about canons. But we have an interval only, and then our place knows us no more, and stuffing that interval with bad writing, in the name of whatever social justice, does not seem to me to be the responsibility of the literary critic.[9]

Bloom links the canon with our mortality, and to some extent this makes sense. We, as humans, only have so much time to interact with texts, giving us a limited number of literary choices to make during our lives about what we want to read. However, the end of this quote also reflects a double-edged sword on Bloom's view of canon. What Bloom disparages as "social justice" really means literature that represents "multiculturalism." Bloom feels that political agendas have diluted the literary canon in an effort to represent diverse voices. Bloom's *Western Canon* thus lays out his own agenda for what the literary world should value, and that agenda can be damaging to the natural evolution of media and the diverse voices that look to contribute to the world of literature.

Given Bloom's critique of "social justice" or multicultural literature, it's easy to extrapolate what Bloom's view of graphic novels and superhero literature would be: literary trash! Bloom would undoubtedly consider the inclusion of superhero texts in the Western canon as being blasphemous. Bloom actually did think that superheroes might eventually become part of the university discourse, but he didn't view this possibility with anything but dread: "What are now called 'Departments of English' will be renamed departments of 'Cultural Studies' where *Batman* comics, Mormon theme parks, television, movies, and rock will replace Chaucer, Shakespeare, Milton, Wordsworth, and Wallace Stevens."[10] This negative view toward the evolution of media and new texts borders on a fear of change where those changes are characterized as being utterly destructive to academic and/or personal growth. Would it really be so blasphemous if Batman stories were read and studied in literature survey courses or in composition courses? Bloom might feel this was a problem, but we would call that progress.

Thus, while we realize there is a certain irony in applying Bloom's ideas to the genre of superhero literature, we do take Bloom at his word when it comes to the idea of people only having so much time to read so many texts. Bloom gets that point right, and thus we do see Bloom's ideas about canon as a way to encourage people to read the best literature available, including the best superhero literature. Yet while we hope developing a canon of superhero literature will encourage people to read more of the great superhero stories, the goal of this canon is not to list all the books a person needs to read before he or she dies. Looking at the canon of superhero literature in that way is both morbid and counterproductive because it can only cause more debate than solidarity. Instead, the goal for creating a canon of superhero literature is to honor the concepts of heroism, bravery, selflessness, and dedication to good for which superheroes are best known.

Superheroes are an old enough concept to merit possession of the affordances and constraints of other genres. These characters are not ones created within the last five, ten, fifteen, or even twenty years. Even the Marvel superheroes, who came twenty years after DC's characters appeared in the late 1930s and early 1940s, have passed fifty years of publication and influence. *Fantastic Four #1*, which marks the beginning of Marvel's superheroes, was published in 1962.

Creating a canon of superhero literature is about privileging the texts and mythologies that have influenced, inspired, and helped construct a part of culture's collective consciousness throughout the twentieth century and into the twenty-first century. Since these characters are ones that most people are already knowledgeable about, presenting a canon of superhero literature is a way of validating the presence of superheroes in cultural, academic, and societal discourses.

A CANON OF SUPERHERO LITERATURE

The canon of superhero literature we are presenting here is not limited to comic books and/or graphic novels. It can't be. Superhero literature has become much too large for such confines, and the nature of multiple continuities necessitates taking a broad view of what the superhero genre encompasses. Every type of media that presents superhero narratives is vital to the overall understanding of superheroes in culture and society, and us. All media have affordances and constraints, but they present superheroes while utilizing their own unique strengths as a medium. Grant Morrison's *Super Gods* makes distinctions between superhero comic books and films saying, "Comics are what they are, and a good comic page can do things that even great movies can't, just as a movie can achieve effects even the best comics are incapable of equaling."[11] We take Morrison's point as encouragement for looking at superheroes through the broadest range of media so as to facilitate a comprehensive exploration of superheroes' strengths, weaknesses, values, and deficits. The way Batman is portrayed in the comic books is vastly different from the way he's portrayed in the films, but both media have powerful ways of representing the character. Spider-Man, Superman, the X-Men, and the Avengers all have been represented in diverse ways through varying media, but these ways are all equally relevant for the goal of creating a rich discourse about superheroes.

A canon is characterized by its identification of texts that are relevant for academic and sociocultural study and discussion. Developing a canon can be subjective in nature since personal experiences influence and affect the value a given person places on particular texts. As already noted, even the traditional literary canon has faced debates by scholars about which texts are relevant and vital for inclusion. There is an inherent deficit in literature's traditional concept of canon, though. Each piece of literature is a story unto itself with its own themes, characters, settings, sociohistorical contexts, and established critics. This creates a situation where the canon is dependent upon the reader being intimately familiar with a singular text in order to contribute to the discourse. In this way, a culture of elitism is developed wherein the value of input is dependent on one's knowledge of countless, specialized texts. This effectively creates a rhetoric constructed strictly on knowledge of specific texts and their ancillary subtexts.

Compare this with a canon of superhero literature. The literature of superheroes is established through repeated exposure to diverse and varying media that develops with a reader as he or she grows. So for children, the literature of superheroes is that of crime fighting and superpowers as portrayed through age-appropriate cartoons, age-appropriate comic books, and storybooks. As a person grows into adolescence and teen years, their exposure to the genre becomes much more diverse, as evidenced by the film versions of superheroes which, presumably, most adolescents and teenagers will have been exposed to. And the film versions of superheroes explore themes that are as broad as possible in order to appeal to wider audiences. This appeases younger audiences with the super-heroism they love and it appeals to older audiences through character deconstructions. The combination of these superhero films is a great springboard for adolescent and teen audiences into more adult superhero stories that either celebrate the superhero or deconstruct that hero. Either way, the reader's exposure to the characters and their themes can be established from an early age and can then mature as the reader/audience member matures.

More importantly, the traditional literary canon is composed of stories that are temporally bound. In other words, *Hamlet* is a contained story with a specific beginning and specific end. All narrative discussions of the characters, setting, politics, and psychology in *Hamlet* are contained within its pages. There is no "other" version of *Hamlet* where authors could have taken liberties with the character such as making Hamlet English instead of Danish or having Ophelia not kill herself; there is no such thing as varying continuities in classical literature. Charles Dickens did not get the chance to write a Hamlet story, but if he had, it would have been subject to different and unique perceptions of the characters. A Dickensian version of *Hamlet* would have been written to fit into the sociohistorical context in which Dickens lived. We've probably missed a lot because Dickens never wrote anything like *Hamlet* but, then again, we are fortunate in that we do have Shakespeare's *Hamlet*, which remains one of the most, if not the most, revered works in all of literature. The point here is not that we need more versions of *Hamlet*, but that superhero literature, unlike traditional literature, does benefit by its lack of constrained storytelling.

Referencing Batman once more, credits in movies, television shows, and comic books will say, "Batman, created by Bob Kane." While this is technically true (Bill Finger notwithstanding), the character is not totally Bob Kane's creation anymore. Part of this is due to comic publishers' style of distribution and composition, which focuses on magazine-style narratives that cater to as many people as possible in a given month. Had Batman been a contained story, say from the years 1938–1942, it would have had its own continuity, sociohistorical context, and author perspective. Instead, the character of Batman has been written and drawn by many other creators throughout the years, and each incarnation has been as unique as the previous one. Batman may "legally" belong to DC, Warner Brothers, and the Kane estate, but many people have added to the character over a long span of time, thereby establishing Batman as a multifaceted creation who has far exceeded the bounds of Bob Kane's original idea.

Who was the best Batman? While the answer to that question will be based on one's exposure to the character, a canon of superhero literature is responsible for that question even existing because the question is not solely rooted in reality. If the question was asked, "Who was the best Hamlet?" the answer has to be in the form of an actor and his interpretation of the character because there is only one Hamlet whose character has not changed since his initial appearance. With "Who was the best Batman?" the question then becomes meta-textual. The answer could be Michael Keaton, Adam West, or Christian Bale, but it could also be "Frank Miller's Batman" or "Alan Moore's Batman" or "Grant Morrison's Batman" or any other creator who had the opportunity to write the character. Each creator took what came before and built a personal vision of the character on previous incarnations, and future creators will continue to do this as well. A canon of superhero literature is meta-textual at multiple levels because the characters have been around for so long, have such complex continuity, and have been reimagined ad nauseam for over seventy years.

Establishing a canon of superhero literature is totally subjective, though, and that must be stressed throughout the following pages. While there are some pieces of superhero literature that most people would probably recognize as being canonical in superhero literature, such as *The Dark Knight Returns* or *Watchmen*, there are works that will be more open to discussion and debate. That is, in fact, one of the beauties of this proposed canon: like the genre of superhero literature, the canon of superhero literature is subject to evolution, change, addition, and subtraction.

MORE THAN A CANON OF GRAPHIC NOVELS

Even beyond the hallowed grounds of traditional literature, into which most would certainly not willingly accept superheroes, superheroes have been marginalized in the developing field of comic studies. Chapter 2 went into this in detail, but for the purposes of discussing canon, it needs to be reiterated: superheroes are not privileged in academic studies of comics or graphic novels. The genre that essentially springboarded comic style narratives into the public consciousness is not as accepted as it should be within comic studies. The limited presence of the superhero genre within comic studies and academia as a whole necessitates the development of a canon of superhero literature to help make superhero literature a larger part of the discourse.

Most of this book has addressed superheroes from Marvel and DC, and to be quite candid, the most popular and recognizable superheroes come from those two publishers. There are of course other publishers such as Image, Wildstorm, Vertigo, Dark Horse, and IDW, but most of the canon will come from Marvel and DC properties. There are instances where other superheroes from publishers not named Marvel and DC are listed, but the vast majority of superhero literature in this canon is from the two major publishers. This is because the canon is built around the stories of superheroes which have impacted fan and public discourses the most.

Superhero literature was born out of what Will Eisner called "sequential art" and continues to thrive in that medium, but for too long the genre has languished in that arena, excluded from more academic discussions. It is our hope that introducing a canon of superhero literature can alter this inaccurate perception that superhero literature is unworthy of serious study.

WHAT CONSTITUTES THE CANON OF SUPERHERO LITERATURE

Let's visit the question of "Who was the best Batman?" once more. However, this time, let's focus on the actors who portrayed him. This question has many different answers including Adam West, Michael Keaton, Val Kilmer, and Christian Bale. We'll take it as a given that the answer "George Clooney" is automatically incorrect. Nevertheless, the subjective answer to this question is reliant on one's date of birth, one's exposure to the character in all of his film and TV incarnations, and knowledge of the movies in which Batman has appeared. One might even give the answer Kevin Conroy, the man who voiced the Dark Knight in *Batman: The Animated Series* and is considered by many fans to be the seminal voice of the Caped Crusader.

Batman has been around for so long that different generations of fans and readers have different memories of the character and his exploits. The question of which actor best portrayed Batman even transcends the film medium itself, as much of what occurs in the films affects the print versions of the character.

What every superhero has is a collection of media over a given number of years that defines who that character is in the sociocultural context. Some heroes have more prominence than others, of course, but the variation in representation of these characters is what constitutes a canon of superhero literature. It is impossible, however, to include any and all representations of one superhero and claim that one superhero represents the entire canon of superhero literature. Again, revisiting Bloom's *Western Canon*, part of his criteria for establishing which pieces are to be a part of the Western canon is "aesthetic value,"[12] or, in other words, whether one thinks a work is good or not. Bloom's "aesthetic value" encompasses that which seems most important when reading literature and/or texts of any kind: whether the story sticks with us. While Bloom's *Western Canon* reflects a traditional view of literature, his selection criteria is at once simple and extraordinarily complex. How does one decide which narratives to read, or at the very least, which to acknowledge in a particular canon? The selection criteria we have chosen to use in developing this canon of superhero literature is the extent to which a work is multimodal, is multigenerational, has "aesthetic value," and is historically significant.

Multimodality refers to a text being able to convey information using varying modes of communication. In a strictly academic/educational sense, this applies primarily to literacy studies where students can communicate a given message using multiple stimuli such as text, sound, pictures, touch, and so on.[13] For the purposes of the superhero canon, multimodal refers to the trend of superhero narratives being told through various media.

The canon being multigenerational reflects a mentality that all of the various incarnations of a superhero are, in their unique ways, valid representations of the superhero in a sociohistorical context. For example, the 1960s *Batman* television show[14] is not reflective of how Batman is perceived or portrayed in today's media. However, simply by being aired the show affected perceptions of the character from that time onward. While that show was and is perceived as funny and/or campy, it is still Batman in the 1960s and therefore a part of the canon. This may cause a generational dissonance, which in turn is really a cultural dissonance where cultures that are separated by time may not hold the same perception of a given character. This is why today's viewers may think of Batman only as a serious character compared with viewers from the 1960s era thinking of Batman as a playful character.

Aesthetic value, which was reviewed a bit already, is of premier importance for superhero literature because there is just so much material for one to read and/or watch. Take Superman and his core titles. *Action Comics* and *Superman* have been in publication since 1938 and 1940 respectively. That gives *Action Comics*, as of May 2012 and including the New 52 reboot, 913 total issues. *Superman*, as of May 2012 and including the New 52 reboot, has 723 issues. These numbers do not include miniseries, crossovers into other books, annuals, or any other type of ancillary stories. The sheer number of Superman comic books necessitates sorting through the narratives to find the ones that best reflect the character and are most worthy of being studied. Also, the 1,636 total issues of *Action Comics* and *Superman* obviously don't include the television, radio, or film adaptations of the character.

Finally, historical significance is also vitally important in superhero literature, but it may conflict with what is considered aesthetically valuable in a piece. For example, the quality of art and writing in the 1940s superhero comic books is not generally on a par with the quality of art and writing today. Part of this is due to changes in technology. Nevertheless, while the quality of some of the texts in the canon of superhero literature may be limited, what those pieces lack in quality they make up for in historical significance. It is not the place of these researchers to identify which pieces they feel are superior or inferior to others. Instead, this canon is meant to reflect a mentality of privileging important texts for a variety of reasons including historical significance. For superhero literature, this is necessary because many of the origin stories of these characters are within texts that may not be of the highest quality, but being exposed to original origin stories allows for developing a better understanding of why characters change and/or remain the same as their sociohistorical contexts change. Overall, though, the majority of texts listed in the canon of superhero literature represent the best the genre has to offer.

ORGANIZATION OF THE SUPERHERO CANON

Categorizing the texts in the canon of superhero literature is useful for representing the best of what each era of superhero literature produced. Therefore this canon is separated into five distinct "Ages" building on the ages proposed and developed by Peter Coogan.[15] Coogan's ages are similar to the Overstreet Price Guide's organizational ages,[16] but Coogan's criteria for describing the ages is socioculturally and sociohistorically focused while Overstreet's is strictly designed for separating comic books into different categories. However, the ages we have settled upon here do have some key differences from Coogan's and Overstreet's.

In this canon, "The Dark Age" is a term that will be used to refer to superhero literature from the 1980s and early 1990s. Coogan kept with a "metal" theme in labeling his eras in superhero literature, but we feel the term "The Dark Age" more closely represents the style of stories told in superhero literature during this time period. In addition, The Dark Age extends past Coogan's 1987 end point, which he says is denoted by the publication of *Justice League International #1.*[17] There is no doubt that *Justice League International* challenged the thematic elements of superhero literature in the 1980s, but at least two key events that followed *Justice League International* seem important to include in this era: Superman's death in *Superman #75* in 1992 and Batman's paralysis in *Batman #497* in 1993. These significant comic events are clearly dark and troubling in nature, and therefore offer an effective closing point for The Dark Age.

A change in direction comes in 1994 with the arrival of *Batman: The Animated Series* and Alex Ross's *Marvels* in 1994. Yes, *Batman: The Animated Series* premiered in 1992, but its subject matter was more adult than previous superhero cartoons had been, and the show ran for four seasons, effectively making it a transitional show. At this time superheroes began to make a shift back toward being more celebratory in nature. Therefore, we use

1994 as the year for highlighting superheroes' transition into what we have labeled "The Heroic Age." This term also relates to Marvel Comics' introduction of the term "The Heroic Age" in 2010. In a press release from that time, Marvel said it was offering this shift in focus for its superheroes: "The Heroic Age ushers in a brighter Marvel Universe and a bold new era for the world's greatest super heroes as they emerge from darkness with a renewed sense of hope and optimism, leading to the formation of all new teams with new members . . . and brand new characters!"[18] Although Marvel's Heroic Age came long after 1994, throughout this later era there was a shifting toward more positive stories following the gloomy focus of the previous era. Thus we use the term "The Heroic Age" for all superhero literature from 1994 onward.

Therefore, the Ages for the canon of superhero literature can be outlined as follows:

The Golden Age: 1938–1956
The Silver Age: 1956–1970
The Bronze Age: 1971–1980
The Dark Age: 1981–1993
The Heroic Age: 1994–Present

The years these "Ages" refer to are based on the original publication dates for any comic books noted. Therefore, a graphic novel printed in the 2000s which reprints a run of comics from the 1940s would still be listed in the Golden Age because that was when the comic stories themselves were originally published. Additionally, the overlap of years in The Golden Age and The Silver Age is due to the publication of *Showcase Comics #4* in October 1956. Since this comic featured the first appearance of DC's contemporary superhero the Flash and the subsequent reimagining of Golden Age comic book superheroes courtesy of Julius Schwartz, the publication of this comic is generally referred to as the beginning of The Silver Age. From this point on, most superheroes began gaining their powers through scientific experiments and/or accidents rather than through magic. The fact that the Flash was both a Golden Age hero and a Silver Age hero leads to this overlap in years.

Even though the "Ages" refer to the publication dates of comic books, other media will be included in these ages as well. This media will include mainly television shows, cartoons, and motion pictures. Since superhero literature is so commonly multimodal, not differentiating between the media better reflects that multimodal nature. However, most of the texts in the canon of superhero literature are comic books or graphic novels in keeping with the genre's origins.

Writers and artists (when available) will be provided with each entry while films, cartoons, and television shows will be credited to their respective directors. It is understood that films, cartoons, and television shows are created by teams, but limiting the accreditation to the director helps link to film studies, where emphasis is typically placed on directors and their creations.

REFLECTIONS ON THE CANON OF SUPERHERO LITERATURE

There will, no doubt, be questions from both casual and hardcore fans regarding this canon. And again, the canon is not designed to be the ultimate unalterable list, subject to no additions, subtractions, or augmentations. During the building of this list, the researchers themselves debated the inclusion and exclusion of many texts. Instead, we see this canon as a valuable starting point for engaging others in a discussion about the importance of superhero literature. This canon is meant to be inviting rather than exclusionary.

As already noted, the selection criteria used to develop this canon were based on works being multimodal and multigenerational and having "aesthetic value" and/or historical significance. For the most part, the canon is made up of Marvel and DC texts with some of the key exceptions being *Spawn*, *Teenage Mutant Ninja Turtles*, *Miracleman*, and *Power Rangers*. There are bound to be fans and/or readers/viewers who consider the inclusion of *Power Rangers* or *Teenage Mutant Ninja Turtles* as blasphemous in a canon of superhero literature, but series like those represent the evolution of the superhero genre beyond its Marvel and DC boundaries. The appeal of these shows may wane as viewers grow older and more mature, but such shows still contributed to the development of morality and cultural values in many viewers.

The same can be said for newer cartoons included in the canon such as *Teen Titans* and *The Super Hero Squad*. These shows represent the continuing evolution of the superhero genre and the potential for the genre to extend beyond themes of dark deconstruction. The prevailing notion that "dark" superhero stories equal "good" superhero stories is challenged by the production of cartoons for children who, quite ironically, were the original focus of the genre. For adult readers of superhero literature, sitting and watching cartoons for children may be perceived as ridiculous, and perhaps it is. But the sole purpose of any canon is not to simply list what people should read. No one is ever expected to read every single text in a given canon. As Bloom notes, there just isn't enough time in anyone's life to do so. Instead, creating this canon is an attempt to recognize what texts have contributed to making the genre of superheroes socioculturally significant.

Another important aspect of this canon is the abundance of "First appearances," which don't always equate to being aesthetically valuable. The sheer abundance of first appearances is necessary for tracking where superheroes come from and why their origins have been changed multiple times. For example, Iron Man's comic book origin is set in the Vietnam War. For a 1960s comic book, this makes perfect sense as the sociohistorical environment warranted such a scenario. In the film version of the character released in 2008, Tony Stark's origin as Iron Man occurred in Afghanistan. Two completely different sociohistorical contexts call for two different origin stories for this superhero. However, the concept of Tony Stark needing the suit to survive because of the shrapnel creeping toward his heart remains intact in both origin stories. If, in another fifty years, the character is rebooted again, the setting will almost certainly change because the world will have changed. Therefore, being familiar with the original origin story as well as its later incarnations is important.

Finally, there is a clear trend in this canon in the way it progresses chronologically. In the Golden, Silver, and Bronze Ages, the vast majority of the canon is made up of single comic book issues. In contrast, the Dark and Heroic ages highlight collections of issues and/or graphic novels. The narrative style of comic books from the 1940s through and up to the late 1970s was aimed at selling single issues to children and adolescents. Therefore, the narrative style of superhero comic books was almost entirely insular. Of course, Stan Lee had begun to break that trend in the 1960s as he started constructing Marvel as a universe of heroes, but superhero comic books, even into the early 1980s, always had caption boxes or dialogue that reminded a reader every issue of who the superhero was and what his or her powers were. This was particularly evident in Marvel Comics, and there are still background pages at the beginning of most Marvel comic books today reminding both veteran and beginning readers who the character is and what the character's ongoing story has been. However, going back to why the early portion of the canon consists of single issues, the reason is because of the narrative style that has been outlined here: single issues were more marketable to children and adolescents during the Golden, Silver, and Bronze Ages. And as was discussed in the chapter on children and superheroes, it was not until the 1980s, when children and teens that had grown up with the characters had themselves become adults, that the demand for more sophisticated, and subsequently longer and more interconnected, narratives became apparent. Thus in these later ages, multiple-issue storylines become more typically the norm, and are listed as such, rather than single comic book issues.

OUR OWN NEVER-ENDING BATTLE

This proposed canon of superhero literature is meant to be a culmination of both this book and superhero literature up to this point in time. As has been covered thoroughly throughout the preceding chapters, superhero literature evolves just as time and culture do; therefore, this canon will also need to evolve with the natural ebb and flow of time. Since it will undoubtedly be added to in the coming years, this canon is presented as the beginning of the legitimization of superhero literature beyond the cramped spaces of comic book shops and the bustling floors of comic book conventions.

Superhero literature is a real and thriving genre that often gets criticized due to its traditional stigma of being nothing more than juvenile and cheap entertainment. Additionally, the tired notion that superhero characters and stories are admired and loved only by grown men who still live in their mothers' basements has become cliché, and the success of superhero films has become a testament of that cliché. Superhero franchises have become some of the most successful films of all time because they matter to more people than just hardcore comic book fans. These stories are as legitimate as any others not only because they offer insight into some of humanity's most pressing issues, but also because people connect to them. Audiences care about superheroes, their actions, their fates, their desires, their triumphs, and even their defeats.

Fortunately for superhero literature, there will always be a next issue, another movie, or a new television series featuring these larger than life characters. This insures that the characters and stories live on beyond the current audiences and inspire new audiences. Since superhero stories build on one another over time, the stories that affected past audiences remain forever relevant to present and future incarnations. The genre of superhero literature is about connecting generations through stories that are simultaneously never-ending yet always familiar.

These characters are not real, but they genuinely affect our real perceptions of the world and how we place ourselves in it. Heroism, crime, bravery, evil, altruism, and many other themes of life are addressed in the superhero canon. Superheroes are a beautiful example of fiction influencing real life. Superheroes don't actually exist, but it's fun to think about what the world might be like if they did.

And perhaps we should be careful about assuming that superheroes aren't real. At the end of *Harry Potter and the Deathly Hallows* (2007), Harry Potter experiences a "death" of sorts. Just like his superhero counterparts, Harry later rises from the dead to finally defeat his nemesis, Lord Voldemort. But before he does so, Harry has one final conversation with his mentor, Professor Dumbledore, in an afterlife setting:

> "Tell me one last thing," said Harry. "Is this real? Or has this been happening inside my head?"
>
> Dumbledore beamed at him, and his voice sounded loud and strong in Harry's ears even though the bright mist was descending again, obscuring his figure.

"Of course it is happening inside your head, Harry, but why on earth should that mean that it is not real?"[19]

That's the true iconography of the superhero. Superheroes are about the central importance of imagination to real life. These stories go beyond mere aesthetics and the embodiment of abstract concepts by brightly costumed figures. Superheroes are real because they represent the best of our thinking, all our hopes and dreams and desires to make the world a better place. We can't save the world like Superman, but we can make the world a better place through our ordinary actions. And every time we do a good deed, we make ourselves into real superheroes, and turn our fictional desires into real-world accomplishments. That's what superhero stories are really all about.

NOTES

1. Agence France-Presse, "'Avengers' third highest grossing film of all time," *Yahoo! News*, http://news.yahoo.com/avengers-third-highest-grossing-film-time-232528940.html (accessed July 8, 2012).

2. Harold Bloom, *The Western Canon: The Books and School of the Ages* (New York: Riverhead Books, 1994).

3. Lee Morrissey, ed., *Debating the Canon: A Reader from Addison to Nafisi* (New York: Palgrave Macmillan, 2005).

4. Art Spiegelman, *The Complete Maus* (New York: Penguin Books Ltd., 2003).

5. Will Eisner, *A Contract with God* (New York: Baronet Books, 1978).

6. Alan Moore and Dave Gibbons, *Watchmen* (New York: DC Comics, 1986).

7. The New London Group, "A Pedagogy of Multiliteracies: Designing Social Futures," *Harvard Educational Review* 66, no. 1: 60—92.

8. Howard Gardner, *Frames of Mind: The Theory of Multiple Intelligences* (New York: Basic Books, 1983).

9. Bloom, *The Western Canon*, 30.

10. Bloom, *The Western Canon*, 484–85.

11. Grant Morrison, *Supergods: What Masked Vigilantes, Miraculous Mutants, and a Sun God from Smallville Can Teach Us about Being Human* (New York: Spiegel & Grau, 2011), 337–38.

12. Bloom, *The Western Canon*, 17.

13. Gunther Kress and Theo van Leeuwen, *Multimodal Discourse: The Modes and Media of Contemporary Communication* (London: Oxford University Press, 2001).

14. *Batman* (20th Century Fox Television, 1966–1968). Show originally aired on ABC and is currently unavailable on DVD.

15. Peter Coogan, *Superhero: The Secret Origin of a Genre* (Austin, TX: Monkey Brain, 2006).

16. Robert M. Overstreet et al., *The Overstreet Comic Book Price Guide: 41st Edition* (Timonium, MD: Gemstone Publishing, 2011).

17. Keith Giffen and J. M. DeMatteis, "Born Again," *Justice League International* vol. 1, no. 1 (May 1987).

18. "Marvel: The Heroic Age," *Marvel Comics*, http://marvel.com/news/story/10914/marvel_the_heroic_age .

19. J. K. Rowling, *Harry Potter and the Deathly Hallows* (New York: Scholastic), 723.

Appendix

The Canon of Superhero Literature

THE GOLDEN AGE CANON: 1938–1956

The canon of superhero literature in the Golden Age represents a place of origin highlighted by the first appearance of many major characters in superhero literature. Most of the comic books in this section are also highly sought in the collectors' markets with many of these comic books fetching hundreds of thousands, if not millions, of dollars. Because of this, most people will only ever be able to read and/or analyze these stories in reprinted volumes, which have become abundantly available in recent years. For the purposes of this canon, the original issue number and the collected volume in which it can be found will be presented. In addition to single-issue numbers, collected volumes will also be in the canon.

Comic Books/Graphic Novels

Action Comics #1 **(First appearance of Superman and Lois Lane)**
    Siegel, Jerry, & Shuster, Joe. (2006). *The Superman Chronicles: Volume 1*. New York: DC Comics.
Action Comics #23 **(First appearance of Lex Luthor)**
    Siegel, Jerry, & Shuster, Joe. (2007). *The Superman Chronicles: Volume 3*. New York: DC Comics.
All-American Comics #16 **(First appearance of Green Lantern, Alan Scott)**
    Finger, Bill, & Nodell, Martin. (1999). *Golden Age Green Lantern: Volume 1*. (DC Archive Edition). New York: DC Comics.
All-American Comics #19 **(First appearance of The Atom, Albert Pratt)**
    Finger, Bill, & Nodell, Martin. (1999). *Golden Age Green Lantern: Volume 1*. (DC Archive Edition). New York: DC Comics.

All Star Comics #3 (**First appearance of the Justice Society of America**)

DC Comics. (1997). *All Star Comics Archives: Volume 1* (DC Archive Edition). New York: DC Comics.

All Star Comics #8 and *Sensation Comics #1* (**First appearance of Wonder Woman**)

Marston, William Moulton, & Peter, Harry G. (2010). *The Wonder Woman Chronicles: Volume 1*. New York: DC Comics.

Batman #1 (**First appearance of the Joker and Catwoman**)

Kane, Bob, & Finger, Bill. (2005). *The Batman Chronicles: Volume 1*. New York: DC Comics.

Batman #47 (**First detailed origin of Batman**)

Finger, B., & Kane, B. (1948). The origin of the Batman! *Batman*, June 1948. No reprint exists.

Captain America #1 (**First appearance of Captain America, the Red Skull, and Bucky Barnes**)

Simon, Joe, & Kirby, Jack. (2005). *Golden Age Captain America Comics: Volume 1* (Marvel Masterworks). New York: Marvel Comics.

Detective Comics #27 (**First appearance of Batman and Commissioner Gordon**)

Kane, Bob, & Finger, Bill. (2005). *The Batman Chronicles: Volume 1*. New York: DC Comics.

Detective Comics #31–33 (**Classic Batman story and first origin**)

Kane, Bob, & Finger, Bill. (2005). *The Batman Chronicles: Volume 1*. New York: DC Comics.

Detective Comics #38 (**First appearance of Robin, Dick Grayson**)

Kane, Bob, & Finger, Bill. (2005). *The Batman Chronicles: Volume 1*. New York: DC Comics.

Flash Comics #1 (**First appearance of the Flash, Jay Garrick, and Hawkman**)

Fox, Gardner. (1999). *Golden Age Flash: Volume 1*. (DC Archive Edition). New York: DC Comics.

Marvel Comics #1 (**Origin of the Submariner**)

Marvel Comics. (2012). *Golden Age Marvel Comics: Volume 1* (Marvel Masterworks). New York: Marvel Comics.

Marvel Mystery Comics #8 (**Fight between the Human Torch and the Submariner**)

Marvel Comics. (2000). *The Golden Age of Marvel Comics: Volume 1*. New York: Marvel Comics.

More Fun Comics #52 (**First appearance of the Spectre**)

Siegel, Jerry. (2003). *The Golden Age Spectre: Volume 1* (DC Archive Edition). New York: DC Comics.

More Fun Comics #55 (**First appearance of Dr. Fate**)

Siegel, Jerry. (2003). *The Golden Age Spectre: Volume 1* (DC Archive Edition). New York: DC Comics.
More Fun Comics #73 (First appearance of Aquaman and Green Arrow)
Miller, J., Fradon, R., & Cardy, Nick. (2003). *The Aquaman Archives: Volume 1* (DC Archive Edition). New York: DC Comics.
New York World's Fair Comic (1940) (First Batman, Superman team-up)
Siegel, J., Shuster, J., Kane, B., & Finger, B. (2004). *Superman: World's Finest Comics Archives: Volume 1* (DC Archive Edition). New York: DC Comics.
Police Comics #1 (First appearance of Plastic Man)
Cole, Jack. (1999). *The Plastic Man Archives: Volume 1* (DC Archive Edition). New York: DC Comics.
Superman #1
Siegel, Jerry, & Shuster, Joe. (2006). *The Superman Chronicles: Volume 1.* New York: DC Comics.
Superman #61 (First story with kryptonite)
Not in any current collected volume.
Superman #76
Various creators. (1999). *World's Finest Comics: Volume 1* (DC Archive Edition). New York: DC Comics.
Whiz Comics #2 (First appearance of Captain Marvel)
Beck, C. C. (1999). *The Shazam! Archives: Volume 1* (DC Archive Edition). New York: DC Comics.

Cartoons/Television Shows

Adventures of Superman: The Complete First Season. (2005). Warner Home Video. DVD.
Max Fleischer's Superman: 1941–1942. 17 Animated, Theatrical Shorts by Fleischer Studios. Warner Home Video. DVD.

Films

Batman: The Complete 1943 Movie Serial Collection. (2005). Sony Pictures Home Entertainment. DVD.
Superman: The 1948 & 1950 Theatrical Serials Collection. (2006). Warner Home Video. DVD.

THE SILVER AGE CANON: 1956–1971

This is an age highlighted by the reaction to the Comics Code Authority and the evolution of the superhero. Marvel started in this age, and though the Golden Age is where the concept of the superhero was born, the Silver Age is where it came into its own. The Silver Age canon of superhero literature is, again, full of first appearances, but it is also a maturation of comic style narratives for superheroes. Unlike the Golden Age, continuity begins to take effect, and characters begin to truly evolve through stories that test the mettle of superheroes and reflect changing social and cultural landscapes.

Julius Schwartz's reimagining of Golden Age superheroes for DC springboarded this age while Stan Lee and Jack Kirby developed a new formula for the superhero that showcased more humanistic characteristics for people with amazing powers.

Comic Books/Graphic Novels

Action Comics #242 **(First appearance of Supergirl)**
   Various. (2001). *The Supergirl Archives: Volume 1.* (DC Archive Edition). New York: DC Comics.
Action Comics #252 **(First appearance of Brainiac and the Bottled City of Kandor)**
   Siegel, J. (2005). *Superman: The Man of Tomorrow Archive: Volume 1:* New York: DC Comics.
Adventure Comics #247 **(First appearance of the Legion of Superheroes)**
   Various. (1997). *Legion of Super-Heroes Archive: Volume 1.* (DC Archive Edition). New York: DC Comics.
Amazing Fantasy #15 **(First appearance of Spider-Man)**
   Lee, S., & Ditko, S. (2009). *Amazing Spider-Man: Volume 1.* (Marvel Masterworks). New York: Marvel Comics.
Amazing Spider-Man #1–10 **(Classic first stories of Spider-Man)**
   Lee, S., & Ditko, S. (2009). *Amazing Spider-Man: Volume 1.* (Marvel Masterworks). New York: Marvel Comics.
Avengers #1
   Lee, S., & Kirby, J. (2009). *The Avengers: Volume 1.* (Marvel Masterworks). New York: Marvel Comics.
Avengers #4 **(First Captain America, Steve Rogers, in the Silver Age)**
   Lee, S., & Kirby, J. (2009). *The Avengers: Volume 1.* (Marvel Masterworks). New York: Marvel Comics.
Brave and the Bold #28 **(First appearance of the Justice League of America)**
   Fox, G., & Sekowsky, M. (1997). *Justice League of America Archives: Volume 1.* (DC Archive Edition). New York: DC Comics.
Captain America #117 **(First appearance of the Falcon)**
   Lee, S., Colan, G., Romita Sr., J., & Buscema, J. (2008). *Captain America: Vol. 4.* (Marvel Masterworks). New York: Marvel Comics.
Daredevil #1 **(First appearance of Daredevil, Matt Murdock)**

Lee, S., & Everett, B. (2010). *Daredevil: Volume 1*. (Marvel Masterworks). New York: Marvel Comics.

Detective Comics #359 (First Batgirl, Barbara Gordon)
Various. (2010). *Batgirl: The Greatest Stories Ever Told*. New York: DC Comics.

Fantastic Four #1-12 (First appearance of Fantastic Four and stories establishing Marvel crossovers and continuity)
Lee, S., & Kirby, J. (2009). *Fantastic Four: Volumes 1 & 2*. (Marvel Masterworks). New York: Marvel Comics.

Fantastic Four #48–53 (Silver Surfer, Galactus, "This Man, This Monster" story, and the Black Panther introduced)
Lee, S., & Kirby, J. (2011). *Fantastic Four: Volumes 5 & 6*. (Marvel Masterworks). New York: Marvel Comics.

Flash #123 (First mention of multiverse in DC Comics)
Broome, J., Fox, G., & Infantino, C. (2002). *The Flash Archives: Volume 3*. (DC Archive Edition). New York: DC Comics.

Incredible Hulk #1 (First appearance of the Hulk, Bruce Banner)
Lee, S., Kirby, J., & Ditko, S. (2009). *The Incredible Hulk: Volume 1*. (Marvel Masterworks). New York: Marvel Comics.

Journey into Mystery #83 (First appearance of Thor)
Lee, S., Lieber, L., Bernstein, R., Kirby, J., & Hartley, A. (2010). *The Mighty Thor: Volume 1*. (Marvel Masterworks). New York: Marvel Comics.

Justice League of America #21–22 (Reintroduction of Justice Society into Silver Age stories subsequently reinforcing the multiverse concept)
Fox, G., & Sekowsky, M. (1998). *Justice League of America Archives: Volume 3*. (DC Archive Edition). New York: DC Comics.

Nick Fury: Agent of S.H.I.E.L.D. #4 (Origin of Nick Fury and his place in S.H.I.E.L.D.)
Steranko, J. (2011). *Nick Fury, Agent of S.H.I.E.L.D.: Volume 3*. (Marvel Masterworks). New York: Marvel Comics.

Showcase Comics #4 (First appearance of the Flash, Barry Allen)
Kanigher, R., Broome, J., & Infantino, C. (1998). *The Flash Archives: Volume 1*. (DC Archive Edition). New York: DC Comics.

Showcase Comics #22 (First appearance of Green Lantern, Hal Jordan)
Broome, J., Kane, G., & Giella, J. (1998). *The Green Lantern Archives: Volume 1*. (DC Archive Edition). New York: DC Comics.

Tales of Suspense #39 (First appearance of Iron Man)
Lee, S., Heck, D., Kirby, J., & Ditko, S. (2010). *The Invincible Iron Man: Volume 1*. (Marvel Masterworks). New York: Marvel Comics.

Tales of Suspense #51–65 (Stories of Iron Man and Captain America, first appearances of Hawkeye and Black Widow, Captain America's first Silver Age solo stories begin)

Lee, S., Rico, D., & Heck, D. (2012). *The Invincible Iron Man: Vol. 2.* (Marvel Masterworks). New York: Marvel Comics.
Wonder Woman #179 (Wonder Woman has no powers and not dressed in traditional suit. Failed attempt to modernize character. Concept went until issue #203)
O'Neil, D., Sekowsky, M., & Novick, I. (2008). *Diana Prince: Wonder Woman: Volume 1.* New York: DC Comics.
X-Men #1–10 (First appearances of the X-Men, Magneto, and various other characters.)
Lee, S., & Kirby, J. (2009). *The X-Men: Volume 1.* (Marvel Masterworks). New York: Marvel Comics.

Cartoons/Television Shows

Batman (1960s television show). Title has never been released on DVD due to legal technicalities. Available only as bootleg or in syndication.

Spider-Man (1960s Cartoon). Title is currently out of print on DVD. As of 5/30/12, available on NetFlix. *Spider-Man: The '67 Collection.* (2004). Walt Disney Video (DVD).

THE BRONZE AGE CANON: 1971–1980

Here is where superhero literature begins to expand its scope both narratively and culturally. This is the age of the X-Men expanding, heroes being challenged by society, and creators aiming for audiences outside of the traditional child and/or adolescent demographics.

The team of Denny O'Neil and Neal Adams bring Batman back to dark roots and make Green Lantern and Green Arrow conscious of society's injustices. John Byrne and Chris Claremont bring the X-Men back from the brink of cancellation. And two young men, Frank Miller and Alan Moore, challenge all previous notions of superheroes and superhero literature. Finally, DC appoints a woman as its publisher expanding the possibilities of the medium like never before.

Comic Books/Graphic Novels

Amazing Spider-Man #121–122 (The death of Gwen Stacy)
Lee, S., Conway, G., Romita, J., & Kane, G. (2007). *Spider-Man: Death of the Stacys.* (Marvel Premiere Classic). New York: Marvel Comics.
Amazing Spider-Man #129 (First appearance of the Punisher)
Various. (2011). *The Amazing Spider-Man: Volume 6.* (Marvel Essentials). New York: Marvel Comics.
The Avengers: The Korvac Saga

Various. (2012). *Avengers: The Korvac Saga*. New York: Marvel Comics.

Batman: Illustrated by Neal Adams: Volume 3 (Denny O'Neil and Neal Adams Stories, and first appearance of Ra's al Guhl)

O'Neil, D., Wein, L., & Adams, N. (2006). *Batman Illustrated by Neal Adams: Volume 3*. New York: DC Comics.

Captain America #176–183 (Fictitious Watergate scandal and Captain America's renouncement of America, becomes NOMAD)

Englehart, S., Warner, J., Buscema, S., Robbins, F., & Trimpe, H. (2007). *Captain America by Steve Englehart, Volume 2: Nomad*. New York: Marvel Comics.

Daredevil #158 (First time Frank Miller on Daredevil title)

Miller F. (2002). *Daredevil Visionairies-Frank Miller: Volume 1*. New York: Marvel Comics.

Green Lantern/Green Arrow Collection: Volumes 1 & 2 (Denny O'Neil and Neal Adams Stories, first John Stewart)

O'Neil, D., & Adams, N. (2004). *Green Lantern/Green Arrow Collection: Volumes 1 & 2*. New York: DC Comics.

Incredible Hulk #181 (First appearance of Wolverine)

Various. (2008). *Essential Incredible Hulk: Volume 5*. (Marvel Essentials). New York: Marvel Comics.

Iron Man: Demon in a Bottle (Collects Invincible Iron Man #120–128)

Michelinie, D., Layton, B., Romita Jr., J., & Infantino, C. (2006). *Iron Man: Demon in a Bottle*. New York: Marvel Comics.

Luke Cage: Hero for Hire #1 (First appearance of Luke Cage)

Various. (2005). *Essential Luke Cage/Power Man: Volume 1*. (Marvel Essentials). New York: Marvel Comics.

Power Man and Iron Fist #50–52 (Beginning of Power Man and Iron Fist Team)

Various. (2008). *Essential Power Man and Iron First: Volume 1*. (Marvel Essentials). New York: Marvel Comics.

Shazam! #1 (First appearance of Captain Marvel since Golden Age, now owned by DC instead of Fawcett Comics. DC can't use name "Captain Marvel" in titles.)

Parker, B., & Beck, C. C. (2008). *Shazam!: The Greatest Stories Ever Told*. New York: DC Comics.

Superman vs. The Amazing Spider-Man (First Marvel/DC crossover, currently out of print. Available on the secondary market.)

Conway, G., & Andru, R. (1976). *Superman vs. The Amazing Spider-Man*. New York: Marvel Comics and DC Comics.

Superman vs. Muhammad Ali: DC Collector's Edition (Superman boxes Muhammad Ali)

O'Neil, D., & Adams, N. (2010). *Superman vs. Muhammad Ali Deluxe*. New York: DC Comics.

Tomb of Dracula #10, 12–13, 17–19 (Blade origin and appearances)

Wolfman, M., McKenzie, R., Colan, G., & Robbins, F. (2004). *Essential Tomb of Dracula: Volume 1*. (Marvel Essentials). New York: Marvel Comics.

Uncanny X-Men: Volumes 1 & 2, Marvel Masterworks (Collects Giant Size X-Men #1, X-Men #94–110, Claremont begins stories, introduction of Jean Grey as the Phoenix)

Claremont, C., Cockrum, D., & Byrne, J. (2009). *The Uncanny X-Men: Volumes 1 & 2*. (Marvel Masterworks). New York: Marvel Comics.

Werewolf by Night #32 (First appearance of Moon Knight)

Various. (2006). *Essential Moon Knight: Volume 1*. (Marvel Essentials). New York: Marvel Comics.

Cartoons/Television Shows

The Incredible Hulk (1970s television show with Bill Bixby and Lou Ferigno). Levi, A. J., & Johnson, K. (2006). *The Incredible Hulk: The Complete First Season*. Universal Studios (DVD).

Super Friends (First animated cartoon depicting the Justice League). *Super Friends! Season 1, Volume 1*. (2010). Warner Home Video (DVD).

Wonder Woman (Lynda Carter television series from the 1970s). Moder, D., & Margolin, S. (2004). *Wonder Woman: The Complete First Season*. Warner Home Video (DVD).

Films

Superman (Richard Donner directed film starring Christopher Reeves and Gene Hackman). Donner, R. (1978). *Superman*. Warner Brothers.

Superman II (Sequel to *Superman*. This film is kept in the Bronze Age despite its release date of 1981 because *Superman* and *Superman II* were filmed simultaneously). Lester, R. (1981). *Superman II*. Warner Brothers.

THE DARK AGE CANON: 1981–1992

The biggest turning point in superhero literature occurs in this decade. Whereas the Silver Age added to the mythology of superheroes with Marvel's complicated stories and interweaving stories, the Iron Age is the deconstruction of the tropes of the superhero. This is the age of Frank Miller, Alan Moore, Kevin Eastman, Peter Laird, John Byrne, and Chris Claremont. This is the age of brutality and graphic novels. This is the age of falls from grace, returns from the depths, reboots, heroes changing attire, and heroes being questioned. This is the Dark Age of superhero literature.

What makes the Dark Age canon unique, though, is the list of cartoons from the era. There were significant cartoons for children in this age that sharply contrast the comic books and graphic novels of the time. The title "The Dark Age" will remain despite this contradiction, given the overwhelming mood of the age, but cartoons such as *Thundercats*, *Transformers*, *Masters of the Universe*, and *G.I. Joe* become significant in the discourse of superhero literature because these were the superheroes for young children at this time. And while they were not DC or Marvel properties, their influence is still significant.

Comic Books/Graphic Novels

Batman: Year One **(Frank Miller's 1986 origin story)**
 Miller, F., & Mazzucchelli, D. (2005). *Batman: Year One*. New York: DC Comics.
Crisis on Infinite Earths **(DC's first "Crisis" and reboot, 1985–1986)**
 Wolfman, M., & Perez, G. (2001). *Crisis on Infinite Earths*. New York: DC Comics.
Daredevil: Born Again
 Miller, F., & Mazzucchelli, D. (2010). *Daredevil: Born Again*. New York: Marvel Comics.
Daredevil: Volumes 1 & 2 **(Frank Miller's run on Daredevil introducing Elektra)**
 Miller, F. (2002). *Daredevil Visionaries—Frank Miller: Volumes 1 & 2*. New York: Marvel Comics.
The Dark Knight Returns **(Frank Miller's seminal work on Batman)**
 Miller, F., & Janson, K. (2002). *Batman: The Dark Knight Returns*. New York: DC Comics.
DC Universe by Alan Moore **(Collects Alan Moore's single issues and short story arcs)**
 Moore, A., & various artists. (2011). *DC Universe by Alan Moore*. New York: DC Comics.
The Death of Captain Marvel **(One of Marvel's earliest graphic novels and an early death in superhero literature)**
 Starlin, J., Englehart, S., Moench, D., & Broderick, P. (2010). *The Death of Captain Marvel*. (Marvel Premiere Classic). New York: Marvel Comics.
The Death of Superman
 Jurgens, D. (1993). *The Death of Superman*. New York: DC Comics.
The Killing Joke **(Alan Moore and Brian Bolland's deconstruction of the Joker, Barbara Gordon is paralyzed)**

Moore, A., & Bolland, B. (1988). *Batman: The Killing Joke*. New York: DC Comics.

Knightfall
Dixon, C., Moench, D. (2012). *Batman: Knightfall: Volume 1*. New York: DC Comics.

The Man of Steel (John Byrne's reboot of Superman)
Byrne, J., & Giordano, D. (1991). *Superman: The Man of Steel*. New York: DC Comics.

Marvel: Contest of Champions (Marvel's first limited series that tied into every title)
Various. (2010). *The Avengers: The Contest*. (Marvel Premiere Classic). New York: Marvel Comics.

Miracleman #1–16 (Alan Moore's take on a classic British superhero)
Currently out of print with past printings being very expensive.

Secret Wars (Spider-Man receives black, symbiotic suit)
Shooter, J., Zeck, M., & Layton, B. (2011). *Secret Wars*. New York: Marvel Comics.

Spawn #1–6 (Image's flagship book, origin of Spawn)
McFarlane, T. (2009). *Spawn Origin: Volume 1*. Berkeley: Image Comics.

Spider-Man Visionaries: Todd McFarlane (Spider-Man wears black costume and the introduction of Venom)
Michelinie, D., & McFarlane, T. (2003). *Spider-Man Visionaries: Todd McFarlane*. Marvel Comics: New York.

Swamp Thing: Saga of the Swamp Thing (Alan Moore's take on the DC horror character)
Moore, A., Totleben, J., & Bissette, S. (1998). *Swamp Thing, Vol. 1: Saga of the Swamp Thing*. New York: DC Comics.

Teenage Mutant Ninja Turtles Ultimate Collection: Volume 1 (Collects the first issues of the series)
Eastman, K., & Laird, P. (2012). *Teenage Mutant Ninja Turtles: The Ultimate Collection* (Volume 1). San Diego: IDW Publishing.

Teen Titans: The Judas Contract
Wolfman, M., & Perez, G. (1991). *The New Teen Titans: The Judas Contract*. New York: DC Comics.

Watchmen
Moore, A., & Gibbons, D. (1986). *Watchmen*. New York: DC Comics.

Wolverine (Claremont and Miller's Wolverine miniseries, Wolverine's first origin)
Claremont, C., & Miller, F. (2009). *Wolverine*. New York: Marvel Comics.

X-Men: The Dark Phoenix Saga

Claremont, C., & Byrne, J. (2012). *The Uncanny X-Men: The Dark Phoenix Saga*. New York: Marvel Comics.

X-Men: Days of Future Past
Claremont, C., & Byrne, J. (2011). *X-Men: Days of Future Past*. New York: Marvel Comics.

X-Men: God Loves, Man Kills
Claremont, C., & Anderson, B. (2011). *X-Men: God Loves, Man Kills*. (Marvel Classic Premiere). New York: Marvel Comics.

Cartoons/Television Shows

Batman: The Animated Series (Bruce Timm and Paul Dini series). Timm, B., Dini, P. (Writers) & B. Timm (Director). (2004). *Batman: The Animated Series, Volume 1*. Warner Home Video (DVD).

The Flash (Live-action television series). *The Flash: Complete Series*. (2006). Warner Home Video (DVD).

G.I. Joe (First episodes). Dixon, B. (Writer). (2005). *G.I. Joe: A Real American Hero*. Shout! Factory (DVD).

He-Man and the Masters of the Universe (First episodes). *He-Man and the Masters of the Universe: Season One, Volume 1*. (2005). BCI/Eclipse (DVD).

Teenage Mutant Ninja Turtles (First 5 episodes of the series, cartoon origin). *Teenage Mutant Ninja Turtles: The Original Series, Volume 1*. (2004). Lions Gate (DVD).

Thundercats (First episodes, origin). *Thundercats: Season 1, Part 1*. (2011). Warner Home Video (DVD).

The Transformers (First episodes, origin). Walker, J. (Writer). (2009). *Transformers: The Complete First Season*. Shout! Factory (DVD).

Films

Batman. Burton, T. (Director). (1989). *Batman*. Warner Bros.

Darkman. Raimi, S. (Director). (1990). *Darkman*. Universal Pictures.

Teenage Mutant Ninja Turtles. Baron, S. (Director). (1991). *Teenage Mutant Ninja Turtles*. AEC One Stop (DVD).

THE HEROIC AGE CANON: 1994–PRESENT

Following the deconstructive period of superhero literature in the 1980s and early 1990s, the Heroic Age is a culmination of the superhero genre as we have experienced it. Not only is this the longest Age in the canon (the Golden Age is eighteen years long as well, but this age is set to continue past 2012), it also has the most texts. This overabundance of texts may come across as catering to the modern age, but there is a genuine quality in the texts listed with some of them harkening back to the Silver Age style, some of them extending the deconstructive style of the Dark Age, and some paving their own path to celebrate the superhero as a cultural and literary achievement.

This is also the age where media outside of sequential art becomes dominant in the superhero's cultural and literary discourse. the flood of superhero films in the last fifteen years has only extended the influence of the superhero beyond its traditional, glossy-papered covers. Much of the Heroic Age Canon is, therefore, rooted in the television shows, cartoons, and films of the time.

Comic Books/Graphic Novels

Action Comics #775
Kelly, J., Mahnke, D., & Bermejo, L. (2001). "What's So Funny about Truth, Justice & The American Way?" *Action Comics, Vol. 1*.

All Star Superman
Morrison, G., & Quitely, F. (2011). *All Star Superman*. New York: DC Comics.

Astro City: Life in the Big City
Busiek, K.., & Anderson, B. (1999). *Astro City Vol. 1: Life in the Big City*. New York: Wildstorm.

The Authority (First Volume)
Ellis, W., & Hitch, B. (2000). *The Authority Volume 1: Relentless*. New York: Wildstorm.

Batman: Hush
Loeb, J., & Lee, J. (2009). *Batman: Hush*. New York: DC Comics.

Batman: The Long Halloween
Loeb, J., & Sale, T. (2011). *Batman: The Long Halloween*. New York: DC Comics.

Batman: Mad Love
Dini, P., & Timm, B. (2011). *Batman: Mad Love and Other Stories*. New York: DC Comics.

Captain America: The Death of Captain America
Brubaker, E., & Epting, S. (2008). *The Death of Captain America, Vol. 1: The Death of the Dream*. New York: Marvel Comics.

Civil War
Millar, M., & McNiven, S. (2008). *Civil War*. New York: Marvel Comics.

Daredevil (Brian Michael Bendis and Alex Maleev run)
Bendis, B. M., Maleev, A., & Mack, D. (2010). *Daredevil Ultimate Collection: Volume 1*. New York: Marvel Comics.

Daredevil: The Man Without Fear

Miller, F., & Romita Jr., J. (2008). *Daredevil: The Man Without Fear*. New York: Marvel Comics.

Daredevil: Yellow
Loeb, J., & Sale, T. (2003). *Daredevil: Yellow*. New York: Marvel.

DC: The New Frontier
Cooke, D. (2004). *DC: The New Frontier, Volumes 1 & 2*. New York: DC Comics.

Emerald Twilight (Currently out of print, issues #48, 49, & 50 of *Green Lantern: Volume 2*)
Marz, R. (1994). *Green Lantern: Emerald Twilight*. New York: DC Comics.

Flashpoint (Last series before DC's New 52, transition to major reboot)
Johns, G., & Kubert, A. (2012). *Flashpoint*. New York: DC Comics.

Hulk: Gray
Loeb, J., & Sale, T. (2004). *Hulk: Gray*. New York: Marvel.

Identity Crisis
Meltzer, B., & Morales, R. (2006). *Identity Crisis*. New York: DC Comics.

Irredeemable: Volume 1
Waid, M., Krause, P., & Cassaday, J. (2009). *Irredeemable: Volume 1*. Los Angeles: Boom! Studios.

Justice League: Tower of Babel
Waid, M. (2001). *JLA: Tower of Babel*. New York: DC Comics.

Kingdom Come
Waid, M., & Ross, A. (1997). *Kingdom Come*. New York: DC Comics.

The League of Extraordinary Gentlemen: Volume 1
Moore, A., & O'Neill, K. (2002). *The League of Extraordinary Gentlemen: Volume 1*. America's Best Comics.

Marvels
Busiek, K., & Ross, A. (2010). *Marvels*. New York: Marvel Comics.

New X-Men: Volumes 1–3
Morrison, G., & Various artists. (2008). *New X-Men: Volumes 1–3*. New York: Marvel Comics.

Spider-Man: Blue
Loeb, J., & Sale, T. (2009). *Spider-Man: Blue*. New York: Marvel Comics.

Spider-Man: One More Day (Spider-Man reboot, erasing of Mary Jane and Peter Parker marriage from continuity, heavily criticized)
Straczynski, J. M., & Quesada, J. (2008). *Spider-Man: One More Day*. New York: Marvel Comics.

Superman for All Seasons
Loeb, J., & Sale, T. (2002). *Superman for All Seasons*. New York: DC Comics.

Superman/Batman: Supergirl
 Loeb, J., & Turner, M. (2005). *Superman/Batman: Supergirl*. New York: DC Comics.
Ultimate Comics Spider-Man: Death of Spider-Man Fallout (Miles Morales becomes Ultimate Spider-Man)
 Bendis, B. M., Hickman, J., Spencer, N., & Bagley, M. (2012). *Ultimate Comics Spider-Man: Death of Spider-Man Fallout*. New York: Marvel Comics.
Ultimates
 Millar, M., Hitch, B. (2010). *The Ultimates: Ultimate Collection*. New York: Marvel Comics.
Ultimate Spider-Man: Volume 1
 Bendis, B. M., & Bagley, M. (2007). *Ultimate Spider-Man: Volume 1*. New York: Marvel Comics.
Wonder Woman: Hiketeia
 Rucka, G., & Jones, J. G. (2003). *Wonder Woman: Hiketeia*. New York: DC Comics.

Cartoons/Television Shows

 Avengers: Earth's Mightiest Heroes. The Avengers: Earth's Mightiest Heroes. Vol. 1–4. (2011). Walt Disney Studios Home Entertainment (DVD).
 Heroes (NBC series). Various. (2010). *Heroes: The Complete Series*. Universal Studios (DVD).
 Justice League Unlimited (Seasons 1 and 2). Timm, B. (Director). (2006). *Justice League Unlimited: Seasons 1 & 2*. Warner Home Video (DVD).
 Mighty Morphin Power Rangers. Winkless, T. H. (Director). (2012). *Mighty Morphin Power Rangers: Season 1, Volume 1*. Shout! Factory (DVD).
 Smallville. (This show ran for ten seasons. While the entire series will be deemed as part of the canon, a complete viewing of the entire series is not necessary.) Various. (2011). *Smallville: The Complete Series*. Warner Home Video (DVD).
 The Super Hero Squad. Gerard, M. (Director). (2010). *The Super Hero Squad: Volume 1*. Shout! Factory (DVD).
 Superman: The Animated Series. Superman: The Complete Animated Series. (2009). Warner Home Video (DVD).
 Teen Titans (Animated series). Various. (2006). *Teen Titans: The Complete First Season*. Warner Home Video (DVD).
 The Tick. Vitello, A. (Director). (2006). *The Tick Season 1*. Buena Vista Home Entertainment (DVD).

Films

The Avengers. Whedon, J. (Director). (2012). *The Avengers*. Walt Disney Studios.

Batman: Mask of the Phantasm (Animated film feature of *Batman: The Animated Series*). Radomski, E. (Director). (1993). *Batman: Mask of the Phantasm*. Warner Brothers.

Batman: Under the Red Hood (Straight to DVD, animated film). Vietti, B. (Director). (2010). *Batman: Under the Red Hood*. Warner Home Video (DVD).

Batman Beyond: Return of the Joker (The Original, Uncut Version). Geda, C. (Director). (2000). *Batman Beyond: Return of the Joker* (original, uncut version). Warner Home Video (DVD).

Blade. Norrington, S. (Director). (1998). *Blade*. New Line Cinema.

The Dark Knight. Nolan, C. (Director). (2008). *The Dark Knight*. Warner Bros.

Iron Man. Favreau, J. (Director). (2008). *Iron Man*. Paramount Pictures.

The Matrix. Wachowski, A., & Wachowski, L. (Directors). (1999). *The Matrix*. Warner Bros.

Spider-Man 2. Raimi, S. (Director). (2004). *Spider-Man 2*. Columbia Pictures.

X-Men. Singer, B. (Director). (2000). *X-Men*. 20th Century Fox.

X-Men 2. Singer, B. (Director). (2003). *X-Men 2*. 20th Century Fox.

Video Games

Batman: Arkham Asylum (Video Game). Dini, P. (Writer). (2009). Batman: Arkham Asylum. Warner Brothers (Video Game).

Batman: Arkham City (Video Game). Dini, P. (Writer). (2011). Batman: Arkham City. Warner Brothers (Video Game).

Bibliography

Abrams, J. J. *Star Trek*. Paramount, 2009.

Agence France-Presse. "'Avengers' third highest grossing film of all time." *Yahoo! News*, http://news.yahoo.com/avengers-third-highest-grossing-film-time-232528940.html

"Alan Moore Profile." *Inside Out East*. BBC, 2008.

All Star Comics Archive. DC Archive ed. Vol. 1. New York: DC Comics, 1997.

Anders, Lou. "A Tale of Two Orphans: The Man of Steel vs. The Caped Crusader." In *The Man from Krypton*, edited by G. Yeffeth, 69–75. Dallas: BenBella Books, Inc., 2005.

Andreeva, Nellie. "Wonder Woman Returning to TV as Series Written and Produced by David E. Kelley." *Deadline*. www.deadline.com/2010/10/wonder-woman-returning-to-tv-as-series-written-and-produced-by-david-e-kelley/.

"As Barry Jenkins, Ohio '69, Says: 'A Person Has to Have Intelligence to Read Them.'" *Esquire*, September 1966, 117.

"The Avengers: Captain America Reborn!" In *The Avengers: Earth's Mightiest Heroes*. Walt Disney Studios Home Entertainment, 2011.

"The Avengers: Heroes Assemble!" In *The Avengers: Earth's Mightiest Heroes*. Walt Disney Studios Home Entertainment, 2011.

"The Avengers: Iron Man Unleashed." In *The Avengers: Earth's Mightiest Heroes*. Walt Disney Studios Home Entertainment, 2011.

"The Avengers: Thor's Last Stand." In *The Avengers: Earth's Mightiest Heroes*. Walt Disney Studios Home Entertainment, 2011.

Baker, Martin. *Comics: Ideology, Power and the Comics*. Manchester, UK: Manchester University Press, 1989.

Barron, Steve. *Teenage Mutant Ninja Turtles*. AEC One Stop, 1991.

Bauer, Karen L., and Ernest Dettore. "Superhero Play: What's a Teacher to Do?" *Early Childhood Education Journal* 25, no. 1 (1997): 17–21.

Beck, C. C. *The Shazam! Archives*. DC Archive ed. Vol. 1. New York: DC Comics, 1999.

Bendis, Brian Michael, and Mark Bagley. "Death of Spider-Man—Part 2." *Ultimate Comics Spider-Man*, June 2011.

———. "Death of Spider-Man—Part 5." *Ultimate Comics Spider-Man*, August 2011.

———. "Powerless." *Ultimate Spider-Man*, November 2000.

———. *Ultimate Spider-Man*. Vol. 1. New York: Marvel, 2003.

Bendis, Brian Michael, and Oliver Coipel. *Avengers vs. X-Men.*

Bendis, Brian Michael, Mike Deodato, Greg Horn, and Chris Bachalo. *Dark Avengers*. New York: Marvel Comics, 2011.

Bendis, Brian Michael, Jonathan Hickman, Nick Spencer, Mark Bagley, and Sara Pichelli. *Ultimate Comics Spider-Man: Death of Spider-Man Fallout*. New York: Marvel Comics, 2012.

Bendis, Brian Michael, Alex Maleev, and David Mack. *Daredevil Ultimate Collection*. Vol. 1. New York: Marvel Comics, 2010.

Berthoff, Ann E., and James Stephens. *Forming, Thinking, Writing*. 2nd ed. Portsmouth, NH: Heinemann, 1988.

"Beyond Batman: Designing the Batsuit." In *Batman*. Warner Home Video, 2009.

Bloom, Harold. *The Western Canon: The Books and School of the Ages*. New York: Riverhead Books, 1994.

Bolt, Robert. *A Man for All Seasons: A Play in Two Acts*. New York: Vintage, 1990.

Branagh, Kenneth. *Thor*. Paramount Pictures, 2011.

Brodsky, Allyn, and Don Heck. "Anything—for the Cause!" *The Invincible Iron Man*, November 1970.

Brooker, Will. *Batman Unmasked: Analyzing a Cultural Icon*. New York: Continuum, 2001.

Broome, John, Gardner Fox, and Carmine Infantino. *The Flash Archives*. DC Archive ed. Vol. 3. New York: DC Comics, 2002.

Broome, John, Gil Kane, and Joe Giella. *The Green Lantern Archives*. DC Archive ed. Vol. 1. New York: DC Comics, 1998.

Brown, Janelle. "Professor Cyborg: Programming Humans" Excerpt. *Endtime News Digest*. www.countdown.org/end/mark_of_the_beast_06.htm.

Brown, Jeffrey A. *Black Superheroes, Milestone Comics, and Their Fans*. Jackson: University Press of Mississippi, 2001.

Brownfield, Troy. "The Reborn Identity: 10 Comics Deaths That Didn't Stick." *Newsarama*. www.newsarama.com/comics/reborn-identity-10-deaths-that-didnt-stick-110711-1.html.

Brubaker, Ed, and Steve Epting. "Civil War: The Death of a Dream, Part One." *Captain America*, April 2007.

———. *The Death of Captain America: The Death of the Dream*. Vol. 1. New York: Marvel Comics, 2008.

———. "The Initiative: The Death of the Dream, Part Two." *Captain America*, July 2007.

Boyle, Rebecca. "Tiny Fractal-Shaped Eye Implants Could Mimic Neurons, Allowing Blind Patients to See." *Popsci*. www.popsci.com/technology/article/2011-05/tiny-fractal-shaped-eye-implants-could-mimic-neurons-allowing-blind-patients-see.

Burgos, Carl, Bill Everett, Paul Gustavson, and Ben Thompson. *Golden Age Marvel Comics*. Marvel Masterworks ed. Vol. 1. New York: Marvel Comics, 2012.

Burroughs, Edgar Rice. *A Princess of Mars*. Chicago: A. C. McClurg, 1917.

Burton, Tim. *Batman*. Warner Brothers, 1989.

———. *Batman Returns*. Warner Brothers, 1992.

———. *Beetlejuice*. Warner Brothers, 1988.

———. *Edward Scissorhands*. 20th Century Fox, 1990.

———. "Shadows of the Bat: The Cinematic Saga of the Dark Knight, Part 1: The Road to Gotham City." In *Batman: Two-Disc Special Edition*. Warner Home Video, 2009.

———. *Sleepy Hollow*. Paramount Pictures, 1999.

Busiek, Kurt, and Brent E. Anderson. *Astro City: Life in the Big City*. Vol. 1. New York: Wildstorm, 1999.

Busiek, Kurt, and Alex Ross. *Marvels*. New York: Marvel Comics, 2010.

Byrne, John, and Dick Giordano. *Superman: The Man of Steel*. New York: DC Comics, 1991.

Campbell, Martin. *Casino Royale*. Sony Pictures Home Entertainment, 2006.

———. *Green Lantern*. Warner Brothers, 2011.

Capra, Frank. *It's a Wonderful Life*. RKO Radio Pictures, 1946.

Cavna, Michael. "The New 52: DC's Dan Didio Shares His Take on Wednesday's Hotly Anticipated Relaunch." *Washington Post*. www.washingtonpost.com/blogs/comic-riffs/post/the-new-52-dcs-dan-didio-shares-his-take-on-wednesdays-hotly-anticipated-relaunch/2011/08/30/gIQAoSKwqJ_blog.html.

Cazden, Courtney, Bill Cope, Norman Fairclough, and Jim Gee. "A Pedagogy of Multiliteracies: Designing Social Futures." *Harvard Educational Review* 66, no. 1 (1996): 60–92.

Chun, Christian W. "Critical Literacies and Graphic Novels for English-Language Learners: Teaching Maus." *Journal of Adolescent & Adult Literacy* 53, no. 2 (2009): 144–53.

Claremont, Chris, and Brent Anderson. *X-Men: God Loves, Man Kills*. Marvel Premiere Classic ed. New York: Marvel Comics, 2011.

Claremont, Chris, and John Byrne. "The Fate of the Phoenix!" *The Uncanny X-Men*, September 1980.

———. *The Uncanny X-Men: The Dark Phoenix Saga*. New York: Marvel Comics, 2012.

———. *X-Men: Days of Future Past*. New York: Marvel Comics, 2011.

Claremont, Chris, Dave Cockrum, and John Byrne. *The Uncanny X-Men*. Marvel Masterworks ed. Vol. 1. New York: Marvel Comics, 2009.

Claremont, Chris, Dave Cockrum, and John Byrne. *The Uncanny X-Men*. Marvel Masterworks ed. Vol. 2. New York: Marvel, 2010.

Claremont, Chris, and Jim Lee. "Rubicon." *X-Men*, October 1991.

Claremont, Chris, and Frank Miller. *Wolverine*. Marvel Premiere Classic ed. New York: Marvel Comics, 2009.

Cole, Jack. *The Plastic Man Archives*. DC Archive ed. Vol. 1. New York: DC Comics, 1999.

Coleridge, Samuel Taylor. *Biographia Literaria*. New York: The Macmillian Company, 1926.

Collins, Max Allan, and Chris Warner. "Did Robin Die Tonight?" *Batman*, June 1987.

Conway, Gerry, and Ross Andru. *Superman vs. The Amazing Spider-Man*. New York: Marvel Comics and DC Comics, 1976.

Conway, Gerry, and Gil Kane. "The Night Gwen Stacy Died." *Amazing Spider-Man*. Vol. 1, no. 121 (June 1973).

———. "The Goblin's Last Stand!" *Amazing Spider-Man*. Vol. 1, no. 122 (July 1973).

Conway, Gerry, Bill Mantlo, and George Tuska. "Showdown with the Guardsman!" *The Invincible Iron Man*, April 1977.

Conway, Gerry, and Don Newton. "Squid." *Batman*, March 1983.

Coogan, Peter. *Superhero: The Secret Origin of a Genre*. Austin, TX: Monkeybrain, 2006.

Cooke, Darwyn. *DC: The New Frontier*. Vol. 1. New York: DC Comics, 2004.

———. *DC: The New Frontier*. Vol. 2. New York: DC Comics, 2004.

Cronin, Brian. *Was Superman a Spy? And Other Comic Book Legends . . . Revealed!* New York: Plume Books, 2009.

Daniel, Tony, and Fabian Nicieza. *Batman: Battle for the Cowl*. New York: DC Comics, 2009.

Daniels, Les. *Batman: The Complete History*. San Francisco: Chronicle Books, 2004.

Dardess, George. "Bringing Comic Books to Class." *College English* 57, no. 2 (1995): 213–22.

"The Dark Knight Box Office Statistics." Box Office Mojo. http://boxofficemojo.com/movies/?id=darkknight.htm.

Dini, Paul. (Writer). *Batman: Arkham Asylum*. Warner Brothers, 2009.

Dini, Paul. (Writer). *Batman: Arkham City*. Warner Brothers, 2011.

Dini, Paul, and Bruce Timm. *Batman: Mad Love and Other Stories*. New York: DC Comics, 2011.

Dixon, Buzz. "G.I. Joe: A Real American Hero: Season 1.1." In *G.I. Joe: A Real American Hero*. Shout! Factory, 2005.

Dixon, Chuck, et al. *Batman: Prodigal*. New York: DC Comics, 1998.

Dixon, Chuck, and Doug Moench. *Batman: Knightfall*. Vol. 1. New York: DC Comics, 2012.

Donner, Richard. *Superman*. Warner Brothers, 1978.

Dyson, Anne Haas. *Writing Superheroes: Contemporary Childhood, Popular Culture, and Classroom Literacy*. New York: Teachers College Press, 1997.

Eastman, Kevin, and Peter Laird. "Teenage Mutant Ninja Turtles." *Teenage Mutant Ninja Turtles*, February 1985.

———. *Teenage Mutant Ninja Turtles: The Ultimate Collection*. Vol. 1. San Diego: IDW Publishing, 2012.

Eco, Umberto, and Natalie Chilton. "The Myth of Superman." *Diacritics* 2, no. 1 (1972): 14–22.

Ede, Lisa, and Andrea A. Lunsford. "Collaboration and Concepts of Authorship." *PMLA* 116, no. 2 (2001): 354–69.

"The 80th Academy Awards (2008) Nominees and Winners." Academy of Motion Picture Arts and Sciences. www.oscars.org/awards/academyawards/legacy/ceremony/80th-winners. html.

Eisner, Will. *A Contract with God*. New York: Baronet Books, 1978.

Elbow, Peter. "Closing My Eyes as I Speak: An Argument for Ignoring Audience." *College English* 49, no. 1 (1987): 50–69.

Elena. "Siri Answers 20 Hilarious Questions." In *freemake.com*.

Ellis, Warren, and Bryan Hitch. *The Authority: Relentless*. Vol. 1. New York: Wildstorm, 2000.

Englehart, Steve, John Warner, Sal Buscema, Frank Robbins, and Herb Trimpe. *Captain America by Steve Englehart: Nomad*. Vol. 2. New York: Marvel Comics, 2007.

Esposito, Joey. "Marvel Wins in Jack Kirby Lawsuit: Marvel Retains Rights to Kirby Icons." *IGN*. http://comics.ign.com/articles/118/1184787p1.html.

Evanier, Mark. *Kirby: King of Comics*. New York: Abrams, 2008.

Favreau, Jon. *Iron Man*. Paramount Pictures, 2008.

Finger, Bill, and Martin Nodell. *Golden Age Green Lantern*. DC Archives ed. Vol. 1. New York: DC Comics, 1999.

"First Look at Adrianne Palicki as Wonder Woman!" *SuperHeroHype*. www.superherohype. com/news/articles/129048-first-look-at-adrianne-palicki-as-wonder-woman.

The Flash: The Complete First Season. Warner Home Video, 1990.

The Flash: Complete Series. Warner Home Video, 2006.

Fleischer, Max. *Max Fleischer's Superman: 1941–1942*, edited by Max Fleischer. Warner Home Video, 2009.

Fox, Gardner. *All Star Comics*, December 1941.

———. *Golden Age Flash*. DC Archives ed. Vol. 1. New York: DC Comics, 1999.

Fox, Gardner, and Carmine Infantino. "Flash of Two Worlds!" *The Flash*, September 1961.

Fox, Gardner, and Mike Sekowsky. *The Brave and the Bold*, February 1960.

———. *Justice League of America Archives*. DC Archives ed. Vol. 1. New York: DC Comics, 1997.

———. *Justice League of America Archives*. DC Archives ed. Vol. 3. New York: DC Comics, 1998.

Fraction, Matt, and Stuart Immonen. "Thor's Day." *Fear Itself*, December 2011.

Gabilliet, Jean-Paul. *Of Comics and Men: A Cultural History of American Comic Books*. Jackson: University Press of Mississippi, 2010.

Gardner, Howard. *Frames of Mind: The Theory of Multiple Intelligences*. New York: Basic Books, 1983.

Geda, Curt. "Batman Beyond: Return of the Joker." Warner Home Video, 2000.

Gerard, Michael. *The Super Hero Squad*. Vol. 1. Shout! Factory, 2010.

Gibson, William. *Neuromancer*. New York: Ace Books, 1984.

Giffen, Keith, and J. M. DeMatteis. "Born Again." *Justice League International*, May 1987.

Goldstein, Claudia. "Comics and the Canon: Graphic Novels, Visual Narrative, and Art History." In *Teaching the Graphic Novel*, edited by S. E. Tabachnik, 254–61. New York: Modern Language Association, 2009.

Goyer, David S., and Miguel Sepulveda. "The Incident." *Action Comics*, May 2011, 70–78.

Gresh, Louis, and Robert Weinberg. *The Science of Superheroes*. Hoboken, NJ: Wiley, 2002.

Gustines, George G., and Adam W. Kepler. "Not All Superheroes Are Equal (at Least the Second Time around)." *New York Times*. www.nytimes.com/2011/10/01/books/for-new-dc-comics-whats-working-and-whats-not.html.

Hajdu, David. *The Ten-Cent Plague: The Great Comic-Book Scare and How It Changed America*. New York: Farrar, Straus and Giroux, 2008.

Hanks, Henry. "The Secret to 'X-Men's' Success." CNN. http://articles.cnn.com/2011-06-03/ entertainment/xmen.legacy.go_1_chris-claremont-dave-cockrum-x-men-franchise?_s= PM:SHOWBIZ.

Harper, Steven. "Supermyth!" In *The Man from Krypton*, edited by G. Yeffeth, 93–99. Dallas, TX: BenBella Books, Inc., 2005.

Harris, Marla. "Showing and Telling History through Family Stories in *Persepolis* and Young Adult Novels." In *Building Literacy Connections with Graphic Novels: Page by Page*,

Panel by Panel, edited by James Bucky Carter, 38–53. Urbana, IL: National Council of Teachers of English, 2007.

Harris-Fain, Darren. "Revisionist Superhero Graphic Novels: Teaching Alan Moore's *Watchmen* and Frank Miller's *Dark Knight* Books." In *Teaching the Graphic Novel*, edited by Stephen E. Tabachnick, 147–54. New York: The Modern Language Association of America, 2009.

Hatfield, Charles. "Defining Comics in the Classroom; or, the Pros and Cons of Unfixability." In *Teaching the Graphic Novel*, edited by Stephen E. Tabachnick, 19–27. New York: The Modern Language Association of America, 2009.

Heer, Jeet, and Kent Worcester, eds. *A Comics Studies Reader*. Jackson: University Press of Mississippi, 2009.

He-Man and the Masters of the Universe: Season One, Volume 1. BCI/Eclipse, 2005.

Hickman, Jonathan, et al. "Ultimate Fallout, Chapter Four." *Ultimate Fallout*, October 2011.

Hickman, Jonathan, and Steve Epting. "Three, Part Five: The Last Stand!" *Fantastic Four*.

Himmelfarb, Gertrude. *The Idea of Poverty: England in the Early Industrial Age*. New York: Vintage, 1985.

Hoffman, Eric. *Magic Capes, Amazing Powers: Transforming Superhero Play in the Classroom*. St. Paul, MN: Redleaf Press, 2004.

Holland, Penny. *We Don't Play with Guns Here: War, Weapon and Superhero Play in the Early Years*. Maiden Head, UK: Open University Press, 2003.

Hood, Gavin. *X-Men Origins: Wolverine*. 20th Century Fox, 2009.

Hudson, Laura. "Answering Dan Didio: The Problem with Having Only 1% Female Creators at DC Comics." *Comics Alliance*. www.comicsalliance.com/2011/07/28/dc-dan-didio-female-creators/.

———. "The Big Sexy Problem with Superheroines and Their 'Liberated Sexuality.'" *Comics Alliance*.www.comicsalliance.com/2011/09/22/starfire-catwoman-sex-superheroine.

Hughes, Jamie A. "'Who Watches the Watchmen?': Ideology and 'Real World' Superheroes." *Journal of Popular Culture* 39, no. 4 (2006): 546–57.

"In-Comic Events: Point One." Marvel Comics. http://marvel.com/comic_books/events/304/point_one.

"Industry Statistics." Diamond Comics. www.diamondcomics.com/Home/1/1/3/237?articleID=100122.

Jacobs, Dale. "Marveling at the Man Called Nova: Comics as Sponsors of Multimodal Literacy." *College Composition and Communication* 59, no. 2 (2007): 180.

Jenkins, Eric. "My iPod, My Icon: How and Why Do Images Become Icons?" *Critical Studies in Media Communication* 25, no. 5 (2008): 466–89.

Joffé, Roland. *Fat Man and Little Boy*. Paramount Pictures, 1989.

Johns, Geoff, Phil Jimenez, and George Pérez. *Infinite Crisis*. New York: DC Comics, 2008.

Johns, Geoff, and Andy Kubert. *Flashpoint*. New York: DC Comics, 2012.

Johns, Geoff, and Reis, Ivan. "Blackest Night, Part 1." *Blackest Night*. Vol. 1, no. 1 (September 2009).

Johnson, Mark Steven. *Daredevil*. 20th Century Fox, 2003.

Johnson, Scott. "Five Things We Love about DC Comics Relaunch." *Comicbook.com*. http://comicbook.com/blog/2011/08/30/five-things-we-love-about-dc-comics-relaunch/.

Johnston, Joe. *Captain America: The First Avengers*. Paramount Pictures, 2011.

Jones, Gerard. *Killing Monsters: Why Children Need Fantasy, Super Heroes, and Make-Believe Violence*. New York: Basic Books, 2002.

———. *Men of Tomorrow: Geeks, Gangsters and the Birth of the Comic Book*. New York: Basic Books, 2004.

Jurgens, Dan. *The Death of Superman*. New York: DC Comics, 1993.

Jurgens, Dan, and Brett Breeding. "Doomsday!" *Superman*, January 1993.

Jurgens, Dan, and Ron Frenz. "Superman . . . Reborn." *Superman*, May 1997.

Jurgens, Dan, Roger Stern, Louise Simonson, Karl Kesel, and David Micheline. "The Wedding Album." *Superman: The Wedding Album*, December 1996.

Kai, O.K. "A Dark Night for Black Superheroes." *40 Acres and a Cubicle*. http://40acresandacubicle.com/2012/07/25/a-dark-night-for-black-superheroes.

Kane, Bob, and Bill Finger. *The Batman Chronicles*. Vol. 1. New York: DC Comics, 2005.
———. "The Batman Wars against the Dirigible of Doom." *Detective Comics*, November 1939.
Kanigher, Robert, John Broome, and Carmine Infantino. *The Flash Archives*. DC Archive ed. Vol. 1. New York: DC Comics, 1998.
Kelly, Joe, Doug Mahnke, and Lee Bermejo. "What's So Funny about Truth, Justice and the American Way?" *Action Comics*, 2001.
Khouri, Andy. "Wonder Woman Costumer from Show You Never Saw Appears on Show You Never Watch, Worn by Actress from Show You Hated." *Comics Alliance*.
Kirby, Jack. "The Capture of X-51!" *2001: A Space Odyssey*, July 1977.
Kirby, Jack, et al. *The Golden Age of Marvel Comics*. Vol. 1. New York: Marvel Comics, 2000.
Kress, Gunther. *Literacy in the New Media Age*. London: Routledge, 2003.
Kress, Gunther, and Theo van Leeuwen. *Multimodal Discourse: The Modes and Media of Contemporary Communication*. London: Oxford University Press, 2001.
Lee, Harper. *To Kill a Mockingbird*. Philadelphia: J. B. Lippincott & Co., 1960.
Lee, Stan, Gene Colan, John Romita Sr., and John Buscema. *Captain America*. Marvel Masterworks ed. Vol. 4. New York: Marvel Comics, 2008.
Lee, Stan, Gerry Conway, John Romita, and Gil Kane. *Spider-Man: Death of the Stacys*. Marvel Premiere Classic ed. New York: Marvel Comics, 2007.
Lee, Stan, and Steve Ditko. *Amazing Spider-Man*. Marvel Masterworks ed. Vol. 1. New York: Marvel Comics, 2009.
———. "The Chameleon!" *The Amazing Spider-Man*, March 1963, 1–10.
———. "Duel with Daredevil." *The Amazing Spider-Man*, September 1964.
———. "The Spider's Web." *The Amazing Spider-Man*, June 1965.
Lee, Stan, Don Heck, Jack Kirby, and Steve Ditko. *The Invincible Iron Man*. Marvel Masterworks ed. Vol. 1. New York: Marvel Comics, 2010.
Lee, Stan, and Jack Kirby. *The Fantastic Four*, March 1963.
———. *Fantastic Four*, November 1962.
———. *The Avengers*. Marvel Masterworks ed. Vol. 1. New York: Marvel Comics, 2009.
———. "Captain America Joins . . . The Avengers!" *The Avengers*.
———. "The Coming of the Sub-Mariner!" *The Fantastic Four*, May 1962.
———. *Fantastic Four*. Marvel Masterworks ed. Vol. 1. New York: Marvel Comics, 2009.
———. *Fantastic Four*. Marvel Masterworks ed. Vol. 2. New York: Marvel Comics, 2009.
———. *Fantastic Four*. Marvel Masterworks ed. Vol. 5. New York: Marvel Comics, 2011.
———. *Fantastic Four*. Marvel Masterworks ed. Vol. 6. New York: Marvel Comics, 2011.
———. "Spider-Man!" *Amazing Fantasy*, August 1962, 1–11.
———. *The X-Men*. Marvel Masterworks ed. Vol. 1. New York: Marvel Comics, 2009.
Lee, Stan, Jack Kirby, and Steve Ditko. *The Incredible Hulk*. Marvel Masterworks ed. Vol. 1. New York: Marvel Comics, 2009.
Lee, Stan, Larry Lieber, Robert Bernstein, Jack Kirby, and Al Hartley. *The Mighty Thor*. Marvel Masterworks ed. Vol. 1. New York: Marvel Comics, 2010.
Lee, Stan, Don Rico, and Don Heck. *The Invincible Iron Man*. Marvel Masterworks ed. Vol. 2. New York: Marvel Comics, 2012.
Lee, Stan, Wallace Wood, Bill Everett, and Joe Orlando. *Daredevil*. Marvel Masterworks ed. Vol. 1. New York: Marvel Comics, 2010.
Leonard, Harris K. "The Classics—Alive and Well with Superman." *College English* 37, no. 4 (1975): 405–7.
Lesnick, Silas. "NBC Passes on Wonder Woman." *SuperHeroHype*. www.superherohype.com/news/articles/167277-nbc-passes-on-wonder-woman.
Lester, Richard. *Superman II*. Warner Brothers, 1980.
"Let's Level with Daredevil." *Daredevil*, October 1966, 21–22.
Levi, Alan J., and Kenneth Johnson. *The Incredible Hulk: The Complete First Season*. Universal Studios, 2006.
Liu, Marjorie, and Mike Perkins. *Astonishing X-Men*, August 2012.
Lloyd, Peter B. "Superman's Moral Evolution." In *The Man from Krypton: A Closer Look at Superman*, edited by Glenn Yeffeth, 181–210. Dallas, TX: BenBella Books, Inc., 2005.

Lobdell, Scott, and Kenneth Rocafort. "I Fought the Law and Kicked Its Butt!" *Red Hood and the Outlaws*, November 2011.

Loeb, Jeph, and Jim Lee. *Batman: Hush*. New York: DC Comics, 2009.

Loeb, Jeph, and Tim Sale. *Batman: The Long Halloween*. New York: DC Comics, 2011.

———. *Daredevil: Yellow*. New York: Marvel, 2003.

———. *Hulk: Gray*. New York: Marvel, 2004.

———. *Spider-Man: Blue*. New York: Marvel Comics, 2009.

———. *Superman for All Seasons*. New York: DC Comics, 2002.

Loeb, Jeph, and Michael Turner. *Superman/Batman: Supergirl*. Vol. 1. New York: DC Comics, 2005.

Lucaites, John Louis, and Robert Hariman. "Visual Rhetoric, Photojournalism, and Democratic Public Culture." *Rhetoric Review* 20, nos. 1–2 (2001): 37.

Lucas, George. *Star Wars*. 20th Century Fox, 1977.

Lunsford, Andrea. "Cognitive Development and the Basic Writer." In *Cross-Talk in Comp Theory: A Reader*, edited by Victor Villanueva, 299–310. Urbana, IL: National Council of Teachers of English, 2003.

MacDonald, Hettie. "Blink." In *Doctor Who: The Complete Third Series*. BBC Worldwide, 2007.

Madrid, Mike. *The Supergirls: Fashion, Feminism, Fantasy, and the History of Comic Book Heroines*. Exterminating Angel Press, 2009.

Marsh, Jackie, and Elaine Millard. *Literacy and Popular Culture*. London: Paul Chapman, 2000.

Marshall, C. W. "The Furies, Wonder Woman, and Dream: Mythmaking in DC Comics." In *Classics and Comics*, edited by George Kovacs and C. W. Marshall, 89–101. Oxford: Oxford University Press, 2011.

Marston, William Moulton, and Harry G. Peter. "Introducing Wonder Woman." *All Star Comics*, December/January 1942.

———. *The Wonder Woman Chronicles*. Vol. 1. New York: DC Comics, 2010.

Martin, Justin F. "Children's Attitudes toward Super Heroes as a Potential Indicator of Their Moral Understanding." *Journal of Moral Education* 36, no. 2 (2007): 239–50.

"Marvel: The Heroic Age." Marvel Comics. http://marvel.com/news/story/10914/marvel_the_ heroic_age.

Marz, Ron. *Green Lantern: Emerald Twilight*. New York: DC Comics, 1994.

McCloud, Scott. *Understanding Comics*. Allenspark, CO: Tundra Publications, 1993.

McDonagh, Maitland, et al. "Look! It's a Bird! It's a Plane! It's Curtains for the Man of Steel." *New York Times*, November 15, 1992, H25.

McFarlane, Todd. *Spawn Origins*. Vol. 1. Berkeley, CA: Image Comics, 2009.

Meltzer, Brad, and Rags Morales. *Identity Crisis*. New York: DC Comics, 2006.

Michelinie, David, Bob Layton, John Romita Jr., and Carmine Infantino. *Iron Man: Demon in a Bottle*. New York: Marvel Comics, 2006.

Michelinie, David, and Todd McFarlane. *Spider-Man Visionaries: Todd McFarlane*. New York: Marvel Comics, 2003.

Michelinie, David, and Paul Ryan. "The Wedding." *The Amazing Spider-Man Annual*, 1987.

Millar, Mark, and Bryan Hitch. *The Ultimates: Ultimate Collection*. New York: Marvel Comics, 2010.

Millar, Mark, J. G. Jones, and Paul Mount. *Wanted*. New York: Top Cow Productions/Image Comics, 2007.

Millar, Mark, and Steve McNiven. *Civil War*. New York: Marvel Comics, 2008.

Miller, Frank. *Daredevil Visionaries: Frank Miller*. Vol. 1. New York: Marvel Comics, 2002.

———. *Daredevil Visionaries: Frank Miller*. Vol. 2. New York: Marvel Comics, 2002.

———. "Last Hand." *Daredevil*, April 1982.

Miller, Frank, et al. "The Men Without Fear: Creating Daredevil." In *Daredevil*. 20th Century Fox, 2003.

Miller, Frank, and Klaus Janson. *The Dark Knight Returns*. New York: DC Comics, 1986.

Miller, Frank, and David Mazzucchelli. *Batman: Year One*. New York: DC Comics, 2005.

———. *Daredevil: Born Again*. New York: Marvel, 2010.

Miller, Frank, and John Romita Jr. *Daredevil: The Man Without Fear*. New York: Marvel Comics, 2008.

Miller, Frank, and Lynn Varley. *Batman: The Dark Knight Strikes Again*. New York: DC Comics, 2004.

Miller, Jack, Ramona Fradon, and Nick Cardy. *The Aquaman Achives*. DC Archive ed. Vol. 1. New York: DC Comics, 2003.

Moder, Dick, and Stuart Margolin. *Wonder Woman: The Complete First Season*. Warner Home Video, 2004.

Moench, Doug, and Jim Aparo. "Knightfall—Part II: The Broken Bat." *Batman*, July 1993.

Moore, Alan. *DC Universe by Alan Moore*. New York: DC Comics, 2011.

Moore, Alan, and Brian Bolland. *The Killing Joke*. New York: DC Comics, 1988.

Moore, Alan, and Dave Gibbons. *Watchmen*. New York: DC Comics, 1986.

Moore, Alan, and Kevin O'Neill. *The League of Extraordinary Gentlemen*. Vol. 1. America's Best Comics, 2002.

Moore, Alan, and Christopher Sharrett. "Alan Moore." In *Alan Moore Conversations*, edited by Eric L. Berlatsky, 46–60. Jackson: University Press of Mississippi, 2012.

Moore, Alan, John Totleben, and Steve Bissette. *Swamp Thing: Sage of the Swamp Thing*. Vol. 1. New York: DC Comics, 1998.

Morrison, Grant. *New X-Men*. Vol. 1. New York: Marvel Comics, 2008.

———. *New X-Men*. Vol. 2. New York: Marvel Comics, 2008.

———. *New X-Men*. Vol. 3. New York: Marvel Comics, 2008.

———. *Supergods: What Masked Vigilantes, Miraculous Mutants, and a Sun God from Smallville Can Teach Us About Being Human*. New York: Spiegel & Grau, 2011.

Morrison, Grant, Tony Daniel, and Lee Garbett. *Batman: R.I.P.* New York: DC Comics, 2010.

Morrison, Grant, J. G. Jones, and Doug Mahnke. *Final Crisis*. New York: DC Comics 2010.

Morrison, Grant, and Frank Quitely. *All Star Superman*. New York: DC Comics, 2011.

Morrissey, Lee, ed. *Debating the Canon: A Reader from Addison to Nafisi*. New York: Palgrave Macmillan, 2005.

Musson, Alex, and Andrew O'Neill. "The *Mustard* Interview: Alan Moore." In *Alan Moore Conversations*, edited by E. L. Berlatsky, 182–206. Jackson: University Press of Mississippi, 2012.

Nama, Adilifu. *Super Black: American Pop Culture and Black Superheroes*. Austin: University of Texas Press, 2011.

"The New Bat Suit." In *The Dark Knight*. Warner Home Video, 2008.

Nolan, Christopher. *Batman Begins*. Warner Brothers, 2005.

———. *The Dark Knight*. Warner Brothers, 2008.

Norrington, Stephen. *Blade*. New Line Cinema, 1998.

O'Neil, Dennis, and Neal Adams. *Green Lantern/Green Arrow Collection*. Vol. 1. New York: DC Comics, 2004.

———. *Green Lantern/Green Arrow Collection*. Vol. 2. New York: DC Comics, 2004.

———. *Superman vs. Muhammad Ali Deluxe*. New York: DC Comics, 2010.

O'Neil, Denny, Mike Sekowsky, and Irv Novick. *Diana Prince: Wonder Woman*. Vol. 1. New York: DC Comics, 2008.

O'Neil, Denny, Len Wein, and Neal Adams. *Batman Illustrated by Neal Adams*. Vol. 3. New York: DC Comics, 2006.

Ordway, Jerry, and Tom Grummett. "Funeral for a Friend—Part 5: Grave Obsession." *The Adventures of Superman*, 1993.

Overstreet, Robert M., et al. *The Overstreet Comic Book Price Guide*. Timonium, MD: Gemstone Publishing, 2011.

Pagnucci, Gian S. *Living the Narrative Life: Stories as a Tool for Meaning Making*. Portsmouth: Heinemann, 2004.

Pak, Greg, and Carmine Di Giandomenico. *X-Men: Magneto Testament*. New York: Marvel, 2009.

Pantozzi, Jill. "Hey, That's My Cape! Marvel Killing Characters for Money?" *Newsarama*.

———. "Kirby Estate Files Appeal in Marvel Lawsuit." *Newsarama*. http://blog.newsarama.com/2011/08/15/kirby-estate-files-appeal-in-marvel-lawsuit/.

"Parallel Universes Theory: The Basics." *Quantum Jumping.* www.quantumjumping.com/articles/parallel-universe/parallel-universes-theory.

Parker, Bill, and C. C. Beck. *Shazam! The Greatest Stories Ever Told.* New York: DC Comics, 2008.

Patterson, Ray, and Carl Urbano. "Trial of the Superfriends." In *Challenge of the Superfriends: Attack of the Legion of Doom.* Warner Home Video, 2004.

Radomski, Eric. *Batman: Mask of the Phantasm.* Warner Brothers, 1993.

Raimi, Sam. *Darkman.* Universal Pictures, 1990.

———. *Spider-Man.* Sony Pictures Home Video, 2002.

———. *Spider-Man 2.* Columbia Pictures, 2004.

Reynolds, Richard. *Super Heroes: A Modern Mythology.* Jackson: University Press of Mississippi, 1992.

Roach, David, Andrew Jones, Simon Jowett, and Greg Hill. "Garry Leach and Alan Moore." In *Alan Moore Conversations*, edited by E. L. Berlatsky, 8–25. Jackson: University Press of Mississippi, 2012.

"Robin's Requiem: The Tale of Jason Todd." In *Batman: Under the Red Hood.* Warner Home Video, 2010.

Robinson, James, and Nicola Scott. *Earth 2*, August 2012.

Robinson, Tasha. "Moore in the *Onion* Edits." In *Alan Moore Conversations*, edited by E. L. Berlatsky, 95–107. Jackson: University Press of Mississippi.

Rogers, Vaneta. "DC Launches Digital Comic Store at DCcomics.Com." *Newsarama.* www.newsarama.com/comics/dc-digital-comics-store-101110.html.

Rollin, Roger B. "Beowulf to Batman: The Epic Hero and Pop Culture." *College English* 31, no. 5 (1970): 431–49.

Rowling, J. K. *Harry Potter and the Deathly Hallows.* New York: Scholastic, 2007.

Ruby-Spears Superman. Warner Home Video, 1988.

Rucka, Greg, and J. G. Jones. *Wonder Woman: The Hiketeia.* New York: DC Comics, 2003.

Sacco, Joe, and Edward Said. *Palestine.* Seattle: Fantagraphics Books, 2002.

Satrapi, Marjane. *The Complete Persepolis.* New York: Pantheon, 2007.

Schmitt, Ronald. "Deconstructive Comics." *Journal of Popular Culture* 25, no. 4 (1992): 153–61.

Schraffenberger, J. D. "Visualizing Beowulf: Old English Gets Graphic." In *Building Literacy Connections with Graphic Novels: Page by Page, Panel by Panel*, edited by James Bucky Carter, 64–82. Urbana, IL: National Council of Teachers of English, 2007.

Schwartz, Gretchen. "Expanding Literacies through Graphic Novels." *The English Journal* 95, no. 6 (2010): 58–64.

Schwartz, Gretchen E. "Graphic Novels for Multiple Literacies." *Journal of Adolescent & Adult Literacy* 46, no. 3 (2002): 262–65.

Schwartz, Shalom H. "A Theory of Cultural Value Orientations: Explication and Applications." *Comparative Sociology* 5, nos. 2–3 (2006): 137–82.

Sharrett, Christopher. "Batman and the Twilight of Idols: An Interview with Frank Miller." In *The Many Lives of Batman*, edited by Roberta E. Pearson and William Uricchio, 33–46. London: BFI Publishing, 1991.

Shooter, Jim, and Mike Zeck. "Secret Wars–Invasion." *Marvel Super Heroes Secret Wars*, December 1984.

Shooter, Jim, Mike Zeck, and Bob Layton. *Secret Wars.* New York: Marvel Comics, 2011.

Siegel, Jerry. *The Golden Age Spectre.* DC Archive ed. Vol. 1. New York: DC Comics, 2003.

———. *Superman: The Man of Tomorrow Archives.* DC Archive ed. Vol. 1. New York: DC Comics, 2005.

Siegel, Jerry, and Joseph Shuster. *Action Comics* 1, no. 1, June 1938.

———. *The Superman Chronicles.* Vol. 1. New York: DC Comics, 2006.

———. *The Superman Chronicles.* Vol. 3. New York: DC Comics, 2007.

Siegel, Jerry, Joe Shuster, Bob Kane, and Bill Finger. *Superman: World's Finest Comics Archives.* DC Archive ed. Vol. 1. New York: DC Comics, 2004.

Simon, Joe, and Jack Kirby. *Golden Age Captain America Comics.* Marvel Masterworks ed. Vol. 1. New York: Marvel Comics, 2005.

Singer, Bryan. "Not Alone." *Superman Returns*. Warner Home Video, 2007.
———. *X-Men*. 20th Century Fox, 2000.
———. *X-Men 2*. 20th Century Fox, 2003.
Slater, Michael. *Charles Dickens: A Life Defined by Writing*. New Haven, CT: Yale University Press, 2009.
Slott, Don, and Steve McNiven. "Brand New Day, Part 1." *The Amazing Spider-Man*.
Snetiker, Marc. "Michael Bay Responds to Fan Outrage about 'Teenage Mutant Ninja Turtles' Alien Debacle." *Popwatch*. http://popwatch.ew.com/2012/03/20/michael-bay-teenage-mutant-ninja-turtles-reponse/.
———. "Michael Bay Says 'Teenage Mutant Ninja Turtles' Are Aliens, Reinvents Origin Story." *Popwatch*. http://popwatch.ew.com/2012/03/19/michael-bay-teenage-mutant-ninja-turtles-aliens/.
"Special Awards and Citations." The Pulitzer. www.pulitzer.org/bycat/Special-Awards-and-Citations.
Spider-Man: The '67 Collection. Walt Disney Video, 2004.
Spiegelman, Art. *The Complete Maus*. New York: Penguin, 2003.
Spielberg, Steven. *Schindler's List*. Universal Pictures, 1993.
"Stan the Man." *Comic Book Men*. AMC, 2012.
Starlin, Jim. *The Death of Captain Marvel*. New York: Marvel Comics, 1982.
Starlin, Jim, and Jim Aparo. "A Death in the Family, Book 2." *Batman*, December 1988.
Starlin, Jim, Steve Englehart, Doug Moench, and Pat Broderick. *The Death of Captain Marvel*. Marvel Premiere Classic ed. New York: Marvel Comics, 2010.
Steinbeck, John. *Of Mice and Men*. New York: Covici Friede, 1937.
Stephenson, Neal. *Snow Crash*. New York: Bantam Books, 1992.
Stone, Oliver. *Wall Street*. 20th Century Fox, 1987.
Straczynski, J. Michael, and Mike Deodato Jr. *Amazing Spider-Man Volume 8: Sins Past*. New York: Marvel Comics, 2005.
Straczynski, J. Michael, and Joe Quesada. *Spider-Man: One More Day*. New York: Marvel Comics, 2008.
Super Friends! Season 1, Volume 1. Warner Home Video, 2010.
Superman: The Complete Animated Series. Warner Home Video, 2009.
Taylor, Aaron. "'He's Gotta Be Strong, and He's Gotta Be Fast, and He's Gotta Be Larger Than Life': Investigating the Engendered Superhero Body." *Journal of Popular Culture* 40, no. 2 (2007): 344–60.
Teenage Mutant Ninja Turtles: The Original Series, Volume 1. Lions Gate, 2004.
Thundercats: Season 1, Part 1. Warner Home Video, 2011.
Timm, Bruce. *Batman: The Animated Series, Volume 1*. Edited by Bruce Timm. Warner Home Video, 2004.
———. *Justice League Unlimited: Season 1*. Warner Home Video, 2006.
———. *Justice League Unlimited: Season 2*. Warner Home Video, 2007.
———. "Requiem and Rebirth: Superman Lives!" *Superman: Doomsday*. Warner Home Video, 2007.
Tolkien, J. R. R. *The Lord of the Rings: The Fellowship of the Ring*. London: Allen & Unwin, 1954.
Truitt, Brian. "DC Comics Turns a New Page This Week." *USA Today*. http://usatoday30.usatoday.com/life/comics/story/2011-08-28/DC-Comics-turns-a-new-page-this-week/50166706/1.
———. "DC Comics Unleashes a New Universe of Superhero Titles." *USA Today*. www.usatoday.com/life/comics/2011-05-31-dc-comics-reinvents_n.htm.
Tucker, Ken. "TV Review: *Smallville* (2001)." www.ew.com/ew/article/0,,181747,00.html.
Tye, Larry. *Superman: The High-Flying History of America's Most Enduring Hero*. New York: Random House, 2012.
Various. *The Amazing Spider-Man*. Marvel Essentials ed. Vol. 6. New York: Marvel Comics, 2011.
———. *Avengers: The Contest*. Marvel Premiere Classic ed. New York: Marvel Comics, 2010.
———. *Avengers: The Korvac Saga*. New York: Marvel Comics, 2012.

————. *Batgirl: The Greatest Stories Ever Told*. New York: DC Comics, 2010.

————. *Essential Incredible Hulk*. Marvel Essentials ed. Vol. 5. New York: Marvel Comics, 2008.

————. *Essential Luke Cage/Power Man*. Marvel Essentials ed. Vol. 1. New York: Marvel Comics, 2005.

————. *Essential Moon Knight*. Marvel Essentials ed. Vol. 1. New York: Marvel Comics, 2006.

————. *Essential Power Man and Iron Fist*. Marvel Essentials ed. Vol. 1. New York: Marvel Comics, 2008.

————. *Heroes: The Complete Series*. Universal Studios, 2010.

————. *Legion of Super-Heroes Archive*. DC Archive ed. Vol. 1. New York: DC Comics, 1997.

————. *Nick Fury, Agent of S.H.I.E.L.D*. Marvel Masterworks ed. Vol. 3. New York: Marvel Comics, 2011.

————. *Smallville: The Complete Series*. Warner Home Video, 2011.

————. *The Supergirl Archives*. DC Archive ed. Vol. 1. New York: DC Comics, 2001.

————. *Teen Titans: The Complete First Season*. Warner Home Video, 2006.

————. *World's Finest Comics*. DC Archive ed. Vol. 1. New York: DC Comics, 1999.

Vaughan, Brian K., and Niko Henrichon. *Pride of Baghdad*. New York: Vertigo, 2008.

Versaci, Rocco. "How Comic Books Can Change the Way Our Students See Literature: One Teacher's Perspective." *The English Journal* 91, no. 2 (2001): 61–67.

Vietti, Brandon. *Batman: Under the Red Hood*. Warner Home Video, 2010.

Vitello, Art. *The Tick Season 1*. Buena Vista Home Entertainment, 2006.

Wachowski, Andy, and Larry Wachowski. *The Matrix*. Warner Brothers, 1999.

Waid, Mark. *JLA: Tower of Babel*. Vol. 7. New York: DC Comics, 2001.

Waid, Mark, Peter Krause, and John Cassaday. *Irredeemable*. Vol. 1. Los Angeles: Boom! Studios, 2009.

Waid, Mark, and Alex Ross. *Kingdom Come*. New York: DC Comics, 1997.

Waid, Mark, and Leinil Francis Yu. *Superman: Birthright*. New York: DC Comics, 2005.

Walker, John. *Transformers: The Complete First Season*. Shout! Factory, 2009.

Ware, Chris. *Jimmy Corrigan, the Smartest Kid on Earth*. New York: Pantheon Books, 2000.

Webb, Marc. *The Amazing Spider-Man*. Columbia Pictures, 2012.

Wein, Len, and Dave Cockrum. "Second Genesis." *Giant Size X-Men*, August 1975.

Wertham, Fredric. *Seduction of the Innocent*. New York: Reinhart and Company, Inc., 1954.

Whedon, Joss. *The Avengers*. Walt Disney Studios, 2012.

Whiston, Daniel, David Russell, and Andy Fruish. "The Craft: An Interview with Alan Moore." In *Alan Moore Conversations*, edited by E. L. Berlatsky, 108–35. Jackson: University Press of Mississippi, 2012.

Wiesel, Elie. *Night*. Translated by Marion Wiesel. New York: Hill and Wang, 2006.

Winick, Judd, et al. *Batman: Under the Red Hood*. New York: DC Comics, 2011.

Winick, Judd, and Shane Davis. "Daedalus and Icarus, the Return of Jason Todd." *Batman Annual*, May 2006.

Winick, Judd, and Guillem March. "And Most of the Costumes Stay On." *Catwoman*, November 2011.

Winkless, Terence H. *Mighty Morphin Power Rangers: Season 1, Volume 1*. Shout! Factory, 2012.

Wolfman, Marv, Roger McKenzie, Gene Colan, and Frank Robbins. *Essential Tomb of Dracula*. Marvel Essentials ed. Vol. 1. New York: Marvel Comics, 2004.

Wolfman, Marv, and George Pérez. *Crisis on Infinite Earths*. New York: DC Comics, 2001.

————. *The New Teen Titans: The Judas Contract*. New York: DC Comics, 1991.

————. "Beyond the Silent Night." *Crisis on Infinite Earths*, October 1985.

————. "A Flash of the Lightning!" *Crisis on Infinite Earths*, November 1986.

————. "The Judas Contract, Book 3: There Shall Come a Titan." *Tales of the Teen Titans*, July 1984.

Wolfman, Marv, and Jim Starlin. "Where Nightmares Begin!" *DC Comics Presents*, October 1980.

Wolk, Douglas. "75 Years of the First Comic Book Superhero (It's Not Who You Think)." *Time*. http://techland.time.com/2010/07/05/75-years-of-the-first-comic-book-superhero-its-not-who-you-think/.

Wright, Bradford W. *Comic Book Nation: The Transformation of Youth Culture in America*. Baltimore: Johns Hopkins University Press, 2003.

X-Men: Pryde of the X-Men. Best Film & Video Corp, 1989.

Yang, Gene Luan. *American Born Chinese*. New York: First Second Books, 2006.

Yost, Christopher, Matt Fraction, Cullen Bunn, and Scot Eaton. *Battle Scars*. New York: Marvel Comics, 2012.

Young, Sheryl. "Superman Becomes World Poster Boy for Political Correctness." *Yahoo!* http://news.yahoo.com/superman-becomes-world-poster-boy-political-correctness-145400775.html.

Zalben, Alex. "New 52 Review: Catwoman." *MTV Geek*. http://geek-news.mtv.com/2011/09/22/new-52-review-catwoman/.

Index

About the Authors

Alex Romagnoli is completing his doctoral studies in Composition and TES-OL at Indiana University of Pennsylvania, where he also serves as a temporary, part-time faculty member. Previously, he was a high school English teacher with three years of teaching experience. Mr. Romagnoli received his B.S. in Secondary Education, as well as his M.Ed., at East Stroudsburg University. His teaching specialties are composition, literacy studies, comic studies, and popular culture. His dissertation study examines best practices for using graphic novels as a teaching tool in collegiate settings. In 2011 he received a Mary Flegal Harte Scholarship to pursue his doctoral work at IUP. He is also a lifelong comic book fan and collector whose favorite superheroes include Superman, Batman, and Daredevil.

Dr. Gian Pagnucci is chair of the Department of English at Indiana University of Pennsylvania. He has also served as director of IUP's Graduate Studies in Composition and TESOL Program. In 2009 Dr. Pagnucci was selected to be an IUP University Professor, IUP's highest academic honor. He has been an English faculty member at IUP for eighteen years. Dr. Pagnucci's teaching specialties are technical writing, composition, technology-based pedagogy, and comic books. He has won a Reflective Practice Teaching Award and an international award for innovative teaching with technology. Dr. Pagnucci is author of *Living the Narrative Life: Stories as a Tool for Meaning Making* and was coeditor for *Re-Mapping Narrative: Technology's Impact on the Way We Write*. In addition, Dr. Pagnucci has published in such leading journals as *Computers and Composition*, *English Journal*, and *English Education*. Dr. Pagnucci is a lifelong comic book collector. His favorite superheroes are Moon Knight, Captain America, and the Justice Society of America.